CONTEMPORARY SOCIAL THEORY
General Editor: Anthony Giddens

This series aims to create a forum for debate between different theoretical and philosophical traditions in the social sciences. As well as covering broad schools of thought, the series will also concentrate upon the work of particular thinkers whose ideas have had a major impact on social science (these books appear under the sub-series title of 'Theoretical Traditions in the Social Sciences'). The series is not limited to abstract theoretical discussion — it will also include more substantive works on contemporary capitalism, the state, politics and other subject areas.

Published Titles

Tony Bilton, Kevin Bonnett, Philip Jones, Ken Sheard, Michelle Stanworth and Andrew Webster, *Introductory Sociology* (2nd edition)
Emile Durkheim, *The Division of Labour in Society* (trans W.D. Halls)
Emile Durkheim, *The Rules of Sociological Method* (ed. Steven Lukes, trans. W.D. Halls)
Boris Frankel, *Beyond the State? Dominant Theories and Socialist Strategies*
Anthony Giddens, *A Contemporary Critique of Historical Materialism*
Anthony Giddens, *Central Problems in Social Theory*
Anthony Giddens, *Profiles and Critiques in Social Theory*
Anthony Giddens and David Held (eds), *Classes, Power and Conflict: Classical and Contemporary Debates*
Geoffrey Ingham, *Capitalism Divided? The City and Industry in British Social Development*
Terry Johnson, Christopher Dandeker and Clive Ashworth, *The Structure of Social Theory*
Douglas Kellner, *Herbert Marcuse and the Crisis of Marxism*
Jorge Larrain, *Marxism and Ideology*
Gerry Rose, *Deciphering Sociological Research*
John Scott, *The Upper Classes: Property and Privilege in Britain*
Steve Taylor, *Durkheim and the Study of Suicide*
John B. Thompson and David Held (eds), *Habermas: Critical Debates*

Forthcoming Titles

Martin Albrow, *Weber and the Construction of Social Theory*
Ali Rattansi and Dominic Strinati, *Marx and the Sociology of Class*

CONTEMPORARY SOCIAL THEORY

General Editor: ANTHONY GIDDENS

Theoretical Traditions in the Social Sciences

This series introduces the work of major figures in social science to students beyond their immediate specialisms.

Wittgenstein
A social theory of knowledge

David Bloor

University of Edinburgh

**MACMILLAN
EDUCATION**

First published 1983
Reprinted 1987

Published by
MACMILLAN EDUCATION LTD
Houndmills, Basingstoke, Hampshire RG21 2XS
and London
Companies and representatives
throughout the world

Printed in Hong Kong

ISBN 0-333-30017-3

For Konrad Alexander Bloor

Contents

Acknowledgements

Five Edinburgh colleagues, Michael Barfoot, Barry Barnes, Celia Bloor, Donald MacKenzie and Steven Shapin, did me the kindness of reading the book in draft. They made extensive, precise and valuable criticisms, and I have done my best to act on them. My debts to my colleagues in fact go far beyond this. Much that is in the book has been learned from them, though the form and occasion of its expression is entirely my own responsibility. Carole Tansley generously undertook the typing of the manuscript and I am most grateful for this enormous help. Throughout the book I have made liberal use of the researches and conclusions of certain historians and anthropologists. I hope that none of them will feel that my borrowing has been too extensive. It is my way of ensuring that this book, unlike some in the area, is not all pots and pans and no pudding.

December 1982   David Bloor

Abbreviations and Referencing Conventions

Wittgenstein's works will be cited using the abbreviations given below. Quotations will be identified by giving the part number of the book (if any), and then the paragraph number. Thus a passage from the *Philosophical Investigations* will be identified as, for example, *PI*, I, 564 – while a passage from *Zettel*, which is not divided into parts, will be just, say, *Z*, 532. In a few cases, such as the *Blue and Brown Books*, which are not divided into numbered paragraphs, it is appropriate to use the more normal method of just citing the page. Where numbers refer to pages this will always be indicated, e.g. *BB*, p.18.

BB   *The Blue and Brown Books*, Oxford, Blackwell, 1969.

CV   *Culture and Value*, ed. G. von Wright and H. Nyman, trans. P. Winch, Oxford, Blackwell, 1980.

LCA   *Lectures and Conversations on Aesthetics, Psychology and Religious Belief*, ed. C. Barrett, Oxford, Blackwell, 1970.

LFM   *Wittgenstein's Lectures on the Foundations of Mathematics, Cambridge, 1939*, ed. C. Diamond, Brighton, Harvester Press, 1976.

NFL   Wittgenstein's Notes for Lectures on 'Private Experience' and 'Sense Data', *Philosophical Review*, vol.Lxxvii, 1968, 271–320.

OC   *On Certainty*, ed. G. Anscombe and G. von Wright, trans. D. Paul and G. Anscombe, Oxford, Blackwell, 1969.

PI   *Philosophical Investigations*, trans. G. Anscombe, Oxford, Blackwell, 1967 (first edn 1953).

RFM   *Remarks on the Foundations of Mathematics*, ed. G. von Wright, R. Rhees and G. Anscombe, trans. G. Anscombe, Oxford, Blackwell, 1964.

RPP *Remarks on the Philosophy of Psychology*: vol. 1 ed. G. Anscombe and G. von Wright, trans. G. Anscombe; vol. II ed. G. von Wright and H. Nyman, trans. C. Luckhardt and M. Aue, Oxford, Blackwell, 1980.

WWK *Wittgenstein and the Vienna Circle*, conversations recorded by F. Waismann, ed. B. McGuiness, trans. J. Schulte and B. McGuiness, Oxford, Blackwell, 1979.

Z *Zettel*, ed. G. Anscombe and G. von Wright, trans. G. Anscombe, Oxford, Blackwell, 1967.

Other abbreviations that are used in the notes and references will be explained as they are introduced.

I am in a sense making propaganda for one style
of thinking as opposed to another.

Ludwig Wittgenstein (*LCA*, p.28)

1

A Problem and a Plan

Ludwig Wittgenstein was born in Vienna in 1889. He trained to be an engineer but his life's work lay in philosophy. After completing his scientific education at Berlin he came to England to do research. His interests turned to mathematics and then to logic, and in 1911 he became a pupil of Bertrand Russell at Cambridge. Returning to Austria with the outbreak of war in 1914 he set about writing his first book. This became known as the *Tractatus Logico-Philosophicus* and was completed in the final stages of the conflict.[1] After the war, in which he had served with distinction, he became a schoolteacher in the villages of lower Austria. In 1929 he returned to Cambridge, cast aside the doctrines of the *Tractatus* and the influence of Russell, and set about tackling the problems of philosophy afresh.[2] It is this late, or mature philosophy, and this alone, which will be my concern.[3]

The centre-piece of the late work is the great *Philosophical Investigations*. The most accessible formulation of it, however, is in the *Blue and Brown Books*, which were written between 1933 and 1935 for private circulation among his pupils. Reflections on more limited and specialised problem areas are to be found in books such as *On Certainty* and the *Remarks on the Foundations of Mathematics*. These writings are impressive for their vigour and profundity and their impact has been considerable. Rightly, Wittgenstein's ideas have been subject to close critical scrutiny, and an extensive literature of commentary and assessment has grown up around them.[4] Recently this detailed analysis has been enriched by an increased awareness of Wittgenstein's cultural roots. He was a professor of philosophy at Cambridge, where he died in 1951, but he was also, and always, a Viennese intellectual.[5]

Of the many aspects of Wittgenstein's writing to which scholars have drawn attention there are two which seem to me of outstanding importance. These might be called the *sociological* and *naturalistic* sides of his thought.[6] He was remorseless in stressing the priority of society over the individual. This is why the concepts of 'culture', 'institution', 'custom' and 'norm' play so prominent a part in his theories. 'To obey a rule, to make a report, to give an order, to play a game of chess', he said, 'are *customs* (uses, institutions)' (*PI*, I, 199). This emphasis on what he called 'forms of life' is part of the naturalistic orientation. 'What we are supplying', he said, 'are really remarks on the natural history of human beings' (*PI*, I, 415; *RFM*, I, 141). His approach to the nature of belief, language, reasoning and action was to see them as natural phenomena. They were to be made intelligible by showing how they arise from human behaviour anchored in its material, biological and cultural setting. 'Commanding, questioning, recounting, chatting', he insisted, 'are as much a part of our natural history as walking, eating, drinking, playing' (*PI*, I, 25). As we shall see, this was the side of his work that was uppermost when he stressed the dependence of our knowledge on patterns of training, and when he developed a bold, naturalistic account of the basis of logic.

It is my intention to give a description and an analysis of all the main themes of the later philosophy in such a way that the sociological and naturalistic Wittgenstein stays clearly in view. Everyone accepts that human beings are social animals and that knowledge is, in some sense, a collective achievement, but it is all too easy to miss the full significance of these facts and to trivialise their implications. Wittgenstein, however, endorsed these ideas without reservation. He treated cognition as something that is social in its very essence. For him, our interactions with one another, and our participation in a social group, were no mere contingencies. They were not the accidental circumstances that attend our knowing; they were constitutive of all that we can ever claim by way of knowledge. Tracing the profound consequences of this insight led Wittgenstein into building up what might be called a 'social theory of knowledge'. I shall show, step by step, how he accomplished this task.

The significance of Wittgenstein's project should not be missed. It represents a determined asssault on some of the most cherished myths of common sense, and on some of the most tenacious elements in our philosophical tradition. If what he says is true, or anywhere near the truth, the great categories of objectivity and rationality can never look the same again. Think how often our polemical appeals to these two things depend on our portraying them as forms of external compulsion. A social theory of knowledge changes all this. Objectivity and rationality must be things that we forge for ourselves as we construct a form of collective life. So the work of Copernicus is undone. Human beings are back in the centre of the picture. Things that had seemed distant become close; product is replaced by process. Apparent universals become variable and relative. The things we had seen ourselves as answerable *to*, we are now answerable *for*. So the body of work that we are about to examine redraws the boundaries of responsibility; it is a subtle attempt to change our cultural self-consciousness.

A social theory of knowledge is not, in itself, a novelty. Durkheim developed a sociological theory about our basic classifications and categories and their hold over us. He theorised about the external, objective character of moral compulsion and astutely noted its connections with logical compulsion. He discussed the idea of truth, our religious experience, and the prevalence of dualistic theories of human nature, all from a sociological standpoint.[7] One important difference, however, between Wittgenstein and Durkheim is the determination and consistency with which this sociologising of philosophy is carried through. For Durkheim a social explanation might be found for primitive systems of classification, but the same could hardly apply to the respected achievements of our own, scientific culture. In the early stages of cultural evolution, he said, a belief may be deemed true because it is socially accepted; but for us it is only socially acceptable on condition that it is true.[8] By succumbing to this seductive idea Durkheim allowed himself to throw away all that he had so painfully won. We shall see that Wittgenstein does not lose his nerve or betray himself in this way. Whether he is dealing with common-sense descriptions of the things and people around us, the esoteric accounts of the scientist, with introspective reports of our mental states, or even with the compelling proofs of the mathematician – whatever the sphere of knowledge – the essentially social character of his analysis does not falter.

Despite its virtues there are undeniable difficulties with Wittgenstein's work. For example, his books do not read like ordinary books. They are collections of remarks, and jump from topic to topic. There is a pressing need to *interpret* his writing. The gaps must be filled in and some underlying order imputed to the fragments so that we can appreciate the connections between them.[9] In saying that Wittgenstein was giving us a sociological theory of knowledge, I am therefore providing a 'reading' of his work. One justification that is often given for offering a 'reading' of an author is that it maximises the consistency of his doctrines. This is not a justification that I would wish to advance. Certainly a sociological and naturalistic reading will allow us to discern a great deal of unity and coherence in his thought, but I do not claim to know whether it makes him out to be more consistent than other possible readings. It seems to me to be a virtue of my approach that it will help to highlight what are, arguably, certain inconsistencies, equivocations and arbitrary elements in Wittgenstein's thought. In particular, a sociological reading points up the ways in which Wittgenstein could have taken his work forward. It makes us wonder why he stopped where he did, and gives us a sense of the next step that must be taken. For example, at a number of points Wittgenstein touched on the role that needs and interests play in structuring a system of belief. Each time he simply dropped the issue. I will make good this deficit by connecting his ideas to a body of historical research that treats precisely this subject. Similarly I shall take up his central theoretical concept, that of a 'language-game', and use empirical material to go beyond what Wittgenstein was willing to do with it. We shall even see what a systematic theory of language-games looks like.

The fact that Wittgenstein's later work has implications for the study of social behaviour and its cultural products is, of course, widely acknowledged. But these implications are usually seen to bear upon matters of sociological method rather than issues of substance. The result is that Wittgenstein is seen as just one more critic of the so-called 'positivist' ideal in sociology. Here the question that is uppermost is whether the student of human behaviour should adopt the same goals and methods as the natural and biological scientist.[10] Part of my aim is to shake off this concern with methodology. It is not that the standard, method-oriented readings are wrong. The problem is that they make the tail wag the dog. There is so much more to learn from Wittgenstein. Furthermore I shall show that much of the anti-positivist argumentation in sociology, and the philosophy of the social sciences, actually runs counter to Wittgenstein's most thoroughly worked out doctrines. This is even true of Winch's book, *The Idea of a Social Science*, which is widely accepted as an account of what Wittgenstein means for sociology and anthropology.[11] Wittgenstein's relation to the positivist tradition in the social sciences is more complicated than is usually allowed.

My plan, then, after examining the main doctrines of the later philosophy, is to link Wittgenstein's work to the sociology of knowledge and to show how it can be developed into a systematic theory of language-games. To those who are already familiar with Wittgenstein's writings, and the conventions that currently surround its interpretation, this may sound like a misguided enterprise. Surely, it will be said, this will distort Wittgenstein's achievements and intentions. Did he not denounce the search for causes and the construction of explanatory theories? 'We are not doing natural science', he insisted. Despite his remarks elsewhere about natural history, Wittgenstein was even prepared to add 'nor yet natural history – since we can also invent fictitious natural history for our purposes' (*PI*, II, xii). He would, for example, bid us imagine a tribe whose customs and concepts are different from ours, or he would imagine that the laws of nature are different, and would ask what effect this might have on our conceptual scheme. Wittgenstein often illustrated his arguments with such thought-experiments, but felt no need to go further. There is no ducking the issue: I will be going against certain of Wittgenstein's stated preferences, his chosen method, and perhaps his deepest prejudices. Nevertheless, I shall argue that this is entirely legitimate. Some purposes may be served by thought experiments, others are not. I shall replace a fictitious natural history by a real natural history, and an imaginary ethnography by a real ethnography. Only in this way can we make a secure estimate of Wittgenstein's capacity to illuminate life, not as it might be, but as it is; and to describe people, not as they might be, but as we find them. There could be no more disciplined way to see just what his work amounts to.

2

From Mental Images to Social Interactions

To do justice to the contribution that society makes to our knowledge, and to understand Wittgenstein's account of these matters, we must first surmount an obstacle. We must learn to expose the habits of mind and the techniques by which social processes are systematically misdescribed or passed over. In some accounts of knowledge they are rendered almost completely invisible. 'There is', said Wittgenstein, 'a kind of general disease of thinking which always looks for (and finds) what would be called a mental state from which all our acts spring as from a reservoir.' He gave a simple illustration. 'Thus one says, "the fashion changes because the tastes of people change". The taste is the mental reservoir' (*BB*, p.143). Notice how the collective phenomenon, the fashion change, is represented in psychological terms. The social event is referred back to the mental states of the individuals who participated in it, and these mental states are then cited as the cause of the change. The emptiness of this particular example is clear, but some explanations of this kind can be difficult to detect. Their common feature is the attempt to analyse characteristically social phenomena in psychological terms. For this reason the 'disease' to which Wittgenstein referred is usually called 'psychologism'.[1]

Wittgenstein took particular exception to this kind of misuse of psychological and individualistic categories when it occurred in discussions about the nature of meaning. Right at the beginning of the *Blue and Brown Books* he asked, 'What is the meaning of a word?' The psychologistic answer would be that meanings are ideas in the mind of the word user. Meanings are mental states accompanying our words. Knowing the meanings of words, e.g. the names of the colours, or the meaning of simple instructions, is, perhaps, a very commonplace and domestic accomplishment. But if we cannot correctly grasp the social character of these cases, we stand no chance with more complicated forms of knowledge. So let us start where Wittgenstein started, with the meaning of simple words. We shall see how he analysed and rejected two theories about meaning which I shall refer to as the theory of images, or mental content, and the theory of mental acts. These served him as typical representatives of the psychological and individualistic analysis of meaning. Wittgenstein became convinced that 'nothing is more wrong-headed than calling meaning a mental activity!' (*PI*, I, 693). However much we may be disposed to agree, it is no good just denouncing psychologism in general terms. We must learn from Wittgenstein how to detect the *precise* point at which the social aspects of knowledge are misdescribed or made to disappear from view.

2.1 Psychologies of act and content

Wittgenstein says that if we want to know what meanings are, we should look at how they are explained (*BB*, p.1). In every language a large number of words must be explained and introduced by ostension, i.e. by pointing to an object or feature of the kind for which the word stands. How does the subsequent employment of the word flow from this act of naming? Supporters of the image theory say that after its first introduction, when it is encountered again, the word will call up an image or picture in the mind. Having the image is what understanding the word amounts to. Similarly with future applications: the use of the word flows from the image. This is what enables us to recognise objects of the kind that have to be given a certain name. Sometimes the image itself is said to be the meaning of the word, otherwise the object or property referred to is said to be the meaning. In this case the mental picture is the user's idea of what is meant. Either way the image is crucial.

This theory has found many supporters. It was particularly favoured by some late nineteenth- and early twentieth-century philosophers and experimental psychologists.[2] Bertrand Russell, at one stage, argued that describing a past event involved picturing it in the mind and choosing our words so as to describe the picture. People are only genuinely apprehending what we say if they manage to construct a picture like ours. Advocates of the image theory are well aware that imagery fluctuates. Habit, for instance, diminishes it. Russell argued that this merely telescopes a sequence of mental events whose full significance must still be spelled out by reference to images. This is why he developed his story in terms of a child's use of language: the word habits are weaker and the images stronger. Even here a verbal exchange may not be accompanied by images, but it is

> the possibility of a memory-image in the child and an imagination image in the hearer that makes the essence of the narrative 'meaning' of the words. In as far as this is absent, the words are mere counters, capable of meaning, but not at that moment possessing it.[3]

The eminent psychologist E. B. Titchener was equally emphatic. He was in no doubt that we can, as he put it, ideate meanings, or that images can be the vehicle for meaning. In his own case he reported that 'In a large measure I think, that is, I mean and understand, in visual pictures.'[4] Titchener insisted that 'the visual pattern does not indifferently accompany, but is or equals, my gross understanding of the matter in hand'.[5]

The second psychological theory that must be considered stresses the role of mental acts such as 'intending' or 'focusing our attention', or 'meaning' something in the sense of referring to it. Here a word or sign has meaning, not because it is accompanied by a mental picture, but because it is accompanied by a mental act – a conscious orientation – actively directed at its object. The symbol is 'meant' in a certain way, and its correct application is governed by an 'intention'. If we introduce the word 'red' by pointing to a red square, the word means what it does because it is accompanied by the intention to refer to the colour rather than the shape. We could, on this theory, say that the redness itself was the meaning of the word, because it is the thing meant. But it is still the mental act that steers subsequent use. Learning takes place when the learner has formed a mental act that corresponds to that of the teacher, so that the word is applied in the way intended by the teacher.

This account received its fullest expression in the Austrian 'act psychology' derived from the work of Brentano and his followers in the phenomenological movement.[6] An example from modern sociology is Alfred Schutz's analysis of everyday experience. We take for granted an intersubjective world, composed of different

types of people, following typical courses of action amidst familiar
kinds of object but, said Schutz, this stable world is the product of
a stream of mental acts. Usually we are unaware of the processes
behind it, but this life-world is only 'meaningful for me in virtue of
those meaning-endowing intentional acts of which I become aware
by a reflexive glance'.[7] On the one hand, said Schutz,

> I can look upon the world presenting itself to me as one that is
> completed, constituted, and to be taken for granted. When I do
> this, I leave out of my awareness the intentional operations of
> my consciousness within which their meanings have already
> been constituted ... *On the other hand*, I can turn my glance
> toward the intentional operations of my consciousness which
> originally conferred the meanings.[8]

Notice that the 'reflexive glance', by which we are to catch ourselves in the act of conferring meaning, is a glance into the *individual* mind. 'Intended meaning', says Schutz, is 'essentially subjective.' It takes place within a 'unique stream of consciousness',
and so it is 'essentially inaccessible to every other individual'.[9]

The justice of calling these theories 'psychologistic' should be
apparent, even though one is based on the psychology of imagery
(or what is called the 'content' of the mind by its advocates), and
the other is based on a psychology of acts. For both of them
meaning is a mental happening within the individual which accompanies the production and reception of words or other features of
our behaviour to which we impute meaning.

2.2   The attack on mental images

Wittgenstein's attack on the image theory looks, at first glance,
rather oblique. He asks us to suppose that *A* shows *B* a sample of
cloth. *B*'s job is to go to a storeroom, examine bolts of material,
and bring back cloth to match the colour of the sample. *B* does not
take the sample with him, but has been trained in such a way that
he can carry out the order successfully. How does he do it? The
image theorist would say that he must have matched the appearance of the bolts to a memory image. The point is that matching an
object to a sample is an act of classification, and so is each applica-

tion of a verbal colour label like 'red' or 'blue'. Any fault in the image analysis of the first case will therefore apply to the second, verbal, case as well. Wittgenstein's criticism is as simple as it is devastating. If, after being shown the sample, *B* had the ability to call up its image, why shouldn't he equally have the capacity to pick up a matching bolt without more ado? 'If the training could bring it about that the idea or image – automatically – arose in *B*'s mind, why shouldn't it bring about *B*'s *actions* without the intervention of an image?' (*PI*, I, 89).

Occurrences of imagery, and our abilities in calling them up, are neither more nor less in need of explanation than the overt performances that are supposed to depend on them. This applies just as forcefully if those overt performances are verbal. Calling up images is neither more nor less problematic than calling up words. It is not a more fundamental process that, by itself, could provide an explanation of verbal behaviour and meaning. Explaining meaning by images is therefore just as circular and empty as explaining changes of fashion by changes of taste.

2.3 The rule of externalisation

Calling up images is an operation that takes place in the mind. That, at least, is how we might typically describe it. We are tempted to settle for pseudo-explanations, of the type that Wittgenstein has just exposed, because we are tempted to assume that mental processes are unproblematic. 'Thought', said Wittgenstein, 'is surrounded by a halo' (*PI*, I, 97). It is as if the mind were a magical entity, and once we have invoked its mysteries all our problems are solved. To offset these tendencies Wittgenstein proposes a useful rule. Whenever we are inclined to say that someone has a picture in his imagination or memory, we should substitute in our account the idea that they are looking at an actual object or sample of the kind pictured. Indeed we can 'replace every process of imagining by a process of looking at an object or by painting, drawing or modelling; and every process of speaking to oneself by speaking aloud' (*BB*, p.4).

This may be called his rule of externalisation. Internal, mental constructions are replaced by external, non-mental counterparts.

In this way we will see more clearly the structure of the explanations that we are discussing. The claim is not that painted pictures are more real than mental pictures, or that samples of coloured cloth are real while images of the sample are fictions. Quite the opposite. The idea is to treat images as just like other objects. The point is to stop us giving them magical powers, and hence highlight the circularities and redundancies that have so often marred the appeal to images. Thus

> as soon as you think of replacing the mental image by, say, a painted one, and as soon as the image thereby loses its occult character, it ceases to seem to impart any life to the sentence at all.

> (*BB*, p.5)

The 'life' of a sentence – that is, its meaning – must come from elsewhere. Something other than our capacity to form images must animate our words.

2.4 The rejection of mental acts

The critical arguments developed so far need not disturb a supporter of the theory of mental acts. Never having accorded much significance to our ability to form mental images, the act-theorist could easily concede Wittgenstein's point that, say, the mental image of a colour sample is very much on a par with the sample itself. Neither carry with them an indication of how they are to be used. This, it would be said, is the prerogative of a mental act. The essence of a mental state, properly so called, is that it possesses intentionality. Non-mental things by contrast, have merely external relations to one another, relations like spatial contiguity or relative movement. As one phenomenologist put it,

> this inner state of reference to and direction upon, this pointing of one thing to another, has no place in the scheme [of the natural sciences]. Physical things stand separate and self-contained; none points beyond itself in that peculiar sense which is made known to us by ideation.[10]

Images are just material to be informed by our intentions. Perhaps they are not even mental things at all, but should be considered as physiological states of our bodies and hence assimilated to physical things.[11] But what are these mental acts of meaning which now carry the theoretical burden? How do they work, and how does their presence alongside the use of a word give it meaning and the capacity to refer?

To throw light on these questions, and reveal the hollowness of the theory, Wittgenstein began by asking us to locate mental acts by introspection. 'Make the following experiment', he says:

> say and mean a sentence . . . Now think the same thought again, mean what you just meant, but without saying anything (either aloud or to yourself).

> (*BB*, p.42)

If meaning is a mental act accompanying our words, then exercises like this ought to separate out the two components. The implication is that they don't.

The second argument against mental acts used one of Wittgenstein's favourite devices: the number sequence. *A* writes down the first few terms of a sequence, say, 2, 4, 6, 8, etc., and tries to get *B* to continue the sequence in the same way. Suppose that *B* writes down 10, 12, 14, etc., until he gets to 1000. Here Wittgenstein considered what would happen if *B* does not then write 1002, 1004, 1006, but produces instead 1004, 1008, 1012, etc. *A* would object and say that this is not what he intended. Such a form of words would be perfectly natural but, to the act-theorist, it looks as if it referred to a specific act of meaning that *A* had engaged in. It suggests that he had thought about *B* putting 1004 instead of 1002, and willed that he should not make such a mistake. Notice that describing *A*'s response in this way requires a specific act of meaning for *each* member of the number series, i.e. for *each* point at which *B* might do other than *A* intended. This is why Wittgenstein's choice of example was so good. The number sequence is infinite, so the act-theorist will be led into saying that *A*'s original intention, though it looked simple enough, must have involved an *infinity* of subsidiary acts. Of course this argument is not logically decisive; the act-theorist might embrace this conclusion, but most of us will feel that something has gone wrong with a theory with these consequences (*PI*, I, 187-8).

The third argument is an application of the rule of externalisation. Let us investigate mental pointing, or intending, by looking at ordinary physical acts of pointing. What gives significance to an act of pointing with our finger? Suppose you point with your finger at a blue jumper and mean to refer to its colour, rather than its shape. How do we do this? (*BB*, p.80). Wittgenstein quickly rejects two answers. If we say that the physical pointing means the colour because it is accompanied by an act of inner, mental pointing, then we have explained nothing. The question once again becomes: how is mental pointing possible? A second possibility is that the act of meaning the colour is accomplished by narrowing our eyes and attending to it, ignoring other aspects of the object. We could make an effort to ignore the shape by deliberately *not* letting our eyes trace its outline. Wittgenstein allows that processes like these may take place, but argues that such recondite contortions of our consciousness cannot constitute something so simple as meaning the colour, but not the shape, of an object (*BB*, p.80).

To find out what is really going on we should ignore the subjective concomitants of the act of pointing and look at the pattern of behaviour into which it fits. To know what is meant by an act of pointing, to know the intention behind it, we need to know what *other* things would be classified alongside the object indicated. Point to a pencil and say 'tove', suggests Wittgenstein. What does 'tove' mean? Does it mean 'pencil', or 'brown', or 'thin', or something else? The only way to find out is to put the isolated act in the context of a protracted exercise in classification which begins to sort the world into 'toves' and 'non-toves'. This is how we would explain the meaning, and this is what enables us to say that something determinate, rather than nothing, is meant by the word. So this is the secret of how we can point to a jumper and mean its colour not its shape. The significance of a piece of pointing behaviour taken in isolation is indeed difficult to discern, but that is not because it is hidden in the mind, but because it depends on the surrounding activity. Its meaning is perfectly open to view, it is on the surface, but it is spread out over time and shared with others (*BB*, p.2; *PI*, I, 33, 34).[12]

2.5 The Würzburg connection

The arguments that have just been examined fit into a definite historical context. By 1900 experimental psychologists in Europe were divided into two opposing camps: one supporting the image theory, the other supporting the act theory.[13] This long-standing rivalry came to a head in what is known as the *imageless thought controversy*, which lasted from about 1900 well into the 1920s. S. E. Toulmin and W. W. Bartley have made the valuable suggestion that Wittgenstein's arguments should be understood in the light of this controversy. I agree, but think that they have misunderstood the relationship. It will be of some importance for my reading to spell out what I think is the real connection. First, I will give the general outlines of the controversy.

The psychology of content was dominated by the work of Wilhelm Wundt. He said that introspection showed that the content of the mind was a stream of sensations, images and feelings. Anything akin to 'pure thought' he rejected. Although Wundt was one of the founders of experimental psychology, he believed that the scope of experiment, and properly controlled introspection, was severely limited. The rigours of scientific method confined them to simple reactions and discriminations. The higher mental processes, Wundt declared, could only be studied by tracing psychological motives through the 'products of the common life ... language, myth and custom'.[14] Anthropology and history took over where the experimental method failed.

Some of Wundt's followers, however, evinced a greater faith in laboratory procedures. Working under the leadership of Oswald Külpe of Würzburg, a group consisting of Ach, Bühler and several others tried to extend the introspective method into the higher processes concerned with thought and meaning. The result was trouble for Wundt's theory, because they generated an anomaly. They gave their subjects tasks involving complex judgements: translating words, doing mental arithmetic, solving problems, and answering questions about the meanings of words or phrases. Their subjects were required to introspect on the mental processes that underlay their answers, describing the sequence of sensations, images and feelings that made up their thinking. It emerged that the answers to the problems set by the experimenter often seemed to come to mind without any accompanying imagery or content at all. In the place of the usual items floating into consciousness Külpe's group claimed to have discovered a new and special state of consciousness. It was not an image, or a feeling, or a sensation, but a kind of pure awareness of meaning: an imageless thought. They called it a *Bewusstseinslage*, or *Bsl* for short. If these *Bsl*s were not exactly acts of meaning they were very close. They were certainly meant to be states of consciousness that heralded an act of grasping or intending a meaning.[15]

Külpe had been a pupil of Wundt's, and the master's reaction to the betrayal was bitter. As far as Wundt was concerned it was a lapse into scholastic prejudices about mental acts. It was a sell-out to Brentano.[16] It would never have happened if the Würzburgers had kept within the proper bounds of the experimental method. Their results, argued Wundt, were mere artefacts caused by making observations under conditions where proper controls were impossible. Wundt turned with particular scorn on Karl Bühler because of the loose, conversational manner with which he gathered introspective data. He used a question-and-answer method which, to Wundt, blurred the crucial distinction between scientific procedures and the casual, unreliable introspections of everyday life:

> These experiments are not experiments at all in the sense of a scientific methodology; they are counterfeit experiments, that seem methodical simply because they are ordinarily performed in a psychological laboratory and involve the cooperation of two persons, who purport to be experimenter and observer.[17]

Despite this onslaught the work continued. Other laboratories said that their observers had also failed to find images when, on Wundt's theory, they should have done. A number of new and useful psychological concepts such as 'determining tendency' and 'set' began to emerge. Defenders of Wundt, like Titchener, said that if you looked carefully you always found some imagery and content. They said that the Würzburgers were making a simple technical error, called the stimulus error: they were not describing their thoughts, but the thing being thought about, so no wonder their reports of mental content were impoverished. Exchanges continued in books and journals, though as Titchener observed, it was throughout 'too warm for either comfort or dignity'.[18]

We can be confident that Wittgenstein knew about the image-less thought controversy. It was discussed in Russell's *The Analysis of Mind*, which contains a chapter giving quotations from the enraged Wundt. This book was one of the few works cited in Wittgenstein's *Blue and Brown Books*. (Russell, whose theory gave a star role to images, sided with Wundt.) As Toulmin and Bartley have pointed out, there were also personal links between Wittgenstein and the Würzburg group. After the First World War Bühler became a leading professor of psychology and pedagogy at the University of Vienna – at the very time when Wittgenstein had left the army and was in Vienna training to be a teacher. Bühler was present at the house of Wittgenstein's sister on the occasion of Wittgenstein's first meeting with the philosophers of the Vienna Circle. He had been invited by Wittgenstein's nephew, who was a pupil of the psychologist. On this basis both Toulmin and Bartley have suggested that we can understand Wittgenstein's criticism of the image theory by seeing him as working in the tradition of Külpe's and Bühler's theory of imageless thought.[19]

This is plausible when we consider the treatment in the *Blue and Brown Books* of what happens when we 'understand' a word. How are we to investigate this? To find out what happens, said Wittgenstein, 'we play this game'. Take a list of words, some familiar like 'house', others less familiar, like 'carburettor'; some from foreign languages, others, perhaps, made-up words:

> All these words are read out to me, and after each one I have to say 'Yes' or 'No' according to whether I understand the word or not. I then try to remember what happened in my mind when I understood the words I did understand, and when I didn't understand the others.

> (*BB*, pp.155-6)

No one who is familiar with the experimental procedures of the Würzburg group will miss their similarity to Wittgenstein's 'game'. We have the same carefully chosen list of stimuli in the form of words; we have the *Aufgabe* or task imposed on the subject; the response is given in the form of a judgement; finally an introspective report is provided to describe the mental processes that underlay the judgement. (The only things missing are those favourite props of early scientific psychology, the voice-key and the Hipp-chronoscope, to measure reaction times). When Wittgenstein summed up the result of this 'game', he actually called it an experiment:

> Now it may surprise us to find that although this experiment will show us a multitude of different characteristic experiences, it will not show us any one experience which we should be in-clined to call the experience of understanding.

> (*BB*, p.156)

To justify this Wittgenstein gave a lengthy, Würzburg-style, intros-pective protocol of the kind he thought would issue from such an experiment. He concluded by reaffirming the basic idea of image-less thoughts: 'There will, on the other hand, be a large class of cases in which I am not aware of anything happening except hearing the word and saying the answer' (*BB*, p.156). These are close and intriguing connections. There can be no doubt that Wittgenstein's language and style came straight from psychologists of the kind who took part in the controversy. Nevertheless it would be wrong to explain what he was doing by presenting him as an advocate of the Würzburg doctrines in general or Bühler's theories in particular. He may have accepted Würzburg-style data about the absence of images, but he certainly did not embrace their positive doctrines. In fact he discussed in detail some of the most characteristic claims of the Würzburg group and dismissed them.

Consider, for example, what Bühler and Ach have to say about following a rule. Bühler claimed that there was something called 'awareness of rule' which he held to be a characteristic state of mind. It involved grasping its meaning and being guided by it. Similarly Ach claimed that there was a specific *Bsl*, or a state of consciousness which was devoid of images, which amounted to an awareness of determination. Wittgenstein never mentioned the names of Bühler or Ach in this connection, but he frequently discussed the case of being guided, and of rule following, and always rejected the idea of any characteristic form of awareness (*BB*, pp.99-100, 118, 122-5; *PI*, I, 175-8). The same goes for the experience of sudden understanding or the dawning realisation of a meaning or a solution to a problem. This was something frequently reported by the subjects in the Würzburg experiments. A question was posed, no pictures came to the mind, but suddenly the answer came into consciousness. The experience of sudden insight was deemed to be a specific *Bsl*, or imageless thought. Wittgenstein frequently reverted to this theme, but always with the idea of diminishing its significance (*PI*, I, 138-9, 151-5, 191, 197, 318, 319).[20] Perhaps the fullest attack on a Würzburg doctrine concerned the question of whether, when words come into our mind, they do so attended by a characteristic state of consciousness. For example, when we name the colours of things, do the colour words come in a particular way? For the Würzburgers there is a special atmosphere, a diffuse *Bsl*. In a passage that anticipates his famous attack on private languages Wittgenstein took issue with this:

> when I say 'red' comes in a particular way ... I feel that I might now give this way a name if it hasn't already got one, say, '*A*'. But at the same time I am not at all prepared to say that I recognise this to be the way 'red' has always come on such occasions.

(BB, p.159)

What, then, was Wittgenstein's connection with the imageless thought controversy? The fact is that he rejected both sides. He was equidistant from both parties. This was because the insight he was looking for was not to be got by taking sides in the debate, but only by stepping back from it. He was challenging the psychologistic assumptions common to both positions and trying to lift the issue out of the psychological realm altogether. His purpose would not be served simply by replacing one psychological account of meaning by another psychological account of meaning.

Now let me sum up, and assess how far these arguments have taken us. Wittgenstein has been clearing the ground and identifying mistakes and circularities in the accepted psychological approaches. When we first posed our questions about the nature of meaning we seemed, said Wittgenstein, to be asking about the states of mind of a person who uttered a word or sentence, 'whereas the idea of meaning we arrived at in the end was not that of a state of mind' (*BB*, p.78). What, though, are we going to say about all the subjective feelings, images and states of consciousness that attend the meaningful use of words and gestures (or what Wittgenstein sometimes called 'signs')? According to the theories that have just been rejected, these inner events were the causes of the outward performances. If they are to be denied this role, then what status do they have? Wittgenstein's answer was that they are mere by-products. They are not the causes of our ability to use words or signs, they are the effects of that ability. Wittgenstein therefore reversed the direction of causality assumed in psychological theories of meaning and said: 'the mental experiences which accompany the use of a sign undoubtedly are caused by our usage of the sign in a particular system of language' (*BB*, p.78). The primary thing, therefore, is the systematic pattern of usage. This is something public and shared, not something that is private.

If the subjective experiences associated with language use are really caused by that use, rather than being causes of it, why do we credit them with strange and extensive powers? Why do our mental images and our acts of intention seem to be endowed with remarkable potency, as if they 'take place in a queer kind of medium' and 'can bring about effects which no material mechanism could' (*BB*, p.3)? To answer these questions Wittgenstein took his hypothesis a stage further. He suggested that these seeming powers are the result of a process of condensation. The properties imputed to mental acts, such as, for instance, the acts involved in pointing and naming, derive from taking the complex body of shared practices associated with the use of the name and concentrating them into that one event. We assume that, somehow, the practices are all contained in the act of naming, like a plant in a seed. The relation of the name to the object then becomes charged with mystery:

A primitive philosophy condenses the whole usage of the name into the idea of a relation, which thereby becomes a mysterious relation. (Compare the ideas of mental activities, wishing, believing, thinking, etc., which for the same reason have something mysterious and inexplicable about them.)

(*BB*, p.173)

No wonder that the mind is an uncanny thing. The strange properties of mental states derive from the fact that they are really properties of groups of people which have been imputed to individuals or individual actions.

The language in which Wittgenstein described the outcome of this process of condensation is intriguing. We have already seen him refer to mental states as 'occult' and as 'life'-giving, and as queer mechanisms that take place in a 'queer medium'. But he also said that we think of them as belonging to 'the upper strata of the atmosphere as opposed to the material phenomena which happen on the ground' (*BB*, p.47). Naming, he said, becomes a 'sacramental act' creating a 'magic relation' (*BB*, p.172). Language itself assumes a dual aspect, with an 'inorganic part' consisting of its physical embodiment in written and spoken signs, and an 'organic part' which is the mental process of understanding and meaning – remember Russell's reference to words without images being mere counters (*BB*, p.172). By consistently using this kind of language, Wittgenstein was surely deliberately invoking the distinction between the sacred and the profane. We can appreciate the significance of him doing this if we place his suggestions in the context of Durkheim's earlier treatment of these themes.[21] Durkheim analysed not 'primitive philosophy' but primitive religion. God, he said, was really the social collectivity. Sacred objects were invested with strange powers because they were symbolic of the power of the social group over the individual. The attributes of divinities are explicable when we see them as descriptions of society: that is why they are everywhere and nowhere, real but invisible, external and yet within us. The strange claims of the believer were not simple errors, Durkheim insisted, because something real answered to them. They were ways of apprehending society, but they required decoding and explaining. In the same way psychologistic theories of meaning represent mythical transfigurations of collective processes. They are perhaps as natural as religion itself. Given, also, the difficulty of apprehending the real character of our own social behaviour, because we are so close to it, it is perhaps no surprise that Wittgenstein's 'disease of thinking' is indeed a general disease.

Whatever the ultimate fate of Wittgenstein's Durkheimean hypotheses, we are now in a position to see that the real source of 'life' in a word or sentence is provided, not by the individual mind, but by society. They are animated with meaning because of the social practices of which they are an integral part. Wittgenstein makes the point explicitly: 'if we had to name anything which is the life of the sign', he said, 'we should have to say that it was its *use*' (*BB*, p.4). It is this idea of use that lies at the heart of his non-psychological approach to meaning. The unit of analysis that he adopted in order to grasp patterns of usage was something that he called a 'language-game'. I shall now explain what a language-game is.

3

Language-Games and the Stream of Life

In the *Blue and Brown Books* Wittgenstein introduced the idea of language-games by saying that they are 'the forms of language with which a child begins to make use of words' (*BB*, p.17). To study them, he said, is to study primitive forms of language, and primitive languages. The point is to ensure that matters of principle stand out clearly. One such principle is that linguistic responses can only be understood if we see how they are integrated into patterns of activity. 'Only in the stream of thought and life do words have meaning' (*Z*, 173). Meaning is located in the function that words have as 'signals' passed back and forth between people in the course of purposeful and shared activity (*PI*, I, 180; *Z*, 601). 'Here the term "language-*game*" is meant to bring into prominence the fact that the *speaking* of language is part of an activity or of a form of life' (*PI*, I, 23). Many of Wittgenstein's examples involve work and labour. One language-game he describes in some detail involves a builder, called *A*, and his helper, *B*.

3.1 Wittgenstein's builders

B's job is to pass *A* stones of various kinds: bricks, slabs, columns, etc. The language-game is one in which *A* communicates with *B*. *A* shouts 'slab!', and *B* passes him a stone of the required shape. Words like 'red' or 'blue' may have a place in the game, so that *A* can shout 'red slab!', and *B* will pass slabs of a certain colour. The game may also contain conventions about the order of words, so that if *A* said 'slab; column; brick', this means that *B* is to bring them in a definite order. Signs having the function of numerals could be introduced. *B* could learn the alphabet off by heart, and when *A* shouts 'd slabs!', *B* could chant the letters a, b, c, d, and bring a slab for each letter. The game could be developed yet further by finding a role for words that act like proper names. Suppose that there is a mark 'H' on the hammer that *A* uses. *A* shows *B* the mark, and *B* fetches the object marked 'H'. Words like 'this' and 'there' could be used in the course of pointing to objects, and moving them from place to place.[1]

This game brings out the different ways that words carry meaning and relate to the world. 'Slab' and 'brick' function quite differently from 'this' and 'there'. They reflect different aspects of *A*'s interaction with *B* and their commerce with the objects around them. The word 'red' mediates a different facet of their behaviour from, say, the counting words: 'by introducing numerals we have introduced an entirely different *kind* of instrument into our language' (*BB*, p.79). The metaphor of words as instruments or tools is one of Wittgenstein's favourites. By reminding us of the variety of objects in a tool-box, the hammers, saws, screwdrivers, glue and glue-pot, ruler and plumb-line, he drives home the theme of functional diversity (*PI*, 11, 12). The point is that a theory that postulates a single, unique relationship between language and the world will never come to terms with the subtle involvement of language and life. It will produce abstract and uninformative generalities – like trying to describe the use of all the different tools by a single formula. We can say, of course, that all tools serve to 'modify' something. The hammer modifies the position of the nail, the saw modifies the shape of the wood, and, presumably, the ruler modifies our knowledge of the wood's length. But nothing worthwhile follows from this way of speaking (*PI*, I, 14).

As an example of a stultifying theory of this kind, Wittgenstein takes the idea that the meaning of a word is what it stands for. The relation of 'standing for' is assumed to be like that between a proper name and the object named. Wittgenstein argued that even if we allow that proper names can be said to have meaning, we still cannot use the formula: meaning equals thing named. The notion of meaning is being used illicitly (*PI*, I, 37-42). Taken seriously, the formula would imply that if *A*'s hammer broke, then the meaning of the symbol 'H' had broken. But when someone dies, we do not say that his name dies too (*PI*, I, 40). The oddity of these locutions suggests that all is not well. What has gone wrong is that something has not even got a name except in the context of a language-game. The emphasis on the word-object link needs to be supplemented by an awareness of the context in which the word is used. We must remember the activities it mediates, then the dominance of the formula will be broken. In place of such theories Wittgenstein puts the idea of 'use'. 'For a *large* class of cases – though not for all – in which we employ the word 'meaning' it can be defined thus: the meaning of a word is its use in the language' (*PI*, I, 43).

Consider the counting words used by the builders: the letters, a, b, c, etc. The naming-theory inclines us to ask: what things do these signs stand for? We might then be tempted to invent quasi-objects, called numbers, for them to name. On the use-theory we do not have this temptation. The only meaning the symbols have is open to view, residing in the use the builders give them. It is possible that interesting feelings attend the use of the counting words. Perhaps the regularity of their use, or the uniformity of the context, creates a strong sense that the words do stand for something. A feeling of thinghood might linger about them. But if this were so, it would just be part of the data to be explained. It would be a problematic fact about the phenomenology of counting. To treat it as if it were a revelation about the essence of number would be a grave mistake (*PI*, I, 254).

3.2   Complete systems of communication

In the example of the builders, each verbal signal has its role, and each facet of activity has all that it needs by way of verbal expression – at least as far as the speakers are concerned. This is the case on which Wittgenstein wants us to concentrate. We are not to think of the builders' language-game as a fragment of language. It is not, he says, an incomplete part of language. We must think of language-games 'as languages complete in themselves, as complete systems of human communication' (*BB*, p.81). To do this he recommends that we imagine the language-game to be the 'entire system of communication of a tribe in a primitive state of society' (*BB*, p.81). We may be inclined to protest at this fiction on the grounds that the builders' language is implausibly truncated: it mainly consists of orders. Wittgenstein would reply: 'ask yourself whether our language is complete' (*PI*, I, 18). His point is that any language could be made out to be incomplete, so that all languages stand on a par with one another in this respect. This being so, we could equally reverse the point and treat any language as complete if it satisfies its users.

It might appear that in making this claim Wittgenstein is trying to push us in the direction of a static picture of language. In fact he does not hold a particularly static view. He is completely at home with the idea that the multiplicity of language-games is not fixed once and for all: 'new types of language, new language-games, as we say, come into existence, and others become obsolete and get forgotten. (We can get a *rough picture* of this from the changes in mathematics.)' (*PI*, I, 23).

The idea of completeness is, in fact, introduced as a device to make us aware of change. It throws into relief what happens when a language-game is modified. It does this by making all change look like an arbitrary act of addition. If something is complete it can have no inner principles of change that require it to be developed in this way or that. Wittgenstein makes the same point by drawing an analogy between the growth of language and the growth of a town. A town, he says, has a maze of little streets and squares at its centre, with old and new houses, and houses with modifications from different periods. Then, as we travel to the outskirts, we find new boroughs with regular streets and uniform houses (*PI*, I, 18). This clearly captures the *ad hoc* nature of the whole, with its growth reflecting historical contingencies. The changing styles speak of changing needs, fashions and circumstances. Extensions and alterations are not simply determined by what is already there. Nor can we say, in abstraction from the purposes of its inhabitants, that a town is ever complete, or that it is intrinsically incomplete.

The point that is being made is central to the later philosophy and its relation to sociology. To fix it in mind it may be useful to introduce a piece of terminology. I shall refer to it as Wittgenstein's 'finitism'. This is the thesis that the established meaning of a word does not determine its future applications. The development of a language-game is not determined by its past verbal form. Meaning is created by acts of use. Like the town, it is constructed as we go along. Use determines meaning; meaning does not determine use. The label 'finitism' is appropriate because we are to think of meaning extending as far as, but no further than, the finite range of circumstances in which a word is used. Beyond these current precedents, meaning, application and reference are not yet determined.[2] Now let us explore some of the ramifications of this thesis.

3.3   Training and translation

Introducing a child to an existing language-game involves shaping spontaneous behaviour by examples, rewards and punishments. It involves training. 'I am using the word 'trained' in a way strictly analogous to that in which we talk of an animal being trained to do certain things' (*BB*, p.77). The success or failure of the enterprise depends on the child's instinctive tendencies to react. Dogs can be taught to retrieve; cats cannot. Children can be encouraged to repeat words and to make verbal responses to people and objects. They then instinctively harness these skills to the expression of their wants; and at the same time these wants are themselves being shaped. The relative uniformity of the responses that children make to training provides the foundation for all language-games. It is one part of the uniformity of judgement upon which communication depends, though as we shall see, it is not the whole of what is involved. 'If language is to be a means of communication', said Wittgenstein, 'there must be agreement not only in definitions but also . . . in judgements' (*PI*, I, 242).

These observations apply not only to language-games, with words like 'pain', which we might readily connect with instinctive responses, but also to language-games that express the refinements of reasoning and inference. These points will all be examined in detail later, but I will give them a first statement now. We must remember, said Wittgenstein, that being sure that someone else is in pain, or doubting the fact, is a natural, instinctive kind of behaviour,

> and our language is merely an auxilliary to, and further extension of, this relation. Our language-game is an extension of primitive behaviour. (For our *language-game* is behaviour) (Instinct).
>
> (*Z*, 545)[3]

(By 'primitive' Wittgenstein here means 'pre-linguistic'.) The same applies to the 'scruples' in our thinking: our sense of logicality, our intuitions about the soundness of our reasoning, and matters of relevance and evidential weight. These, too, have to begin with instinct and emerge from something non-linguistic. Hence, 'a language-game does not have its origins in *considera-tion*. Consideration is part of a language-game' (*Z*, 391). Training and instinct, then, provide the starting point of all our expla-nations, and the terminus of all our justifications. Explanation is only possible, insists Wittgenstein, after training has been success-ful (*Z*, 419).

The fundamental character of training, and the derivative character of explanation, may seem obvious. In practice it is easy to lose track of the point. One reason is that processes of pointing, or ostension, play a role both in training and in explaining. Sup-pose a child knows the names of some colours but not others. He asks: 'What colour is Prussian Blue?', and gets the answer, 'That is' – accompanied by a pointing gesture towards a passing Prus-sian. This would be a genuine ostensive definition, but of course the framework which makes the explanation possible could not itself have been acquired in the same way: 'the ostensive definition explains the use – the meaning – of the word when the overall role of the word in language is clear' (*PI*, I, 30). Confusing ostensive training with ostensive definition makes it look as if all language learning is a form of translation:

> as if the child comes into a strange country and did not under-stand the language of the country; that is, as if it already had a language, only not this one. Or again: as if the child could already *think*, only not yet speak. And 'think' would here mean something like 'talk to itself'.
>
> (*PI*, I, 32)

Here is the source of the illusion that the doctrine of finitism was meant to banish. I am referring to the illusion that meaning deter-mines subsequent usage, and that these future applications are already implicit in what has gone before. This is an idea that would derive support from the assumption that language-users *already* possess a language in advance of the creation of language-games: as if all our unknown, future experience had already been linguisti-cally processed. Then we would just read off the correct application of our concepts as our experience unfolds. Our response to the world would be a response to a text, and our verbal rendering of experience would be a process of translation. But, insists Wittgenstein, 'words are not a translation of something else that was there before they were' (Z, 191). The point is not that there is nothing in the world but words. The point is that words are ultimately connected to the world by training, not by translation.

If the semantics of finitism is to be taken seriously the rival view must be attacked directly. At the heart of the rival view is the idea that predicates have associated with them a 'reference class' or 'extension'. The extension of a word is the class of all things of which it may be truly predicated. The extension of 'water' is everything, known and unknown, that could truly be called water. The extension of a word is generally assumed to stretch far beyond the finite boundary of existing applications. It is therefore necessary to see if the idea is tenable or whether it should be rejected. This issue is best approached by looking at language-games that are concerned with the important activity of classification.

3.4 Extensions and frontiers

How do we learn to apply labels to things and group them into kinds and classes? Clearly we are trained by the use of examples selected by our teachers. As spokesmen of the local culture they convey to us that this, and similar things, are to be counted as the same for the practical purposes of the language-game. We learn that *this* and *this* is water, while *that* is wine. All that the learner has access to are a few representatives of the class to be picked out by the word. When he learns to co-ordinate these samples with representatives of other classes that are to be discriminated from them, here again, he only has a few cases to work with. Wittgenstein points out that in this respect the position of the pupil is not fundamentally different from that of the teacher. When the teacher points to a sample and says that this and similar things are water, he knows no more than this himself (*PI*, I, 69 and 208-9). He may know a greater number of locally accepted examples but, like the pupil, he has no access to the totality of things that might come to be deemed 'water'. The extension of the class, as such, can play no role in the proceedings. The teacher's knowledge, we might be tempted to say, is incomplete, just like that of everybody else.[4]

From the fact that usage is established and transmitted on the basis of 'this and similar', Wittgenstein concluded that the concepts in a language-game are 'uncircumscribed' (*PI*, I, 70). They work in the absence of known boundaries to their extension or reference class. He expressed this by saying that 'the extension of a concept is not closed by a frontier' (*PI*, I, 68). This way of putting the matter disguises the radical character of the point. Wittgenstein was not simply modifying the concept of extension; he was destroying it. The picture that goes with the idea of an extension is that of an idealised, closed sphere enveloping everything to which a word properly applies. And from this point of view, an 'enclosure with a hole in it is as good as *none*' (*PI*, I, 99).[5]

By blithely assuming that we can make reference to the totality of objects that will, or should, belong to a class, the real problem is ignored. This is the problem of describing and explaining the contingent step from one accepted application of a word to the next accepted application. Instead of seeing this transition as problematic, we treat ourselves to the vision of the future applications of a word – its extension – stretching ahead of the limited scope of actual usage. In our imagination we move to the completed task of classification, as if we can accomplish in thought what we will never achieve in practice. But, as Wittgenstein put it, 'the assumption of a shadow of a transition does not get us any further, because it does not bridge the gulf between it and the real transition' (*BB*, p.143). Wittgenstein explored the contingencies of this 'real transition' by means of a number of devices: the doctrine of family resemblances, the interaction between what he calls 'criteria' and 'symptoms', and some brief remarks about the various 'needs' that may be expressed in language-games and symbolic notations. I shall now examine each of these in turn.

3.5 Family resemblances

There are a number of standard and traditional accounts of how a word comes to be applied to new cases. For example, the transition to the new application may be said to result from our apprehending a 'universal' that is present in the new particular that is awaiting classification. Or we may be said to grasp the 'essence' of the new case. These theories suppose that we can come to know that diverse things share a common ingredient, or a common property, and this explains our grouping them together under the same heading. Wittgenstein's aim was to make the idea of universals, essences, ingredients and properties as problematic as possible. His theory of concept application was based on judgements of similarity made within a language-game, and it was meant to replace the traditional accounts. He therefore tried to show how we can co-classify objects, reapply our predicates, and make the transition from old to new cases, without recourse to any common properties in the explanation. First I shall outline the main ideas in his alternative account and then show how it can be generalised. The question of the generality of his theory has prompted a number of objections and I shall have to confront these difficulties as I go along.

If we examine the instances that fall under our concepts, said Wittgenstein, we often find that there is not a property common to all the members in virtue of which we grouped them together. Instead we see 'a complicated network of similarities overlapping and criss-crossing: sometimes overall similarities, sometimes similarities of detail'(*PI*, I, 66). He said that he could think of no better way of describing the basis of the grouping than by the metaphor of 'family resemblances'. The various members of a family who resemble one another do not necessarily do so because they all possess a single feature in common, like a snub nose. More often the impression of resemblance comes from the fact that, say, a daughter has her father's chin, while her son has her nose but an uncle's hair, and so on.

As an example Wittgenstein cited the case of games. He asked us to look at board games and to notice all the similarities and differences between them; then to look at card games, ball games, children's street games, and so on. Notice how some features drop out and others appear. A second, strategically chosen, example was the concept of language itself. Don't think of language as having an essence. It is made up of a number of different language-games. These

> phenomena have no one thing in common which makes us use the same word for all, – but ... they are *related* to one another

in many different ways. And it is because of this relationship, or these relationships, that we call them all 'language'.

(*PI*, I, 65)

Notice the careful phrasing. We count different language-games as instances of the concept 'language', so that we could, if we wish, say that they all had something in common: they are all uses of language. The point, though, is that they have no one thing in common 'which makes us use the same word for all'. Their common property is the *result* of their being assigned to the same class, not the *cause*.

Family-resemblance concepts abound in the classificatory language of history, especially the history of culture and art. Think, for example, how philosophers are grouped into schools, or paintings into styles. This field provided Wittgenstein with an early application of the idea. Instead of saying, with Oswald Spengler, that all the cultural manifestations of an epoch shared the same 'spirit', which might be construed as a rather mysterious common feature, Wittgenstein declared,

> Spengler could be better understood if he said: I am *comparing* different cultural epochs with the lives of families; within a family there is a family resemblance, though you will also find a resemblance between members of different families . . . we have to be told the object of comparison, the object from which this way of viewing things is derived.

(*CV*, p.14)[6]

Despite the plausibility and utility of the idea of family-resemblance concepts there have been objections raised against the whole idea. It has been claimed that there are, in fact, no concepts at all that have this structure. Nothing, it has been said, could answer to this description, because any such concept would suffer from a fatal defect that would make it unusable. It would face the 'problem of wide-open texture'. The point is that if we allow ourselves to exploit all kinds of criss-crossing similarities, and if we shift the respect in which things are judged similar, then our groupings would eventually include everything. A knife is like a fork because they are both used for eating; but they are both like a screwdriver because they are metallic and rather sharp; but then a screwdriver is like an umbrella because it is long and thin and has a handle; and an umbrella is like a parachute; and so on. Such concepts would have no constraints and register no discriminations. This objection was first formulated by the psychologist L. S. Vygotsky, who arrived at the idea of family-resemblance groupings at about the same time as Wittgenstein. He said that they were pseudo-concepts, characteristic of a particular stage of child development. The genuine concepts used by adults, Vygotsky declared, classify things in a disciplined fashion, avoiding chain-like connections and syncretic groupings. Single, unitary properties are used, or orderly and fixed combinations of these.[7]

This criticism is not to be dismissed, but it is not correct. If our groupings were, indeed, purely the result of our fluctuating sense of similarity, then there probably would be no order in them. But Wittgenstein's theory is not just a resemblance theory: it is a *family*-resemblance theory. His comments on Spengler brought out this fact. This means that as well as resemblance there should be some other factors which play the role of ancestral connections.[8] Something must link the resemblances through time, and differentiate 'within-family' from 'cross-family' resemblances. There are in fact two things in the account that do this. First, judgements of resemblance are focused around accepted paradigm cases. These are the 'objects of comparison' referred to in the comment on Spengler. Second, resemblances are always judged in the context of a particular language-game. These provide a horizon and a sense of relevance that reinforces some, but not other, similarities. The words 'knife' and 'fork' have a use that is integrated into the rituals of eating. The word 'screwdriver' is part of another activity and another language-game. So ancestral links are tacitly present in the precedents and purposes built into specific language-games. We must not forget the matrix of non-linguistic action.

While there is certainly a strong element of open-texture in Wittgenstein's family-resemblance theory it does not, then, fall into the trap of 'wide-open texture'. It is saved from this mistake by the social conventions that are implicit in every language-game. Whereas the traditional accounts of concept application seek to avoid the chaos of wide-open texture by the idea that we can grasp properties or essences, Wittgenstein avoids it by assuming that language-users are trained in a body of conventionalised practice. The concept-user must learn how a similarity here trades off against a difference there. The untidy, criss-crossing of resemblances between the cases that are to be classified clearly shows the need for decisions and judgements. Communication requires that these be aligned, and for this purpose locally accepted standards of relevance must be used. What the family-resemblance theory does, therefore, is to bring out in a clear and simple way the social and conventional aspects of concept application.

3.6   How general is this theory?

Do all concepts have a family-resemblance structure? Critics of Wittgenstein say that they do not, and they conclude from this that the idea of family resemblances has a very limited power to illuminate the process of concept application.[9] Surely, they say, we can and do locate common properties, and we can and do use them in our classifications and in the application of concepts. Two sorts of counter-example feature prominently in this argument. First, there are the common properties that we seem to intuit directly, for example the colours of things. Here our perceptual apparatus seems to reveal the essence of blueness or redness in a direct and unproblematic way. Second, we seem to grasp some of the properties and essences of things through what may, loosely, be called the workings of the intellect. Don't the methodical operations of science reveal some of the ultimate ingredients of things to us? In other words: some common properties we can just see, others we discover. I shall look at each of these claims in turn and assess their significance for the theory of family resemblances. What is at stake in this discussion is, of course, the generality of the claim that concept application has a conventional character of a deep and significant kind. If the transition from one application of a concept to another can be mediated by our perceptual or intellectual apparatus, without crucially depending on local conventions, then the project of building a social theory of knowledge had better be abandoned.

Consider, first, the argument from science. Family-resemblance concepts, it is said, may be tolerated in daily life or cultural affairs, but they are not good enough for the scientist. They are vague and allow exceptions, and this would make it impossible to formulate laws of nature. As an example take the law of constant proportions in chemistry. This says that all samples of a given chemical compound will combine their ingredients in the same proportions. The law has the general form: All As are B. But if all As are B, then all the members of the class A have a common property, namely B. By Wittgenstein's own definition this means that A is not a family-resemblance concept. Therefore not all concepts have this structure. QED. As one critic has put it, in chemistry 'there has been a long search for adequate replacements for the family resemblance predicates picking out natural substances'. The observed patterns on the surface of phenomena must be referred to a 'natural ground' and this means finding concepts where 'all members of the reference class have something in common'. That we can move towards this goal, says the critic, is 'our faith', and he concludes by telling us that 'we should not rest content until family resemblance predicates . . . have been banished from our science'.[10]

Clearly, not every concept, at every point in its history, has a family-resemblance structure. That cannot be the way to claim generality for Wittgenstein's picture. We must stick to the point about the conventional character of concept application. And this is just the point that is in danger of getting lost amid the calls to banish family-resemblance concepts from science. As an attempt to limit the scope of the family-resemblance doctrine, it rests on a quite unrealistic picture of scientific procedure. To show this I shall take some material from Ludwik Fleck's pioneering study *Genesis and Development of a Scientific Fact*.[11] This deals with the emergence of the modern concept of the disease entity we call syphilis.

The idea of the disease can be traced back to the fifteenth century when it emerged from a jumble of facts and beliefs about chronic illnesses and skin complaints. Looking back we see that the early concepts did not distinguish between syphilis and leprosy, scabies, tuberculosis, smallpox, gonorrhoea, soft chancres and a variety of other conditions, some of which are still counted as non-specific. Eventually, however, there emerged a concept with two main components: one quasi-moral, the other empirical. The idea developed of a disease that was at once a carnal scourge and also a condition that could be treated by mercury compounds.

We now know that gonorrhoea does not respond to mercury, so it does not surprise us to find ancient authorities remarking on the irregularity of the response of the disease to treatment.[12] In the eighteenth and early nineteenth centuries there were extensive debates about the classification of the disease. Experimental evidence introduced further complications and more permutations and combinations of symptoms. Nevertheless, said Fleck, there was a search for a single, common factor. This focused on the allegedly befouled blood of the syphilitic patient – an idea that was derived from the old theory of humours.[13] Blood-tests became the goal. Time and again the claim was made that the specific character of syphilitic blood had been isolated, and time and again others failed to repeat the result.[14] This situation changed in 1905 with the detection of *Spirochaeta pallida* and the conclusion that here was the causative agent in syphilis. The concept of the disease then became organised around this discovery. For instance, finding this organism in the lymphatic ducts of patients soon after infection meant that, even in its early stages, syphilis could no longer be regarded as a localised disease. An issue that had long been disputed could now be settled. In this and in many other ways, order was made out of chaos.

If we were to follow the critics of the family-resemblance theory who appeal to the workings of science, this is where the story ought to stop. We have seen the early classifications with their loose groupings based on a criss-cross of superficial similarities. We have seen the triumphant search for common factors and reliable generalisations. We have seen the emergence of clear categorisations based solely on the presence of *Spirochaeta pallida* as the common factor. This is not, however, where the story really stops, and it was one of the aims of Fleck's book to show why. As a scientist trained and working in this field, Fleck spoke with some authority.

Instead of thinking of the discovery of *Spirochaeta pallida* as representing a natural finishing point, we should see that it is merely the beginning of the same process all over again. How do we know, for example, that the presence of the spirochaete isn't a symptom of the disease rather than its cause?[15] What are we to make of the fact that some persons can be carriers of the spirochaete without any signs of clinical illness? Again there is the significant fact that *Spirochaeta pallida* are biologically very like

Spirochaeta cuniculi, *Spirochaeta pallidula*, *Spirochaeta dentium*, and others. How are they to be distinguished? Animal tests have to be used. But that means that *Spirochaeta pallida* is being defined by syphilis, rather than the other way round – which was supposed to have been the outcome of the research. If we try to avoid this circular procedure by resort to a classification of spirochaete species we run into other serious trouble. Bacteriological species are very problematic and their lines of classification show no convergence with those of pathology.[16]

It therefore cannot claimed that syphilis is definable epistemologically solely on the basis of *Spirochaeta pallida*. The idea of the syphilis agent leads into uncertainties attending the concept of bacteriological species as such and will thus depend upon whatever future developments there may be in this field.[17]

As the concept of syphilis changed, said Fleck, new problems arose and new fields of research were established – which had all the same features as the old ones. Just as Wittgenstein indicated that our language is not 'complete', so Fleck concluded that 'nothing here was really completed'.[18]

The overall picture is one of oscillation. Complexity gives way to simplicity, only to give way again to complexity. Family-resemblance concepts give way to concepts that pick out common properties, which in turn give way to more family-resemblance concepts. Each stage counts as progress. Scientists may indeed strive to remove family-resemblance concepts in their search for causes and laws, but their research is ever revealing the similarities between different kinds of thing, and differences between things of the same kind. So the idea that science is governed by the principle that family-resemblance concepts are to be progressively eliminated is, at best, only half the story. In fact, says Fleck, every scientific theory goes through two phases. The first is the 'classic' phase when everything seems to fit. The second is when anomalies come to the fore again.[19] The observation is indeed a general one. There is nothing in my choice of example that is particularly unfavourable to Wittgenstein's critics. Instead of medical science I could have chosen, say, chemistry. Exactly the same pattern applies to the law of constant proportions: chaotic origin, order and success, and then more counter-instances.[20]

The injunction to banish family-resemblance concepts is really the injunction to stop doing science. This is why, despite the thrust of the previous argument, some of the most obvious examples of non-family-resemblance concepts are to be found in daily life. We can say that all brothers are male, and use the common property of maleness as proof that brother is not a family-resemblance concept. This is because we allow ourselves to stop at the habits and conventions of everyday usage. But once the concept of 'maleness' becomes involved in speculation or research about the nature of sexuality, its simplicity vanishes like the morning dew.[21] Exactly the same gradient from complexity to simplicity can be found within science itself. Practitioners at the research front have to engage with endless troubles of the kind that Fleck portrayed so well. By the time their work reaches the textbooks, and the esoteric has become the exoteric, the subtleties have been excluded. Certainty and simplicity, says Fleck, increase with distance from the reality of scientific practice.[22] So when we come across concepts that do not possess the characteristic family-resemblance structure we must not assume that, at last, a conventional classification has given way to a concept that reflects the natural division of things, or corresponds to their 'natural ground'. All concepts could easily come to assume a family-resemblance structure, and a further study of their instances will often reveal, quite readily, the criss-crossing of similarities and differences to which Wittgenstein drew our attention. The point could, perhaps, be expressed like this: until they become protected by habit and routine, the concepts that pick out common properties have to be actively sustained in the face of complexity. The work that maintains this cognitive order is, of course, the very same work that maintains social order. This is because common-property concepts are as dependent on convention as family-resemblance concepts; they too have no life other than that given to them by the language-game.

The clash between Wittgenstein and his critics may, in some measure, reflect rival metaphysical assumptions. Recall that the critic of family-resemblance theory declared that it was 'our faith' that we could align our concepts with the 'natural ground' of things. But suppose that nature provided no anchor-points and no natural divisions. Then we would have to see all boundaries as artefacts and wonder how we contrived to keep them in place. We would always expect counter-examples and be puzzled if people managed to keep them at bay. This is a 'faith' very different from the one that was said, rightly or wrongly, to underlie our science. All essences would then be the result of convention, and we might be tempted to say that the natural state of all concepts would be that of a family-resemblance grouping. There is some evidence that this is how Wittgenstein saw things. He certainly spoke of reality as something dark and unfathomable: 'Why should not order proceed, so to speak, out of chaos?' (Z, 608). In a similar vein he wonders whether 'an organism might come into being even out of something quite amorphous' (Z, 608). Fortunately we are not obliged to reach any decision on the truth of these metaphysical faiths. We can, though, assess them for their methodological significance. One useful consequence of Wittgenstein's stance is that it provides a way of distancing ourselves from any set of knowledge claims; it robs them of their self-evidence and finality, and this can often help to make their social components more visible. This, of course, does not mean that it is true. Perhaps reality is rigidly law-like and structured by essences, but it might be so complicated that, for many purposes, the deductions from Wittgenstein's view turn out to be correct. Such a stance certainly seems to make sense of the history of science.

3.7   Patricians and plebeians

There is just one more point about family resemblances that must be dealt with. In a sense, family-resemblance concepts actually presuppose the existence of non-family-resemblance concepts. If we group things according to a criss-cross of overlapping features, rather than a common feature, we still have to be able to pick out the features in question. So what about the concepts that refer to these? These pick out a single property, so we might be tempted to say that, underlying family-resemblance concepts, there is a layer of simple or basic concepts. We have already seen that, in principle, this does not blunt the important point that Wittgenstein was making, because the level at which we stop drawing distinctions and discriminations – the level at which we find simplicity – is itself a matter of convention. This is why, when Wittgenstein broke down the concept of 'game' into a set of instances with overlapping features, he immediately dissolved each of these features into a set of non-identical particulars. Some games involve skill and others don't, but skill in chess is different from skill in tennis. So perhaps the feature referred to as 'skill' could, if we cared to build up the discriminations, be broken down into a set of instances related in a family resemblance fashion.

Wittgenstein won't even allow to the traditional theory the idea that the relation of 'similarity' is a unitary, homogeneous thing that might have a determinate essence. This, of course, is the point at which the traditional theory tries to creep in at the back door. Those who try to get rid of universals by using the idea of similarity are told that they are really presupposing at least one universal, namely the idea of similarity itself. Not so, said Wittgenstein: 'We use the word "similar" in a huge family of cases' (*BB*, p.133). Think of the similarity of a tune and its variations; then the similarity of two states, like physical and mental strain; then the similarity of two processes like searching the park for a friend and searching the memory for a word.

The argument that we can always make further discriminations within our existing, classificatory groupings is a powerful way to bring home their conventional character. There is, however, an objection to be overcome. To give the objection maximum plausibility consider perceptual discriminations. These seem to have a natural rather than a conventional stopping-point. Because our capacity to make ever-finer perceptual discriminations must come to an end, this would appear to commit us to a class of naturally simple concepts. It suggests that there might be a 'data language' whose elementary concepts are given by experience alone. This is why family-resemblance concepts have been contrasted with other concepts like 'red' or 'blue' which are said to be based on simpler and more straightforward resemblances.[23] We need to see how Wittgenstein handled cases like these.

It might seem obvious that all shades of the colour we call 'blue' must have a common ingredient, their blueness, that explains why we classify them together. When we see that they are similar, doesn't the experience consist in noting the similarity which there *is* between them (*BB*, p.133)? Wittgenstein rejects this: it is a tautology dressed up as a statement about essences. Saying that 'blue' indicates what all the different shades have in common, just means that we use the same word for all these cases (*BB*, p.135).

The real basis of co-classification lies in the language-game that exploits their resemblances in some particular way. Imagine a game, says Wittgenstein, where *A* shows *B* patches of different colour and asks what they have in common. *B* is to answer by pointing to a particular primary colour. If *A* shows him pink and orange, *B* is to point to pure red. If *A* produces two shades of greenish-blue, *B* points to pure green or pure blue. If *A* produced light blue and dark blue it is clear what *B* is to answer. Similarly, if *A* pointed to pure red and pure green, *B* would have to say that they had nothing in common (*BB*, p.134). The meaning of these questions and answers is, however, relative to the game. Alter the game and the same words, 'what do these colours have in common?', would call for different responses. Wittgenstein points out that a culture need have no common expression for light and dark blue. They might call one 'Cambridge' and the other 'Oxford'. So there could be language-games in which the question 'what do these colours have in common?' would correctly elicit the answer 'nothing' (*BB*, p.135). Conversely, it is easy to imagine a game in which pure red and pure green were said to be colours that certainly had something in common.

> Imagine a use of language (a culture) in which there was a common name for green and red on the one hand and yellow and blue on the other. Suppose, e.g. that there were two castes, one the patrician caste, wearing red and green garments, the other, the plebeian, wearing blue and yellow garments.

> (*BB*, p.134)

In this culture, he goes on, both yellow and blue would always be called plebeian colours, and green and red would always be referred to as patrician colours. Now imagine a variant of the game between *A* and *B*. Asked what a red patch and a green patch had in common, *B*, as a member of this culture, would not hesitate: he would say that they were both patrician. If it is objected that we can literally *see* that red and green are different, we must remember that we can see that light and dark blue are different. If it is objected that 'patrician' isn't the name of a single, real colour, we must remember that the same could be said about blue: it is just a juxtaposition of 'Oxford' and 'Cambridge'.

So even if there are subjectively straightforward resemblances, and perceptually simple features, this carries no immediate implications for the proper application of concepts. Without the sanction of a language-game we cannot even rely on the move from light blue to dark blue being a legitimate one. Nor is there any reason why we should not attach a colour label to what we call a 'red' object, and then promptly apply it to what we call a 'green' object. So the conclusion about the conventional character of concept application, so strongly supported by the family-resemblance theory, and so strongly resisted by its critics, remains intact after all.

3.8 Symptoms and criteria

One of the most explicit ways in which Wittgenstein brings out the conventional structure of our language-games is by his notion of a criterion. A criterion, as Wittgenstein uses the word, is an identifiable cue whose presence is taken to justify the use of a word or classification. It is often the sort of thing that is used in training. Once the significance of the cue has been established it can then be used in more sophisticated ways to prompt or assess verbal responses. Wittgenstein gives the example of toothache:

> When we learnt to use of the phrase 'so and so has toothache' we were pointed out certain kinds of behaviour of those who were said to have toothache. As an instance of this kind of behaviour let us take holding your cheek.
>
> (*BB*, p.24)

The best way to understand criteria is to see them as social institutions. This accords well with the various things that Wittgenstein says about their role in a system of belief. It explains, for example, why the onus of proof is always on the sceptic if a conclusion based on a criterion is challenged. It also fits with the fact that a criterial relation is not treated as if it were an hypothesis. Anthropologists routinely talk about alien cultures in a way that highlights procedures of the kind that Wittgenstein would describe by his idea of a criterion. For example, a man's wife falls ill, his cattle sicken and die, so the Azande say he is bewitched. They will look for the neighbour whose malicious gossip may betray the fact that he is the witch who is responsible. Then the poison-oracle will be consulted about the suspect. Poison is administered to a chicken and the oracle gives its answers by determining whether the creature lives or dies. The fate of the chicken is decisive: it is the criterion for the identification of the witch.[24]

Similar moves will be found in every branch of knowledge. There is nothing essentially primitive about them. Chemistry, physics or Newtonian mechanics could furnish examples. Historians of science can find taken-for-granted cues operating as criteria among the physicists who first studied beams of X-rays, just as easily as anthropologists can find them among believers in witchcraft. Typically in these cases there is no sense that an inferential step is involved. Habit ensures that, psychologically, those who use a criterion feel themselves to be in the immediate presence of whatever it is presumed to indicate, whether this be a toothache, an act of witchcraft, or a new physical radiation.[25]

When anthropologists and historians of science describe the workings of these processes in detail, it is apparent that they are more subtle than the stereotypes of reasoning that have been abstracted and codified in deductive and inductive logic. The link between a cue and the meaning attached to it is certainly something other than an inductively supported generalisation. This is because criteria are taken, for all practical purposes, to convey certainty. They are authoritative. Also, in many cases, their users are in no position to observe the repeated conjunctions or correlations needed to prompt and support inductive generalisations. This applies to the theoretical entities assumed by the physicist, but we need only think of the case of toothache. When we learn to impute toothache to others, we are only witness to one side of the connection that is asserted (or seems to be asserted). But it will not do to jump to the opposite conclusion and say that we must be dealing with a deductive link, or a definition. Again the point could be argued with a scientific example, but an aching tooth will suffice. Putting our hand to our cheek is neither a necessary nor a sufficient condition for pain. We accept the fact that people may feign pain, or stoically hide it.

It is because criteria operate as conventions in a language-game that they cannot be assimilated, without difficulty, to idealised accounts of inductive generalisation or context-free definition. Criteria are institutionalised formulae that are to be used in the light of a mass of background knowledge: definitions to be used with discretion. Thus a child may apply the word 'toothache' to anybody who looks, superficially, as if he might have toothache. A more sophisticated understanding makes the usage contingent on a wider knowledge of the ways of the world. The usage becomes more sensitive to context, and to the knowledge that a range of contingencies may upset its applicability in any given case.

Wittgenstein develops his account by introducing the notion of a 'symptom'. A symptom is also a cue for the application of a word, but one that is used because it has been observed to correlate with a criterion. Suppose, says Wittgenstein, that whenever you saw someone holding his jaw, and hence whenever you would say that he had toothache, you noticed a red spot on his cheek. This could act as a symptom of toothache. Now we could attribute toothache to someone, even if we did not see him holding his jaw. Symptoms and criteria have different statuses. It makes sense to ask for the justification of a symptom but not a criterion. A symptom can be challenged, and the challenge met by indicating the correlation that exists between it and the criterion. You can ask and answer the question: how do you know that somebody with a red spot on his cheek has toothache? This takes you back to the criterion. But if someone says: how do you know that someone who holds his jaw really has toothache? – then we have run out of justifications. A more realistic case would be the witchcraft-detecting practices of the Azande. The oracle is the criterion; the display of malice that might put someone on the list of suspects is just a symptom. Ask an Azande why bad neighbours are suspects, and the reply would be that frequently the oracle has revealed such people to be witches. Ask why the oracle's pronouncements are taken to show that someone really is a witch, and the conversation would probably be at an end. We strike rock-bottom said Wittgenstein, 'that is we have come down to conventions' (*BB*, p.24).

In fact the full story is a little more complicated. First, if the use of a criterion is challenged it is sometimes possible to make a justificatory show. The Azande accept that sometimes the oracle does not give them the right answer. They say that this happens if it is not consulted properly, and if the correct ritual conditions are not satisfied. A given pronouncement can then be defended on the grounds that nothing is known about this case to raise any doubts. In general we use a criterion in conjunction with a number of known disqualifying conditions. Pain behaviour provides a criterion for imputing pain, but learning to operate with this criterion also means learning when to say that someone isn't really in pain – because they are cheating or rehearsing their part in a play. It is in this way that our greatest certainties co-exist with uncertainties. We feel no conflict because we do not average our degrees of belief; we parcel them out, contextualise them, and cope with particular problems in an *ad hoc* way. In learning to live with the fact that our certainty-giving criteria can, on occasion, be defeated, we even allow that new, unpredictable reasons for disqualification may appear. 'No one thought of *that* case' – we may say (*Z*, 118). These problems can never be repaired, and yet we do not experience them as problems. The absence of doubt, said Wittgenstein, is of the essence of a language-game (*OC*, 370).

A second complication is that symptoms and criteria are not really as separate in practice as the account so far may have suggested. Something that acts as a symptom on one occasion may be treated as a criterion on another: 'what to-day counts as an observed concomitant of a phenomenon will to-morrow be used to define it' (*PI*, I, 79).[26] Wittgenstein referred in this connection to 'the fluctuations of scientific definitions' (*PI*, I, 79). An example would be, perhaps, the relationship between force and acceleration in mechanics, but the practice is declared to be quite general: 'Nothing is commoner' (*Z*, 438). As we might expect from Wittgenstein's finitist premises, his position is that the roles of symptom and criterion are not in fact defined in advance of particular decisions:

> if you were asked which phenomenon is the defining criterion and which is a symptom, you would in most cases be unable to answer this question except by making an arbitrary decision *ad hoc*.
>
> (*BB*, p.25)

Doctors, said Wittgenstein, choosing an example that takes us back to Fleck's material, often talk about diseases 'without ever deciding which phenomena are to be taken as criteria and which as *institutional/practice rules*

symptoms'. He stresses that this must not be assumed to be lack of clarity. Rather than being deplorable it is in the nature of discourse.

Bringing the notion of a criterion under the heading of 'institution', and showing how the family-resemblance doctrine highlights the conventional character of concept application, throws us back on our understanding of institutions and conventions. It might be argued that until these sociological concepts have been sharply defined our understanding of Wittgenstein has not advanced at all. This would be to overlook a number of important facts. Even without a rigorously defined theory of institutions and conventions, the identification of, say, a criterion a thing of this general kind, is highly significant. It indicates what kind of investigation would help to illuminate them, and what kinds of connection must be explored if we are to deepen our understanding. And, of course, there is much that we do know about these things.

To appreciate this point it is salutary to remember just how determined some Wittgenstein scholars are that we should keep empirical material at arm's length. Consider, for example, Baker's paper 'Criteria: A New Foundation for Semantics'.[27] This contains a valuable exposition and clarification of the idea of criteria. Baker rightly wants us to be fascinated by the way in which criteria convey certainty, and are yet defeasible. Nevertheless he is adamant that we should not approach the topic in an empirical and naturalistic frame of mind. He goes out of his way to tell us that we should not treat the idea of a criterion as a theoretical concept in anthropology or psychology. (He actually says *intuitive* anthropology and *armchair* psychology, but that is rhetoric.) What he objects to is our understanding what Wittgenstein says about criteria as if it were 'an empirical statement about how we do in fact treat claims to knowledge'.[28] He will not brook using the idea of a criterion as a

> description of how we do in fact justify claims to knowledge and of what we accept [as] a justification for them *or* in the description of how we do in fact learn to use language and of how we teach it to children.[29]

If we look for why this sweeping restriction is imposed we find that Baker is less forthcoming. Indeed he gives no significant justification at all, only a few passing remarks that do not stand up to examination. He says that the empirical approach has its 'special difficulties' – which are unspecified – and it 'conflicts with Wittgenstein's claim' that the criterial relation 'belongs to grammar and determines sense'. But does it conflict with this claim? Surely the empirical study of criteria would just *be* the empirical study of how words are given sense. Wittgenstein's use of the word 'grammar' refers to the conventions of word-use in a given context, or roughly, the rules of a language-game (e.g. *BB*, pp.10, 15, 23). No reason is given why grammar, in this sense, should not be investigated empirically, or why the concept should not be given a role in some (empirically based) anthropological or psychological theory about the contingencies of actual word-use. In fact these phenomena have been subject to empirical study. Fleck's book is an example, and so is the ethnography of the Azande. Anthropology and the history of science are replete with relevant material and with plausible generalisations.

3.9   Needs of the greatest variety

There is an important element in Wittgenstein's theory that I have not so far mentioned. It is not as obvious as the other parts of his analytical apparatus, and has certainly received less attention. Running like a *leit motiv* through Wittgenstein's argument are references to the 'needs' of those who develop and change language-games. Thus:

> we sometimes wish for a notation which stresses a difference more strongly, makes it more obvious, than ordinary language does, or one which in a particular case uses more strongly similar forms of expression ... Our mental cramp is loosened when we are shown the notations which fulfill these needs. These needs can be of the greatest variety.
>
> (*BB*, p.59)

We are given some examples. One concerns our choice of psychological terminology. We may describe one person's behaviour towards another by saying that although *A* does not know it, really he despises *B*. Alternatively we may say that *A* doesn't really despise *B*, he merely behaves as if he does. A second example is from geometry. Nothing seems more clear-cut than saying that either a straight line intersects a circle or it doesn't. If it doesn't then it must be at a definite distance from doing so. But exactly the same options may be described in quite different terms. We can say that a line *always* intersects a circle, but sometimes at real and sometimes at imaginary points. (The word 'imaginary' has a technical meaning here. If we write down the equation of a circle and the equation of a line, then solving the equations will reveal the points that the figures have in common. Algebraically, however, there will always be two roots or solutions, though they may contain the symbol $i = \sqrt{-1}$. Those that do contain $\sqrt{-1}$ will give the 'imaginary' points of intersection.) The first formulation emphasises the difference between intersecting and not intersecting, the second gives a unified description of the two cases by using the idea of imaginary numbers. It therefore makes the difference between intersecting and not intersecting less conspicuous (*BB*, pp.29-30).

These examples show that patterns of similarity and difference can alter without our perceptions being altered or refined. We don't have to stare at the behaviour of *A* or *B*, or pore over diagrams of lines and circles, trying to pick out hitherto unnoticed details, in order to give the redescription something upon which to hang. What is perceptually simple can always become conceptually complicated by our theories and imputations. So here is more evidence for the conventional character of judgements of similarity. But what is it that prompts us to give redescriptions of this kind, and to modify our classifications and notations? Wittgenstein speaks of needs. Indeed, he refers to needs of the greatest variety; but what are these needs? Elsewhere Wittgenstein imagines a tribe who classify in a different way to us. It is not that they fail to perceive what we perceive; the question he says, is whether certain similarities are important to them (*Z*, 352, 380; *RPP*, vol. *II*, 727). So what is it that makes similarities important or not? Knowing this would surely bring us close to the stream of life that pulses through the language-game. But any reader of Wittgenstein who looks in his writings for the answers to these important questions will find to his dismay that they have not been provided. Search as we may, the references to needs are never properly explained.

Wittgenstein indicates a subject that is clearly central to his theory, and then does not bother to explore it.

The scandal is compounded by his followers and commentators. With a unanimity that is remarkable, they too stop short here. Consider, for example, E. K. Specht's *The Foundations of Wittgenstein's Late Philosophy*.[30] This is one of the best available treatments of the subject. Beneath the surface of Wittgenstein's work Specht discerns a powerful and general theory. He enjoins us to carry the work forward, but what does he do when he comes to the question of why new language-games are created, or old ones modified? He invokes the category of 'spontaneity'. In drawing up a new language-game, says Specht, 'the rules of language are not read off from the objects but are drawn up spontaneously, i.e. somehow freely and without determination'.[31] What is being denied here is correct and useful; but what is being asserted comes dangerously close to obscurantism. Of course, Specht is only following Wittgenstein, who also invoked the mysterious category of spontaneity.[32] But this is no defence because elsewhere he declines to follow Wittgenstein.

Why, then, has the idea of 'need' not been pursued? How can it have seemed adequate to cloud over the issue with vague references to spontaneity and freedom from determination? I suspect that the reason is because the idea of 'need' calls for an empirical investigation. It brings us face to face with contingency. It leads the enquiry into the nature of knowledge into an area where philosophers have neither the qualification nor the inclination to go. This explains the uniformity of the response: the boundary at which curiosity stopped short was a disciplinary boundary.

I shall proceed in a different way and try to draw attention to the role of needs. To do this I shall put forward a simple hypothesis about what they are and how they work. What Wittgenstein was referring to by 'needs' were the very things that sociologists refer to under the heading of social interests. Needs are not individual appetites but are best construed as collective phenomena. When we detect a change in a language-game we must look for a shift in the goals and purposes of its players which is sufficiently widespread and sufficiently uniform to yield that change. Confronted by competing usages we should look for rival groups and track down the causes of the rivalry; if we see language-games merging with one another we must look for, and try to explain, the continuities and alliances between their players. So when, to take up Wittgenstein's example of 'despising', we find one group of people who stress outward forms, and another who stress inner states, we must ask what sustains this difference in emphasis. What institutions are best served by deflecting attention away from individual intentions, and which can be most easily justified by emphasising them? Who gains advantage in the one case or the other? These are the kind of questions that will lead us to the interests that structure language-games

I have now given a systematic account of Wittgenstein's theoretical apparatus. I have identified and related together all the main components of his theory of language-games. These components are: functional diversity, finitism, training, the rejection of extensions, family resemblances, the interaction of criteria and symptoms, and the role of needs. I have argued that all these features serve to emphasise the conventional character of concept application. At the same time we have seen how the social dimension of the theory appears to be arbitrarily truncated. As a first step in repairing this fault I have suggested that we should equate Wittgenstein's 'needs' with social interests. In subsequent chapters I will be introducing some badly needed empirical material in order to show how sociological and historical investigations can illuminate the issues that have been raised. But having now examined the general principles that apply to all language-games, the next step must be to study particular cases taken from different areas of our life. In the next chapter I will discuss the language-games of everyday psychological discourse. After that I will move to the extremely revealing language-games associated with mathematical reasoning and logical inference.

4

The Social Construction of Mental States

The language-games of commonsense psychology include reporting bodily sensations, describing feelings, imputing motives and intentions, engaging in mental skills such as reading, and telling our dreams. We shall be concerned with how these topics are handled outside the laboratory, but for purposes of comparison we must sometimes don the white coat of the specialist. Before plunging into details it may be useful to say how these issues bear upon the enterprise of building a social theory of knowledge. What we will be talking about is the mind and the ego. This is the part of ourselves that is often assumed to be known most intimately. It seems to be the location and source of our identity and individuality. There is therefore a sense in which this is the keep of the individualist's castle. At least, there is much in what we are tempted to say about the mind, and there is much in traditional philosophies of mind, that can be used to support the idea that a theory of knowledge must begin with the individual and, so to speak, work outwards. Wittgenstein took the opposite approach. Instead of approaching public knowledge via individual experience, he approached the intimacies of the self via the public categories with which they must be grasped. The Self was to be understood through the Other. In this way he constructed a social theory of those things which might appear to be most irreducibly individual. As we shall see, his social theory of mind was derived from his social theory of meaning. This is why he attended to issues that are sometimes passed over as if they were unproblematic, such as the question: how do we come to attach names to our sensations?

4.1 Naming sensations: Wittgenstein and Skinner

Wittgenstein asked: 'how does a human being learn the meaning of the names of sensations? – of the word 'pain' for example (*PI*, I,

244). The problem is that sensations are private: my headache leaves you without a twinge. Is the reference of a sensation word, therefore, something that each person can know only in his own case? How, then, can their names ever be taught? The process would seem to involve the teacher in a hopeless inference, or require him to be a mind-reader. Wittgenstein's response to these long-standing problems had a negative and a positive part. Negatively he argued that their peculiarly puzzling character is because the terms in which we formulate them contain subtle distortions of language. In real life we never feel that, while we know our own pain 'directly', we have no access to the reality of the pain of others (*PI*, I, 303). Nor do we think that the sensation of a blue sky on a sunny day in any way belongs just to us. It is only when we philosophise that there seems to be an 'asymmetry in the use of . . . all words relating to personal experience' (*NFL*, p. 278).[1] Positively, Wittgenstein began the job of offering a rival analysis of psychological concepts, for example the naming of sensations. One possibility, he said, to explain how we learn the meaning of the word 'pain', is that 'words are connected with the primitive, the natural, expressions of the sensation and used in their place' (*PI*, I, 244). A child who hurts himself and cries is comforted by adults who provide a vocabulary for expressing the pain. The word 'pain' does not mean 'crying', but takes over from it. The newly acquired verbal behaviour, he says, is itself a form of pain behaviour.

Elsewhere, in lecture notes, Wittgenstein gave an example that explains why this is only 'one possibility'. The example in question does not actually deal with pain, but with what Wittgenstein called an 'indirect' method of teaching colour words. Nevertheless, the principle involved is the same. Instead of pointing to coloured samples, and labelling them, a teacher could give the pupil coloured spectacles and ask him to look at a piece of white paper through them. To help the teacher, said Wittgenstein, suppose that the different-coloured lenses are different shapes. The teacher sees the round spectacles on the pupil's nose and calls 'red', then gives him the elliptical ones, and calls 'green' (*NFL*, p. 285). The indirect method works because of a reliable contingent connection between the different cues available to the pupil and the teacher. In a sense, on this method, what the teacher teaches is different from what the pupil learns: but he does learn. The word-shape association, used by the teacher, enables the pupil to acquire a word-colour association.

Wittgenstein must have realised that this example could be the basis of interesting developments, because underneath it he wrote in his notes the words 'mind reading'. This forges the link with the natural-expression theory of sensations and, indeed, the general problem of the knowledge of other minds. These examples and theories were not, however, developed. Fortunately, the psychologist B. F. Skinner has argued along very similar lines in an acute paper called 'The Operational Analysis of Psychological Terms'.[2] By following his argument we can see what Wittgenstein's ideas might have looked like had they received a fuller statement.

Skinner assumes that organisms are always initiating behaviour or, as he says, emitting 'operant responses'.[3] The task is to show how these responses become shaped by rewards, or 'reinforcements', and hence come under the control of specific stimuli. The main principle is that a response must be rewarded in the presence of a stimulus, though empirically it emerges that it does not have to be rewarded every time. Verbal behaviour, for Skinner, just consists of responses like any other behaviour; and private sensations, like headaches or toothache, are to be treated as stimuli just like any others. Exactly the same laws apply. In adopting this approach we see that Skinner is conforming to a procedural rule of the kind that I referred to as the rule of externalisation. To see how we name sensations all we have to do, on Skinner's theory, is to work out how the 'verbal community' manages to set up a 'reinforcement schedule'. This must impinge systematically on the required stimulus-response relation. So here is a direct attack on Wittgenstein's question by a thinker who shares his rejection of the 'asymmetries' fostered by traditional theories of mind.

The problem, of course, is that a training schedule requires publicly observable cues. Skinner solves the problem by outlining four possible mechanisms by which a private stimulus can be made subject to a public reinforcement schedule. First, a child's use of 'it hurts' could be brought into line with public usage by making reward contingent on an observable event like a smart blow or tissue damage. It could be rewarded by comfort if, and only if, it produced the verbal responses under these circumstances. Notice that, even so, the response would eventually come under the control of any private stimulus that was reliably connected with the public one. Skinner likens this case to the sighted teacher teaching a blind man the name of various shapes. The teacher uses visual cues, but the result is that the responses come under the control of tactile cues. This is the exact analogue of Wittgenstein's indirect method, with the shaped and coloured spectacles.

In Skinner's second case the reward is given on the basis of a collateral response to the private stimuli. By rewarding, say, a verbal response to toothache on the basis of groans and jaw-holding, we could attach the verbal response to the stimuli that provoked the jaw-holding in the first place. This is Wittgenstein's natural-expression theory, or very like it. There are however two other cases to be considered that Wittgenstein did not discuss.

The third case is where verbal responses begin their careers as descriptions of public behaviour, and then become attached to a covert or incipient part of that behaviour. A reward schedule could be set up on the basis of the behaviour, and could result in attaching a word to, say, the proprioceptive cues that arise from the behaviour but are known only to the actor. For example, the word 'ravenous' denotes both food-seeking behaviour and a mental state. Wittgenstein went out of his way to deny that this applies to the word 'pain' – it doesn't mean 'crying' – but he omitted to say that this analysis might well apply to other cases.

Finally, there is what Skinner calls 'stimulus induction'. A response rewarded for one kind of stimulus naturally generalises itself to stimuli that are subjectively similar. There are many experimental studies of these natural propensities to generalise. This could account for the use of words like 'calm' or 'agitated' to describe mental states and feelings.

It is fashionable to criticise Skinner's theories of language, but whatever their shortcomings there is much that can be illuminated by these clearly stated ideas.[4] For example, they explain why introspective reports are indeed possible, but vague and limited. Our discriminations are crude because of the problems of establishing a reinforcement schedule. Skinner's theory implies that in 'the absence of the "crisis" provided by differential reinforcement ... private stimuli cannot be analysed'. An individual achieves awareness 'only after society has reinforced verbal responses with respect to his behaviour as the source of discriminative stimuli'. So, like Wittgenstein, Skinner concludes that the individual must always be approached via the verbal community: 'being conscious, as a form of reacting to one's own behaviour', says Skinner, 'is a social product'.[5]

The most intriguing conclusion that Skinner arrives at, is that there is no way of conditioning a response entirely to the private aspect of a complex of stimuli. No differential reinforcement schedule could be made contingent on privacy alone. The private, as such, can never be prized apart from the public. This follows from the principles of reinforcement theory. It explains, Skinner points out, why we cannot simply 'assign names to the diverse elements of private experience and then . . . proceed with consistent and effective discourse'. As Skinner rightly says, this is a crucial fact in evaluating traditional psychological concepts. It is also the very issue that Wittgenstein discusses under the heading of 'private languages'. I will now turn to this topic, keeping Skinner in mind when I come to assess Wittgenstein's argument.

4.2   Private languages

In order to prove that there is an indissoluble link between the public world and the mental life of the individual, Wittgenstein attacked the idea of what he called a 'private language'. A private language would be a vocabulary of pure introspection for recording the innermost aspects of our experience. We often introspect using our ordinary language, but in a private language the words are to refer 'to what can only be known to the person speaking; to his immediate private sensations. So another person cannot understand the language' (*PI*, I, 243). This is why Wittgenstein says that in so far as our words for sensations are tied to their natural expressions, as they are in ordinary language, they are not private in the special sense that he intends (*PI*, I, 256). The word 'pain', for example, does not in these terms refer to our immediate private sensations: as we ordinarily use the word, others can be properly said to know that we are in pain (*PI*, I, 246). The concepts of a private language, therefore, if they are to record what can only be known to the person speaking, would have to be somewhat different from our normal ones.

Wittgenstein's argument to show that there can be no private languages has two main parts. The first deals with the conditions that must be satisfied if a word is to function in a genuine language. Here the discussion covers words that refer to sensations of an everyday kind. The second part of his argument focuses on the nature of privacy and the idea of immediate private sensations. This is meant to reinforce and deepen the earlier conclusions. The passages in which these themes are discussed are concentrated between sections 243 and 317 of the *Investigations*. They represent Wittgenstein at his best and his worst. The argument is over-compressed and lacks a clear structure, but at the same time it is enormously suggestive.

Wittgenstein imagines someone saying 'But I can (inwardly) undertake to call THIS "pain" in the future' (*PI*, I, 263). The speaker might strike himself on the breast while saying this, as if the emphatic stress on the word 'this' would capture the identity of the thing being referred to (*PI*, I, 253). To counteract this assumption we need to remember all the problems connected with ostension and mental acts. Merely saying a word in the presence of a sensation will not suffice to give it a role. Indeed, the role is presupposed by the act of ostension if that ceremony is going to give the word a meaning. So the initial reply to the advocate of a private-language theory is that he has left out what Wittgenstein calls the 'stage-setting' that is necessary for defining the words of a language (*PI*, I, 257 and 264). Without this the response 'pain' cannot have meaning, let alone signify what we ordinarily mean by it. Is there anything to stop someone providing the stage-setting for his own performance? The straightforward reply is that this is ruled out because it is beyond the capacity of the individual. A single mind would have to accomplish a task that is, in reality, distributed among a multitude of people. According to this view, the idea of a private language is not logical nonsense, but it is so far removed from reality that it is totally impossible. It is ruled out by the nature of human beings.[6]

Wittgenstein did not give this straightforward answer, or, rather, he only gave it by implication and in an oblique manner that obscured the empirical character of many of his claims. He considers a very simple linguistic act and shows that if it is performed privately there is an important ingredient of language that will be missing. We are to forget the idea of building up in our heads a complicated counterpart of a real language, and think merely of setting up a consistent association between a sensation and a response. Suppose, says Wittgenstein that I want to keep a diary of the recurrence of a certain sensation. 'I associate it with the sign "S" and write this sign in a calendar for every day on which I had the sensation' (*PI*, I, 258). In the effort to ensure consistency I concentrate my attention on the sensation. I impress it upon myself and in this way 'inwardly *undertake* to use the word in such and such a way' (*PI*, I, 262).

In this example Wittgenstein simply spoke of recording a 'sensation', and used the word without any special qualification. For this reason the privacy of the diarist's undertakings can be assumed to be contingent rather than necessary. In other words we could, for the purposes of this part of the argument, substitute a socially isolated individual who is classifying not his sensations, but some entirely public set of objects. But, of course, any negative conclusions that apply to a contingently private performance will apply with even greater force to a necessarily private one. What, however, is supposed to be dubious about the diary entries that register sensations? Wittgenstein's explanation is terse:

> But 'I impress it on myself' can only mean: this process brings it about that I remember the connexion *right* in the future. But in the present case I have no criterion of correctness. One would like to say: whatever is going to seem right to me is right. And that only means that here we can't talk about 'right'.
>
> (*PI*, I, 258)

These critical comments are about the conditions for making appraisals of our judgements. Wittgenstein is talking about the nature of right and wrong, and the circumstances under which standards and criteria can be said to exist. The diary-keeper's predicament is one where the processes of classifying something as an 'S', and remembering that it is an 'S', have been collapsed together. There is, therefore, no difference for the diarist between his remembering the classification of his sensation correctly, and thinking that he has remembered it correctly. So he has no way of grounding the idea of right and wrong, or accuracy and inaccuracy.

I will shortly come back to this example, but some idea of the scope of Wittgenstein's comments may be gathered by making a comparison. The points that Wittgenstein raised also apply to moral standards and criteria. Just as there can be no private language, so there can be no private morality. The subjective creation of meaning is just as much of an illusion as the subjective creation of moral right and wrong. I cannot bring moral principles into being by, say, attending to my feelings of pleasure and pain and declaring: henceforth I will call *this* 'good'. If, as here, there is no difference between something seeming good to me and it being good, then I cannot talk about 'good' at all. The individualist does not see the force of this: he thinks a state of inner conviction will suffice. For him the good can be felt in the heart. What he fails to grasp is that morality is distinct from inclination because it is a social institution. An isolated individual cannot, for example, place himself under an obligation. It would be a sham because obligations are institutional phenomena, and hence supra-individual. Right and wrong are external to the individual: 'justification consists in appealing to something independent' (*PI*, I, 265). They are public standards, and their authority comes from their being collectively held. That this is the form of argument that is being advanced is clear from Wittgenstein's analogy between endowing a word with meaning and the institution of gift-giving. Why, he asks, can't my right hand give my left hand money?

> My right hand can put it into my left hand. My right hand can write a deed of gift and my left hand a receipt – but the further practical consequences would not be those of a gift. When the left hand had taken the money from the right, etc., we shall ask: 'Well, and what of it?' And the same could be asked if a person had given himself a private definition of a word; I mean, if he had said the word to himself and at the same time has directed his attention at a senation.
>
> (*PI*, I, 268)

The argument so far may be summarised in the claim that there can be no private languages because languages are institutions, and a private language would not be an institution. Its rules, being private 'would hang in the air; for the institution of their use is lacking' (*PI*, I, 380). Wittgenstein's position fits snugly into the Durkheimean tradition. Durkheim argued that although individual inclinations and impressions possess some degree of natural orderliness, they lack any quality of moral coercion or impersonal objectivity. This, he said, comes from the social group. In developing this position Durkheim was, quite self-consciously, giving a sociological interpretation of the traditions of Kantean philosophy.[7] The claim, running from Kant, through Durkheim, and clearly present in Wittgenstein, is that sense-experience, as such, lacks objectivity. The deliverances of our sense-organs are to be distinguished from our concepts of the things we experience. It is in this spirit that Wittgenstein tells us not to believe that we have the concept of colour within us just because we look at a coloured object (*Z*, 332).[8] The older, Kantean, versions of this argument tried to ground the distinction between experience and concepts in different faculties of the mind – the sensibility and the understanding. Durkheim and Wittgenstein locate the source of objectivity outside the mind altogether, in society.[9]

Now let me return to the diary example. Exactly what has Wittgenstein established? Has he really shown that the performance of registering sensations in this way is a sham? This is certainly the impression that he gives. He imagines the diarist protesting that, at least, he *believes* it is the same sensation again, even if he has no objective criterion to which he can appeal. To this Wittgenstein coolly replies that perhaps the diarist merely believes that he believes this. In other words: not even this subjective stance really has any meaning.

> Then did the man who made the entry in the calendar make a note of *nothing whatever*? – Don't consider it a matter of course that a person is making a note of something when he makes a mark – say, in a calendar.
>
> (*PI*, I, 260)

The conclusion that we are meant to draw is that the whole exercise is a charade: 'sounds which no one else understands but which I "*appear to understand*" might be called a "private language"' (*PI*, I, 269). This is difficult to swallow. So far, all that Wittgenstein's argument has done is to deny the diarist the public *concept* of a specific class of stimuli referred to by the sign 'S'. There is a step missing. This is the proof that the diarist *needs* a full-blown, publicly sanctioned concept in order to pull off the feat of making regular responses. (After all, machines can interact in a regular way with their surroundings, and they don't possess concepts.) In order to clarify this point it will be useful to make another comparison. Let us return to the earlier discussion of Skinner.

How would Skinner analyse the diary episode? To begin with he would refer to stimuli rather than to sensations. The diarist has a stimulus of type S_1 and makes his response. We have already seen, however, that Skinner's working assumption is that responses which are not innately connected with a stimulus – his 'operant responses ' – are likely to be produced in the presence of other kinds of stimuli as well, say type S_2. This is the nature of complex organisms. If we assume that there is no reinforcement schedule to differentiate S_2 from S_1, then nothing will keep the response under the control of S_1 alone. Skinner's theory, therefore, really does give us a reason to believe that the diarist's performance is a sham. If the theory is true then the diarist will not be able to keep his responses aligned with a given kind of stimulus. For Skinner this incapacity is not a matter of logic but a fact about organisms. It would be perfectly possible for them to be built differently. They might innately discriminate their responses to the stimuli in question. The fact is, however, that lacking any feedback they will generalise their responses and shift the basis of their outer performances without realising it.

The Skinnerian counterpart of the public concept is the external sanction of the reinforcement schedule. Wittgenstein does not spell out any comparable theory about the mechanics of reinforcement and association. This gives him even less reason than Skinner for saying that the diarist must have a concept of what he is doing and cannot, without it, set up an association between his diary entry and a specific kind of sensation. What we find, however, is that by a route of his own Wittgenstein converges on a conclusion that is remarkably similar to Skinner's. This is the outcome of the second part of the anti-private language argument to which I shall now turn.

Wittgenstein asks us to suppose that the diary-keeper discovers that whenever he believes himself to have a particular sensation a manometer shows a rise in his blood-pressure. This, he notes, enables the diarist to say that his blood-pressure is rising without using the instrument. Here is a useful result and a use for the sign

'S', something that it lacked up till now.

> And now it seems quite indifferent whether I have recognized the sensation *right* or not. Let us suppose I regularly identify it wrong, it does not matter in the least. And that alone shows that the hypothesis that I made a mistake is mere show. (We as it were turned a knob which looked as if it could be used to turn on some part of the machine; but it was a mere ornament, not connected with the mechanism at all.)
>
> (*PI*, I, 270)

Once again the argument is disconcertingly brief. What Wittgenstein is doing is following the principle that he formulated elsewhere: always get rid of private objects by imagining that they vary but the fact is not noticed (*PI*, I, xi, p.207). He is trying to show that the diary-keeping episode really was a sham because one term in the supposedly regular association between sensation and outer response can be got rid of entirely. The sensation drops out of the story. The trouble is that the argument is stated in a thoroughly confusing way. Wittgenstein is telling us that it makes no difference if the sensation is identified incorrectly, just when the supposed ability to predict the manometer makes it look as if the diarist was doing something coherent after all.

The best way to analyse the argument is to adopt a very down-to-earth reading of the manometer example. I take it that what the introduction of the manometer shows is that, without realising it, the diarist had been responding to his blood-pressure. With one small qualification that I will explain shortly, we can say that the sensation 'S' must have been the sensation of blood-pressure. Although the fact was not known in advance, the capacity to predict the manometer reveals that the sensation was not an immediate private sensation but a common-or-garden sensation of the kind dealt with in ordinary language. This follows from the fact that other people can know if we are having the sensation, because it can be identified with and through an observable physiological state. So what the diary-keeper's successful predictions establish is that the claims of the diarist were not really those of a private linguist. The ability to predict the manometer therefore vindicates the diarist's belief in his own consistency, but it only does so in the case where the sensation that is being registered turns out to have been contingently private rather than necessarily private. The advocate of a private-language theory will stress that the diarist didn't know that his sensation would turn out to be a sensation of a public thing like a physiological state. It might have turned out differently. If no physiological explanation was ever found for his diary entries wouldn't the diarist, at least, still know in his own mind that he was responding to the same kind of sensation? This is precisely the thing that he doesn't know. He might in fact be right, but he wouldn't know he is right.

Now for the step in the argument where Wittgenstein asks us to imagine that the sensation is frequently identified wrongly. How can he conclude that it makes no difference? If we keep to our simple reading of the manometer case then the sensation in question is the sensation of a rise in blood-pressure. The diarist can predict the rise in the manometer because he can actually feel his blood-pressure. If we suppose that he frequently identified *this* sensation wrongly we would be saying that he would frequently make incorrect manometer predictions. That would be to reject the terms of the example. What seems to have happened in the argument is that Wittgenstein should be talking about immediate private sensations rather than ordinary sensations. The argument works, and it only works, if it is applied to immediate private sensations. The assumption of unnoticed change in our sensations is a technique for getting rid of redundant parts of an explanation. He is trying to show that no explanatory work can be done by making reference to immediate private sensations *as well as* ordinary sensations in our accounts of human behaviour.

Wittgenstein's discussion of the manometer predictions was meant to remind us that once we have located the physical and public basis of a puzzling piece of behaviour (like the diary entries), then our ordinary use of the word 'sensation' will refer the behaviour to those conditions. The language-game carries an implied reference to the public anchor-points of behaviour. That is why it was natural to say of the diarist that his sensation must have been the sensation of the blood-pressure. We feel relief because we have at last identified the sensation. The step that Wittgenstein wanted to avoid was that of decoupling our idea of a sensation from this public framework. There are a number of reasons why we may do this. We may, for example, be tempted to duplicate our reference to sensations and insert extra steps in our explanations. Impressed by the fact that our diarist did not know that his sensation was a sensation of blood-pressure, we may say that he wasn't really responding to his blood-pressure at all, but to something else, for example to the subjective experience of it; something that was fully known to him and to him alone. We may be tempted to treat the appearance of a thing as if it were another thing, detachable from the first like a membrane. The inner face of an object then becomes yet another object. As well as the senation of blood-pressure we now have another entity to cope with: the sensation-as-it-appears.

Moves of this kind subvert the normal language-game that we play with the word 'sensation', unless, that is, we can find a genuine role for the refinement. Sometimes, indeed, we might want to talk about the sensation felt by the diarist as distinct from the physical state of his blood-pressure that appears to be the ultimate cause of the behaviour. We might want to say that the diarist does not respond 'directly' to the blood-pressure but to something else. This can be perfectly in order, because there is no reason to assume that just because someone can predict their blood-pressure on the basis of their sensations, that the sensations have to be sensations of blood-pressure. They might be sensations of a quite distinct physiological state that was regularly connected to the rise in pressure. But of course this kind of intervening object is not a necessarily private one. It simply represents a more refined way of anchoring the responses in the public world.

The temptation towards redundancy that Wittgenstein was particularly keen to root out was the idea that when we respond on the basis of a sensation we confront the sensation and, as it were, designate or name it. This, he suggests, is the model that inclines us to treat the appearance-to-us of a public object as if it were another object, only this time a private one. His point was that 'if we construe the grammar of the expression of sensation on the model of "object and designation", the object drops out of consideration as irrelevant' (*PI*, I, 293). This is what was supposed to be happening in the rather too-rapid analysis of the manometer case. If we must think of the diarist responding to an object when he wrote the letter 'S', we should think of him responding to the public object. His response does not stop short at the sensation: it is not, so to speak, addressed to the sensation but to the cause of the sensation. That this is the way to analyse matters would have been brought out more effectively if Wittgenstein had been more realistic in his handling of his example. He should have thought, as Skinner always thinks, of the process of learning and adapting. Wittgenstein quietly assumes that the diarist is always able to predict the manometer. Suppose, however, that we think of him *learning* to predict, or of him *improving* his predictions. If this were possible at all it would be done by using the manometer readings to give him positive and negative feedback. In Skinnerian terms we would reinforce the correct predictions. In this way the diarist might improve his discriminations. But we would gain nothing by saying that he improved his discrimination of his sensation of blood-pressure. That would just mean: he improved his discrimination of his blood-pressure. As Wittgenstein insisted: if we construe the expression of sensation on the model of object and designation, the private object drops out.

There is much to be said for using the idiom of stimulus-response (S-R) theory, in order to reconstruct Wittgenstein's ideas. The idea of a stimulus has built into it the presupposition that it will someday be identified with a physical and public state. Even where the proponent of S-R theory is led to theorise about inner states we have seen that he avoids the redundancies that Wittgenstein opposed. The idea of a stimulus also helps us from the outset to avoid dogmatic commitment to the object-name model. To respond to a stimulus is not, in itself, to name it. Wittgenstein said that we don't *know* our sensations, we just *have* them. The same could be said of a stimulus. Its relation to a response has just that automatic, unreflective quality that Wittgenstein wanted to convey.

We are now in a position to see the similarity between Skinner's assumption that, without reinforcement, a response will move from stimulus to stimulus, and Wittgenstein's idea that we can get rid of private objects by supposing them to vary without our noticing it. Skinner's idea is that our responses are all held in place by external constraints, but reinforcement cannot reach down to anything that is necessarily private. There can be no control over responses to the purely private aspects of a stimulus. So if the private stimulus is a reality it is an idle cogwheel in the machinery of our explanations. Any behaviour based on it would appear as randomness against a background of order. Wittgenstein reaches the same conclusion from the opposite direction. Instead of working inwards and showing that anything purely private would be left spinning and disconnected, he asks us to turn the suspected cogwheel and notice that nothing in the machine depends on it. One varies the response to the private stimulus, the other varies the private stimulus to a stable pattern of public responses. The claims have the same functional significance in their two accounts. There is just one twist to Wittgenstein's argument that takes him beyond Skinner. If we cannot condition any public response to something that is necessarily private, then we have no basis for calling what is private a 'sensation' or even a 'something'. These are, after all, words whose meaning comes from their role in our ordinary, public language-games (*PI*, I, 261).

Now let me take stock. I have no reservations about the first part of the anti-private language argument, but the second part called for clarification. As it stood there was some confusion between sensations and the real target of the attack – the idea of the necessarily private inner object, or the immediate private sensation. Once this equivocation is put right the argument can be seen to be sound. The essential conclusions stand fast, though I needed the help of tough-minded thinkers like Durkheim and Skinner to convey them. The point is that even introspective discourse is a public institution which depends on conventions and hence on training. We have no immediate self-knowledge and no resources for constructing any significant account of a realm of purely private objects and experiences.

In the next section I will examine the attempts that have been made to apply the anti-private language argument to dream reports.

4.3   Dreaming

Here is how Wittgenstein handled dreams. People tell us about certain incidents on awakening and we teach them to preface their narrative by the words 'I dreamt'. Then we can ask if they dreamt last night and they can say 'yes' or 'no', and perhaps give an account of the dream. 'That' says Wittgenstein 'is the language-game' (*PI*, II, vii). The contours of the concept of dreaming can then be traced by studying the moves that are considered proper to the game. For example: we often speak of dreams as if they were events that happened during sleep and were then remembered on awakening. Wittgenstein expressed doubt about whether the language-game of dream-telling is really based on any assumptions about these matters. As the game is normally played there is no significant role for, say, the distinction between really having certain images while we sleep, and merely seeming to have had them when once we wake. On the other hand he doesn't think that it is nonsense to raise these questions: 'It will turn on the use of the question' (*PI*, II, vii).

In his book, *Dreaming*, Normal Malcolm hardens this position into the bold claim that *not* raising questions of this kind is essential to the concept. Anyone who thinks that dreams are composed of thoughts, feelings and images occurring in sleep is just wrong.[10] The argument is that we can only impute these things to people on the basis of their behaviour. It follows that we can never verify that anyone had, say, images while they slept, because the behaviour called 'sleeping' precludes all the other behaviour needed for the imputation. The dreamer's own waking testimony makes no difference. Once awake the dreamer stands to his sleeping self in the same position as everybody else. All he has is the impression of having had imagery, but no criterion to check the impression. There is therefore no difference between remembering correctly and thinking that one remembers. He is in the position of the private diary-keeper. Of course it makes sense to say that someone has dreamt. There is a language-game, and the criterion is dream-telling. The dreamer's testimony verifies the fact, but the fact is not what we might take it to be. If we *can* verify that someone dreamt, but *not* that they had images whilst asleep, this proves that dreams aren't made up of images. Dreams are constituted by, and in, the discourse that makes them a public phenomenon.[11]

At first sight this new, linguistic emphasis would seem to be the ideal prelude to a broad-ranging discussion of all the different ways the language-game of dream-telling might proceed. We could examine how, and why, dreams were differently constituted in different cultures, and examine their historically changing role in our life. The heuristic potential of this approach, however, is ignored. Indeed, Malcolm draws only negative conclusions, and ignores what might be called the anthropological dimension of Wittgenstein's thinking. Nevertheless, he uses the ideas to considerable effect in his criticism of psychological research into dreaming.

Psychologists have taken over our commonsense assumption that if a sleeping person or animal makes sounds, or moves, they must be having a dream. They have refined it by monitoring very delicate 'movements', like those of the eyes behind the closed lids, or even electrical activity in the brain. They have discovered that there are regular phases when the sleeper is more agitated than at other times, and when the eyes make rapid movements. People who are woken during these phases tend to say they were dreaming. They do this more frequently than do people woken during quieter sleep. There is even some evidence that, where the eye movement is predominantly vertical or horizontal, this corresponds to the geometry of the events reported in the dream (say, the back-and-forth movements of a ball in a tennis game). The obvious hypothesis supported by these results is that questions about how long, or how frequently, people dream do make sense, and that a dream really is a sequence of images and feelings, and involves processes rather similar to waking acts like watching or observing.[12]

Malcolm makes no attempt to deny these facts but launches a vigorous attack on their significance. To prepare the ground he goes back to the commonsense idea behind the psychological methods. A young man murmurs 'Mabel' in his sleep, and we say that he is dreaming of Mabel. What does this really mean? Strictly, says Malcolm, either the sighing is a new criterion for dreaming, or it is being treated as evidence that the sleeper will tell a dream about Mabel when he awakens. In fact, we are told, usage is unclear on this point: our words do not fall definitely into either alternative, and indeed have no clear sense'.[13] This is an adroit move. At the point where our ordinary discourse might blossom into science, Malcolm detects in it the defects of obscurity and lack of sense.

The main attack, however, lies in the claim that the psychologists are not really investigating dreams at all. They have introduced a new concept with new criteria. They are not making discoveries about dreams, but promulgating new definitions.[14] They use the old label, but their concept only remotely resembles the old one.[15] To show this, consider the relation of the ordinary concept of dreaming to measures of time. We talk of being woken 'during' a dream, or having a dream just 'before' wakening, but Malcolm insists that our ordinary language-game attaches no real significance to the temporal words: 'It is no part of the concept of dreams to provide a translation of this impression into physical time.'[16] But such a translation is just what the psychologist is looking for. He measures the length of rapid-eye-movement sleep, and draws conclusions about the length of dreams.

The crucial piece of evidence, for Malcolm, is this: with the psychologists' concept, someone can be told whether they had a dream. If a sleeper awakens but says he did not have a dream, the psychologist can consult his polygraph recordings and tell him that he must have forgotten. Telling a dream by the dreamer is no longer the last word on the matter.[17] For Malcolm this proves that a different concept is involved. Malcolm acknowledges that the introduction of a new concept of dreaming might be tempting. He even allows that it might be 'overwhelmingly natural'.[18] But the failure to mark the gulf between the two concepts, and hence the tendency to see the psychologist's results as being about dreams in the ordinary sense, is just 'confusion'.[19]

Malcolm's Wittgensteinean analysis has proven extremely controversial, and I shall now look at one systematic line of response that it has evoked. This is the argument of Putnam's 'Dreaming and "Depth Grammar"'.[20] Putnam argues for the continuity of the everyday and scientific concepts of dreaming. They may not have the same criteria, he says, but it is plausible to think of them as being references to the same thing. It is entirely natural to take the psychologist's work as a progressive unveiling of a hidden reality, while keeping our criteria of identification revisable and fluid. This is how science always proceeds and it is also in accord with common sense. Science does not call for the point-by-point verification of its theories, so there is no reason to think that it is nonsense to impute images to sleeping persons. What matters is whether the claim coheres with our overall understanding. Our concepts form a system and are to be judged as a whole. Part of this system, shared by psychologists and laymen, is that all the various episodes of dream-telling, sighing in our sleep, rapid eye-movements and electrical agitations of the brain, are indicators of an underlying dream experience. On this basis Putnam is 'convinced' that most speakers would not find the psychologist's innovations at all puzzling. These uses 'were always there in the language'.

Although this is a persuasive picture of discourse, it is less than decisive against Malcolm, and Putnam knows it. He announces that he won't be able to *prove* that Malcolm is wrong,[21] and declares that his and Malcolm's views form two 'circles': 'We *could* learn to speak with Malcolm, and say that the term ['dream'] is *given* a series of new uses. But this obscures just what we want to stress'.[22] Exactly: what is at issue is what the two parties 'want to stress'. Malcolm wants to stress the autonomy of commonsense language-games: no one, he says, is 'required' to follow the example of the scientist.[23] By contrast, what Putnam wants to stress is the authority of the scientist. This is why he slides from a description of scientific practice to a normative conclusion about its legitimacy. This fallacious transition is obscured by appeal to the 'natural' character of the procedures described.[24] In the last analysis Putnam simply hands over to the scientist the question of how we ought to proceed, and lets him be judge in his own case:

> On our view, whether scientists at t_1 and scientists at t_2 are or are not talking about the same thing when they use a term is . . . to be ascertained by examining the relevant scientific theory (the latest available!).[25]

In the same way, the proper method for finding out what the word 'dream' has all along referred to, is to look at the latest available scientific theory.

What does the philosophical argument between Malcolm and Putnam really amount to? It amounts to two rival recommendations about the use of a concept where, in the end, both sides come close to admitting that it could be used as their opponent suggests. They have divergent preferences, but unable to refute their opponents, they display authorities and affirm allegiances. The authority of science lends credibility to one side; the authority of commonsense usage and daily practice lends credibility to the other. Now let us look at another case with a remarkably similar structure.

4.4   Who is to define 'reading'?

Not long after its publication Paul Feyerabend wrote a detailed review of the *Investigations*.[26] This has rightly become a standard analysis of the content and argument of that book. Feyerabend expounds the whole of Wittgenstein's position in terms of one important example: the concept of 'reading'.[27] Suppose, said Feyerabend, that a physiologist were to declare that reading was essentially a physiological process of a certain kind in the brain. Ignoring all the complexity of our everyday use of the concept, the scientist asserts that a person is really reading if, and only if, these special events are taking place in his nervous system. For Feyerabend this claim would be inadmissible and, we are given to understand, it would be inadmissible for Wittgenstein too.

To demonstrate this, Feyerabend poses a problem. What would happen if the neural process identified with reading was found in the brain of somebody who, by normal standards, was *not* reading? Suppose a subject is connected to the physiologist's apparatus and, though he is looking idly out of the window, his brain is undergoing the changes said to be characteristic of reading. Would we declare that here was a hitherto undiscovered case of reading? No, says Feyerabend emphatically. We would alter the physiological hypothesis. Conversely, suppose that during the course of reading aloud, the nervous process allegedly characteristic of reading only occurred during the pronunciation of one of the syllables of each of the longer words. Would we say that the subject was only really reading for a brief second, whilst the rest of his utterance was not in fact a case of reading? No, says Feyerabend, and insists that this would be quite meaningless.

The same arguments are repeated with a mental process substituted for a physiological process. Mental processes, says Feyerabend, 'are subject to the same kind of criticism as material processes'.[28] If we said that reading was really a characteristic feeling (say, the feeling of one's consciousness being determined by the symbols on the page), then what if the subject reported the feeling when he was not, in the ordinary sense, reading? Is this a new case of reading? No. Conversely, says Feyerabend, if someone were to read aloud, in the ordinary sense, we would not allow this description of his behaviour to be overruled by the report that the special feeling was not present. The same arguments refute both a mental and a physiological criterion of reading, because both 'cling to the same scheme of explanation'.[29]

If this is indeed Wittgenstein's position, then Wittgenstein is wrong. This will be easier to see if we accept Feyerabend's point that physiological and psychological theories are in the same boat. We can then concentrate on the physiologist. The question is: what is supposed to be wrong with the physiologist saying that he has discovered a hitherto unknown case of reading? If we really press the point we find that there is no decisive and general objection to such a response. We may also note that Feyerabend doesn't actually advance any argument. He poses the question rhetorically, and answers it dogmatically. So let us explore the option that Feyerabend foreclosed. What might tempt a physiologist to identify reading with a brain process? Such a proposal would only be credible if a rough correlation could be established between reading in the ordinary sense of the word and the brain event. This proves the historical priority of the everyday concept. But if there were a rough correlation, it would not be silly to advance the hypothesis that reading was to be identified with the brain event. All that would be happening is that what started out as an observed concomitant of a phenomenon is taking over as the definition. We have Wittgenstein's word for it that this is a commonplace process. Symptoms can become criteria (*PI*, I, 79).

Feyerabend focused on what would happen if the physiological correlates were detected on their own. He assumed that this would refute the identification. But the idea of a hitherto unidentified case of reading is not really laughable. It is a natural thing to say if we want to preserve the law that identified reading with the brain process. It simply involves modifying the scope of the concept. The isolated occurrence of the brain process would then be treated as a problem calling for research. Perhaps physiologists would refer to these events as cases of pseudo-reading, or unconscious reading, or brain-reading. They could theorise about them, and test their theories, and perhaps interesting results would emerge. Here are some of the theories that could be tried. Recall that Feyerabend had our subject staring out of the window (to emphasise that he is in no wise reading). The physiologist might wonder if his subject's preoccupation was caused by his silent rehearsal of something he had previously read. Perhaps one part of the brain is replaying the sensory experience of reading, while another part is responding to these internal stimuli – just as it had earlier responded to the external stimuli from the page. This would explain the recurrence of the physiological processes normally detected during reading – one part of the brain was reading messages from another part.

If further research supported this idea then it would make sense to congratulate the physiologist on discovering a new case of reading. The revised usage would be no more an outrage than talking about 'imaginary' numbers in mathematics. These, it will be recalled, were offered by Wittgenstein as entirely acceptable cases where our notation is modified in order to highlight certain similarities and play down others. As in these cases, the extended application of the word 'reading' reclassifies phenomena and modifies the application of words to accord with the direction of scientific research, and the 'needs' of the scientist.

The same applies to the other side of Feyerabend's argument. This dealt with the absence of the crucial physiological process during episodes that would normally count as reading. Clearly, any gross disparity would remove credibility from the usage but, as before, a few anomalies would provoke a flurry of research, not a rejection of the idea. Perhaps the momentary occurrence, rather than continual presence, of the physiological process implies a 'snap-shot' theory of the intake of information. Perhaps reading without the physiological process – or, for that matter, without the characteristic feelings – is detectably different from reading with it, say in degree of comprehension or retention.

The point of these flights of fancy does not lie in their details or plausibility. They are to remind us that our classificatory decisions depend on our purposes and the overall pattern of our activity. Feyerabend's discussion is defective because it fails to put the physiologist's and psychologist's choices into a proper context. They are made to look silly by being presented in an unrealistic way. If there was no inductive basis for the proposed identification in the first place, if there was no likely pay-off in terms of the coherence of the new usage with the results of further enquiry, then indeed there would be nothing to recommend it. But there can be sound reasons for doing the kind of thing that Feyerabend treats as wrong in principle.

Although it would be possible to contest the point, I am taking it for granted that Feyerabend is faithful in his portrayal of the Wittgensteinean position. There are differences between the two writers, but these are mainly the differences between caution and equivocation on the one hand, and clarity on the other hand. Wittgenstein was obviously treading rather carefully on these top-ics, as well he might. But Feyerabend has certainly caught the anti-scientific spirit of the argument. This means that the defects in his position can reasonably be laid at Wittgenstein's door too.

4.5   Agency and action

The extensive vocabulary of words that we use to frame everyday accounts of action include 'reason', 'desire', 'intention' and 'motive'. Wittgenstein's work is full of intriguing comments about the language-games in which these words feature. He tells us, for example, that the 'game of giving the reason why one acts in a particular way does not involve finding the causes of one's actions (by frequent observations of the condition under which they arise)' (*BB*, p.110). What, then, is the game? It consists in making our actions intelligible by relating them to an accepted pattern of conduct and expectation. These patterns are known to all competent social actors and so they are readily available for the purposes of explanation and justification. They do not require statistical evidence before they can be cited. For this reason an intention is something that is, as Wittgenstein put it, embedded in human customs and institutions (*PI*, I, 337).

One of the great contributions of Wittgenstein's followers has been to develop these ideas into a detailed analysis of our everyday psychological language-games. Of the various statements of this position I shall select for discussion A. I. Melden's book, *Free Action*.[30] The starting-point of our everyday language-games, says Melden, is the assumption of agency. We take it for granted that we are dealing with people, not things, and that people have certain primitive abilities. Consider the notion of desire or want. We can learn something, says Melden, by seeing how we apply these ideas to animals. Here 'wanting is exhibited transparently in the very character of the doing itself'.[31] This uninhibited wanting reminds us that observable behaviour provides our ultimate criterion. 'It is by reference to such doings that the rudiments of the concept of wanting can be grasped.'[32] The point of imputing wants in more complex cases is to use the simple case as an object of comparison, and make a pattern visible despite inhibitions, disguises and sophistications.

To explain an action means finding a classification in terms of wants or motives or intentions which can be sustained through an ever-widening circle of circumstances and consequences. It is like finding the reading of a text that is consistent with what follows. Melden is at his best when he is showing how the categorisation of an act comes to implicate its context. He proceeds dialectically, starting from simple movements and showing how understanding them requires us to move outwards until the whole system of surrounding convention is involved.[33] What makes the raising of an arm an act of signalling a right turn? Obviously, that it is done by the occupant of a car, on a road, against a background understanding of the conventions of signalling. It is 'conditions or circumstances', he says, that '*constitute* or *define* the bodily movement as the action that it is'.[34] For Melden, 'conditions or circumstances' are structured by 'social and moral institutions, conventions, statutes, etc.'[35] Social intercourse is between people who relate to one another as specific sorts of person, as 'employers and employees, sellers and purchasers, motorists, strangers, friends'.[36] In practice we never work with the category of action or agent as such, but only with this or that sort of action and agent, particularised within a 'complex network of social and moral conventions'.[37]

Melden does not hesitate to draw radical conclusions. If our mental states do not progressively *reveal* themselves, but are progressively 'constituted and defined' by ever-broader social contexts, then as that context changes, so too will their essential meaning. (As the social 'text' unfolds, so we may decide a certain sentence must have meant, all along, something different.) If the same behaviour is placed within, or viewed from, a different context, so its essential nature will be differently accounted. What is judged as 'voluntary' here will be judged 'involuntary' from there, says Melden. These issues are not to be settled by a return to the inner nature of the action. These have no determinate form other than that which is socially imputed.[38]

The stress on institutions and conventions is quite characteristic of Wittgensteinean work. Melden's book is not at all idiosyncratic. Indeed, others are even more explicit. R. S. Peters, for example, analyses the imputation of motives in the same anti-psychological, but pro-sociological, way. The question 'Why did X do that?', he says, is usually the request 'for an elucidation of the whole pattern of conventions', and then adds:

> I would go so far as to say that anthropology or sociology must be the basic sciences of human action in that they exhibit the systematic framework of norms and goals which are necessary to classify actions as being of a certain sort.[39]

One might pause at the words 'exhibit' and 'classify', and wonder what has happened to the goal of explanation, but the general point seems clear. Nevertheless there is a problem. That problem may be epitomised by a single but intriguing fact. In 1940 the sociologist C. Wright Mills wrote a well-known paper called 'Situated Actions and Vocabularies of Motive'.[40] This argued exactly the thesis developed many years later by Peters and Melden. However, none of the philosophical writers who developed Wittgenstein's ideas have made any reference to it. Furthermore, a comparison with Melden's work, over thirty years later, shows no advance in either positive content or programmatic level over Mills's pioneering effort. Had Mills's paper been an isolated production, and had it borne no connection with subsequent lines of empirical enquiry, then it would be easy to see how it could have been overlooked. In fact it belongs to a prominent body of work in sociology devoted to a study of practical psychological reasoning.[41] It is therefore difficult to allay the suspicion that, unlike sociologists, philosophers don't really want to study practical reasoning at all. They do not seem fascinated by it for its own sake. Could their professed concern with it be just a means to another end? Their goal is, surely, something quite other. They are erecting a barrier to stop, or contain, the advance of causal, deterministic models of mind and action of the kind developed by psychologists and physiologists. Everything else is subordinate to this concern:

> Common-sense, which is incorporated in the concepts of ordinary language, has creamed off most of the vital distinctions. Psychology has the task of systematizing what is already known and adding bits of special theory to supplement common-sense.[42]

In psychology, the role of Galileo, we are told, must be forever unoccupied.

4.6 Causes and redescriptions

Melden says that the causal idiom of the sciences is 'wholly irrelevant to the understanding we seek' in our everyday description of
behaviour.[43] Can this be true? When we say we act because of a
reason, what other sense of 'because' do we have except a causal
sense? And what other causal sense is there, but one that ultimately reduces to that used by physicists and physiologists? This,
in essence, is the reply given to Melden by Davidson in his paper
'Action, Reasons and Causes'.[44] Notice, he says, how Melden's
analysis takes for granted that agents act for reasons. This by-
passes the crucial question of how we should analyse the link
between reasons and actions. Again, when Melden discusses the
signalling episode, what he really explains is what makes the
movement a signal, not why the agent raised his arm. The explanation of why someone raises his arm might be: he is driving,
wants to make a turn, notices the turn approaching, and knows the
proper procedure. Why not treat these states of readiness, and
these inputs of sensory experience, as causes? Perhaps this will
even turn out to be consistent with most of the rest of what Melden
wants to say.

One obvious bias in Melden's analysis comes from his tendency
to over-simplify the character of causal thinking in science. This
gives a spurious credibility to the contrast he wants to draw
between causal and everyday explanations. It removes all the
subtle interpretative work that goes into making causal links visible in science. Thus we find Melden saying that whereas motives
explain by giving a fuller characterisation of an action, a causal
explanation is not concerned with the identity or character of the
effect. A causal explanation leaves the description of the phenomenon unchanged. As a comment about science this is ill-informed.
It implies that scientific discoveries are superficial pieces of natural
history, with no theoretical component. Many examples could be
cited to show that important discoveries amount to a new way of
looking at the world.[45] It would be nearer the truth to say that
redescription is *more* prominent, and *more* radical in science than
elsewhere. We may, perhaps, usefully redescribe a man's anger as
'anger at losing in cards' (in preference to the face-saving description favoured by the irritable player), but this in no way matches
the enormous conceptual changes that take place in science.[46]

The issue of redescription is really the hinge upon which the whole argument turns. Consider, for example, the question of scientific generality. The contrast between the generality of scientific law, and the particularity of non-scientific modes of understanding, has always been central. We say of a particular person on a particular occasion: 'He married her for her money.' This neither means nor implies that he does everything for money, or is always marrying for money. It is a statement about a unique event. Even if we offer an explanation in terms of the scoundrel's character, that would not, apparently, be an embryonic statement of a law. This is shown, says Melden, by the fact that we know that people can act out of character, but we don't treat these events as refutations of the imputation. The concepts do not have the same logic as scientific ones. So while we can, if we wish, say his desire for her money, or his rotten character, were the 'causes' of his behaviour, they are certainly not causes in the scientist's sense.[47] Davidson's reply is to invoke the possibilities of redescription. We also make statements about singular causal occurrences, he says, when describing events in the physical world. We see a stone break a window. We as good as see the causal link, but physics textbooks don't contain laws about bricks and windows. Nevertheless we have sufficient experience of deplorable events of this kind to be confident that *some* causal laws exist of which these cases are instances. In other words, we are confident that there exists a vocabulary (of mass, velocity, momentum, force, stress, etc.) that differs from our everyday vocabulary, so that if the event were redescribed in these terms, its law-like characteristics would be unveiled.

Stated intuitively, the point is that we believe there are underlying regularities in phenomena, and while these may not be either explicit or open to formulation in an existing vocabulary, they could be formulated in a new set of terms. It is arguable, for example, that men knew there must be *some* regularity connecting the behaviour of light and shadows before they hit on the principle of rectilinear propagation and the methods of representation used in geometrical optics.[48] In the same way, the stability and utility of our commonsense understanding of behaviour might be held to offer the strongest presumption of, at least some, underlying causal laws.[49]

If redescription offers hope to the believers in a causal science of behaviour, then we can appreciate why their opponents have tried so strenuously to block, or simply obscure, that same process. The strategy adopted by opponents of scientific redescription has two parts to it. First, it is shown that any redescription involving the idea of causes and laws is incompatible with our existing common-sense descriptions. Second, our existing descriptions must be shown to be preferable. Here the goal is to convince us that commonsense descriptions are uniquely equipped to capture the true character of our behaviour. They, and they alone, convey its essence, or draw their conceptual boundaries along the same lines as reality itself. In short, they fit so snugly onto the world, that nothing could improve on them. The privileged character of commonsense descriptions is conveyed by treating them as simply equivalent to the facts of the case. They are not the facts as seen in a certain light; they just are the facts. They define the very subject-matter, so any other description is an irrelevance or a distortion. Thus, says Melden,

> it must appear problematic at best that the physiological psychologist who purports to be attempting to explain human action is addressing himself to his ostensible subject-matter.[50]

Here are some of the typical arguments adopted by those who are pursuing this strategy. To show that commonsense and causal descriptions exclude each other it has been argued that talk about desires and motives has a teleological or goal-oriented structure. Desires are directed at objects, whereas, says Melden, 'physiological occurrences are blind'.[51] For this reason no mere happening in the natural world, which is the province of the scientist, could have the required logical features.[52] To show that commonsense descriptions simply define the 'subject-matter', some authors try to capture the phenomenology of action, with its felt experience of purposiveness, so that we can see how faithfully it is reflected in everyday discourse. This, they conclude, must constitute an 'original and inescapable language'.[53]

Let us grant all these points, rather than tangle with the issues of detail that they raise. The important thing is how little follows from them, and how they fail to establish the conclusion they are meant to establish. First, they do nothing to clarify the relationship between everyday discourse and such scientific descriptions of behaviour as already exist. In ordinary parlance, I raise my arm. For the physiologist the arm rises, and certain events take place in nerves and muscles. Melden asserts, rightly, that it is 'the very same thing that is the rising of my arm that is also describable as my raising my arm'.[54] The descriptions can meet in the same event, but the descriptions are said to exclude one another. This spells trouble. Davidson puts his finger on the difficulty. Melden says that actions can be identical with movements. He allows, to the physiologist, that bodily movements have causes, but he denies that these are the causes of the actions. 'This, I think', says Davidson, 'is a contradiction.'[55]

Second, even if we grant complete incompatibility, or incommensurability, between scientific and everyday descriptions, that does not preclude the displacement of one by the other and the redescription of the phenomenon. Indeed, this is typical of the theoretical changes that take place during scientific revolutions. The oxygen theory of combustion, for example, was logically incompatible with the older phlogiston theory, but this did not preclude its introduction.[56] This comparison shows just how comic these defences of commonsense descriptions of action really are. Imagine defenders of the phlogiston theory trying to fend off Lavoisier by a philosophical argument of the following kind: our theory defines the facts, they say, the 'subject-matter' of any theory of combustion. Logical scrutiny of the oxygen theory proves that it could never yield conclusions about phlogiston. Therefore: 'it is problematic at best that Lavoisier, who purports to be attempting to explain combustion, is addressing himself to his ostensible subject-matter'. This is not, I think, a mode of argument that would carry much weight. It amounts to saying: we got there first.

Third, suppose we grant that the ordinary language of action and motive and reason has every kind of phenomenological, historic, or pragmatic priority that we care to claim for it. Let us suppose that it is indeed an 'original and inescapable language'. From this it follows that all the scientific studies that might be used to justify a mechanistic redescription of human behaviour must be conducted in this language. The experiments are done by people who think of themselves as agents, and they are done on people who are also treated as agents. (Think of how they are persuaded to act as subjects, how their duties and tasks are explained, how they are thanked, and the next appointment made.) From this it follows that the causal conclusions that are drawn from the experiments must be, in some sense, parasitic.[57] The question is: in what sense? I suggest that it is the same sense as that in which a physicist's understanding of atoms and molecules must be parasitic upon his prior understanding of tables, chairs and billiard balls. If theoretical concepts like 'atom' and 'molecule' are subject to a logical analysis, it is evident that their meaning must be constructed out of concepts which have reference to observable entities. A plausible account of how this construction takes place is that observable objects provide models and metaphors with which to think and talk about minute and unobservable objects. Concepts like 'billard ball' can be learned by ostension and then displaced and refined and used in new ways to form an idea of gas molecules.[58] In this way the concept of 'molecule' is parasitic on that of, say, 'billiard ball'. With regard to its meaning, therefore, a concept like 'molecule' has a secondary status. It does not follow from this, however, that from an explanatory and ontological standpoint it cannot be deemed to be primary. We can still say that we must explain the behaviour of macro-objects by appeal to the micro-objects of which they are composed. The concept of a molecule is built out of the concept of a billiard ball; but billiard balls, as objects, are built out of atoms, as objects. The fallacy committed by those who oppose the enterprise of redescription is to present arguments that are pertinent to questions of logical analysis, and draw conclusions about questions of explanation and material composition. Analysis and explanation are two different relations, and the patterns of dependence they refer to point, so to speak, in different directions. It is no impediment to a causal and mechanistic theory of behaviour to say that its concepts are logically secondary.[59]

4.7 What game are we playing?

The positive accomplishments of the Wittgensteinean analysis of our everyday, psychological language-games have been considerable. We now understand their detailed mechanics far better than before. In particular, we can see how different they often are from neighbouring scientific language-games. Furthermore, these differences are made intelligible by noting the purposes the language-games are meant to serve, and the purposes they are not meant to serve. This is a descriptive achievement of no mean order, and it has considerable explanatory potential. It must be admitted that the descriptions that philosophers have offered are of an impressionistic nature, innocent of the controls that would be expected of similar descriptions offered by anthropologists, historians or sociologists. Nevertheless a valuable start has been made.

Unfortunately, we have seen another issue raise its head. Instead of saying 'commonsense proceeds like this', and then going on to explain its structure, we have found that philosophers have said: 'and this is right and this is wrong'. They have turned the exercise into a debate between science and commonsense. Description has become subordinated to apologetics. Think, for example, of Malcolm's debate with Putnam over dreams, or Feyerabend's discussion of the physiology of reading. They were just rehearsing actual or potential conflicts between the layman and the scientists. The real points under debate were: who *owns* the concept of dreaming? and who *owns* the concept of reading? That is: what body of persons shall decide the proper pattern of use of these concepts? What skills and preoccupations will be most prominently reflected in their applications? Feyerabend and Malcolm back the parent and schoolmaster; Putnam backs the scientific specialist. This is disappointing. The real duty of the analyst is not to be an advocate of the interests of this or that social reference group. It is to make clear that we have a choice and to spell out its ramifications. Ideally the task would also include a study of the factors that underly the conventions of the different groups involved. The social practices of both specialist and layman are perfectly viable. No wonder that Putnam invoked the picture of closed circles, that Malcolm conceded the naturalness of his opponent's practices, and that Feyerabend advanced no real arguments against his imaginary physiologist.

The effect of this decision to take sides has brought the whole enterprise perilously close to disaster. It has not only threatened its descriptive accuracy, it has threatened to overturn Wittgenstein's basic insight: that usage determines meaning. The result of taking sides has been to tempt philosophers into arguments that move, fallaciously, from premises about the meaning of concepts to conclusions about their proper usage. Meanings are turned into essences and used to measure the legitimacy of proposed uses. The physiologist can't say this: it would betray the concept of 'reading'. The psychologist can't say this: it would betray the concept of 'dreaming'. We can't redescribe behaviour causally, or begin to construe our ordinary talk of desires and motives causally: it would betray the essential character of our understanding. And the fallacies of one party have, as we have seen, sometimes tempted the other party into a corresponding error.

Let me take a single example that brings out the point with particular clarity. Recall what Melden, and other philosophers, have said about explanations that appeal to 'character'.[60] They say that we do not treat it as if it were an embryonic scientific theory about the causes of a person's behaviour. We do not see it as a kind of 'force' impelling certain kinds of action. The reason they give to justify their claims is that we do not treat out-of-character behaviour as a scientist would treat counter-instances to his laws, or anomalies in his theories. They are neither treated as refutations of a character imputation; nor do they lead us to complicate our model. We don't postulate counter-vailing 'forces' that on some occasion prove stronger than the 'force' of character. Subject to the qualifications mentioned above this seems reasonably well observed. At least, we may grant that it is. What follows from it? We may indeed conclude that the concept of character is not a 'scientific' concept. It is, after all, what usage makes it. The fact that we let it co-exist with anomalies in a way that is (arguably) untypical for concepts used by scientists is sufficient evidence. The important point, though, is that nothing whatsoever follows about how the concept *ought* to be used, or about how it *might* come to be used. There is nothing in any of the observations that are made about the concept of character to show that we could not begin to take anomalies much more seriously. We could begin to change our practice and this would then change the logic of the concept, and therefore, in a sense, its meaning. If philosophers were simply describing usage they would be right. If they were simply making that usage intelligible by relating it to a given pattern of 'needs', thresholds of importance, and structures of relevance, then they would be right. If they were simply guessing that the concept will never be usefully refined, then they might be right. But when they try to legislate, their position is groundless.

The question is: what game do we want to play? Do we want to take sides in the battle between science and commonsense, or do we want to understand and explain that potential conflict? I shall opt for the latter course. I propose to take seriously the Wittgensteinean invitation to be descriptive. I shall not construe this to mean 'describe but don't build theories.' I shall take it to mean 'describe, don't evaluate.'

> In describing reality I describe what I come upon among men. Similarly, sociology must describe our conduct and our valuations just like those of the Negroes. It can only report what occurs. But the proposition, 'Such-and-such means progress', must never occur in a sociologist's description.
>
> (*WWK*, pp.115-16)

I shall now look at how Wittgenstein applies these widely ignored precepts to some of the most intriguing problems facing the sociologist of knowledge. In the next two chapters I shall discuss Wittgenstein's ideas about mathematics and logic. My aim will be to show how he opens these subjects to sociological scrutiny, and to give some examples of the kind of work that can be built upon these insights.

5

Mathematics: An Anthropological Phenomenon

Wittgenstein had been a schoolteacher, and when he spoke of the 'foundations' of mathematics he gave the word an appropriately robust meaning. Elementary instruction is the foundation for later learning. The foundations of mathematics are the psychological, social and empirical facts upon which the structure of knowledge is actually raised. A child has got to the bottom of arithmetic when he has learned how to apply numbers, 'and that's all there is to it' (*LFM*, p.271).[1] This is a deliberate rejection of the idea of 'foundations' as it is used by logicians such as Russell and Frege. They say that logic is the foundation of mathematics. They want to start with logically primitive concepts and exhibit an unbroken chain of deduction that leads up to mathematics proper.[2] But, asks Wittgenstein, 'Why hanker after logic?' (*LFM*, p.271). Mathematics and logic are two language-games on a par with one another: both equally the product of instinct, training and convention. One is no more a foundation for the other 'than the painted rock is the support of a painted tower' (*RFM*, V,13).[3] To look at mathematics through the eyes of the logician will be to overlook all the techniques of inference that are special to it, and all the differences between those techniques (*RFM*, IV,24).

If we are going to adapt a truly descriptive approach, if we are going to see mathematics as 'an anthropological phenomenon', then we must strip away some to the myths that protect it from scrutiny (*RFM*, V,26). One such myth is the doctrine of mathematical realism or 'Platonism', and I shall begin by looking at Wittgenstein's attack on it.

5.1 How the thread runs

Platonism is the view that mathematical results are discoveries about a special realm of objects that exist prior to our knowledge of them. Arithmetical propositions are true because they correspond to facts about entities called 'numbers'. Geometry informs us of the relations between idealised entities called 'points' and 'lines'. Advocates of this view have never fully explained the mode of being, of, say, numbers, or clearly described how they intermingle with ordinary material objects. All they do is stress that they are different, more basic, and never change. On this view, mathematics becomes a kind of natural history of these strange entities. The more recondite areas of mathematics, for example those dealing with infinite numbers, then hold for us the same charm as those branches of natural history that deal with exotic species (*LFM*, p.140).

This view may sound naive, but we often fall back on it because it answers to some of our deepest feelings about the objectivity of theorems and proofs. Eminent and creative mathematicians have held variants of this theory. Wittgenstein's Cambridge contemporary G. H. Hardy said:

> I believe that mathematical reality lies outside us, that our function is to discover or *observe* it, and that the theorems which we prove, and which we describe grandiloquently as our 'creations' are simply our notes of our observations.[4]

The noted logician Kurt Gödel similarly claimed we 'have something like a perception ... of the objects of set theory', as witnessed by the fact that its premises 'force themselves upon us as being true'. Gödel did not mean that the objects that mathematical theories are about act on our sense-organs. He thought that we had another kind of intuitive relation to them that was equally objective. The presence of these perceptions, he said, 'may be due to another kind of relationship between ourselves and reality'.[5]

These ideas were anathema to Wittgenstein. He was to try again and again to 'show that what is called a mathematical discovery had much better be called a mathematical invention' (*LFM*, p.22). The trouble with Platonism is that it encourages us to respect the air of mystery that lingers around some mathematical concepts, instead of immediately realising that this indicates an error in our understanding (*RFM*, IV,16). Nevertheless, Wittgenstein is sensitive in his portrayal of Platonism and its temptations. He describes how, though the mental process of multiplying 25 by 25 happens at a certain moment in time, we feel that in the mathematical realm 25 × 25 is *already* 625 (*LFM*, p.145). The Platonist speaks as if we have merely traced out what was already faintly written down. We do not think of it as a peculiarity of *our* nature, that we get *this* result. The fact does not seem a psychological one. A person playing our language-game of calculation is:

> under the impression that he has only followed a thread that is already there, and accepting the How of the following as something that is a matter of course; and only knowing *one* explanation of his action, namely: how the thread runs.
>
> (*RFM*, V,4)

Compelling as it is, the impression is wrong. To see why, Wittgenstein selects a very simple example of a mathematical inference: the continuation of a number sequence like 2, 4, 6, 8 . . . Suppose we are told the rule of the sequence: we are to add 2 each time. We are to reflect on the nature of this simple mathematical act of thought, and ask what is going on and how it is to be explained. The example is so simple that if Platonism fails here, then it fails everywhere.

Superficially, the Platonist has no trouble describing this example in terms of his theory. After all, the correct continuation of the sequence, the true embodiment of the rule and its intended application, already exists. We just continue the sequence in the *same* way, and we can do this, and know what it means, by stating the rule of the sequence to ourselves. The feeling imposes itself that there is only one right way to go on. This arises from our capacity to observe, or directly intuit, features of mathematical reality, in the way that Hardy and Gödel indicated.

Wittgenstein's counter-argument shows us that this reply hides the real problem. The Platonist is actually presupposing the very competence that he is meant to be explaining. In a typically compressed passage the argument is stated like this:

> And if I know it *in advance*, what use is this knowledge to me later on? I mean: how do I know what to do with this earlier

knowledge when the step actually has to be taken? . . . 'But do you mean to say that the expression '+2' leaves you in doubt what you are to do e.g. after 2004?' – No; I answer '2006' without hesitation. But just for that reason it is superfluous to suppose that this was determined earlier on. My having no doubt in face of the question does *not* mean that it has been answered in advance.

(*RFM*, I,3)

Obviously this argument is connected with the earlier criticisms of the mental-image and mental-act theories and the idea of 'extension', but it is of such importance that it deserves to be analysed step by step. The Platonist assumes that we have access to some kind of archetype of the number series. This seems to explain our continuation of the series because we know the answers in advance. But now, says Wittgenstein, the original problem just repeats itself. How does the person following the archetype know that it really is the correct embodiment of the rule he wants? To know that the archetype is correct requires exactly the knowledge that was considered problematic in the first place: namely, knowledge of how the rule goes.

The trouble with Platonism is not that its ontology is obscure (which it is), but that its epistemology is circular. Suppose we follow Wittgenstein's rule of externalisation and give mathematical reality an entirely clear status. Let us suppose mathematical objects can be quite literally perceived. Suppose the answers are indeed already written down faintly, and continuing the series just means copying them out. The objection of circularity still holds. This cannot explain how we know that what we are copying is the correct answer. The Platonist's problem is like that of the schoolboy who cheats. He has to know who has the right answers to copy from. This is brought out in the even more compressed version of the argument that Wittgenstein gave in his 1939 *Lectures*. The Platonist says that 25×25 is *already* 625, but 'then it's also 624, or 623, or any damn thing'. The problem is picking out the *right* archetype from all the other wrong, but possible, archetypes which are, so to speak, adjacent to it. If, with the Platonist we postulate a shadow world of mathematical reality, we must not forget that this is no help because there are 'an infinity of shadowy worlds. Then the whole utility of this [assumption] breaks down, because we don't know which of them we're talking about' (*LFM*, p.145).

These arguments are very strong ones. Unfortunately there is one loophole in them that must be blocked before we can declare Platonism refuted. Hardy's talk of 'observing' mathematical reality, and Gödel's hints about 'another kind of relationship between ourselves and reality' could, I think, be reconstructed in a way that by-passes Wittgenstein's charge of circularity. Suppose the Platonist said: 'But I don't mean that what I do now ... determines the future use *causally* ... but that in a *queer* way, the use itself is in some sense present' (*RFM*, I,126).[6] For example, suppose we assumed a natural tendency of the mind to select the right archetype: a natural tendency to move towards a truth that is 'in some sense present'. Grant a teleological premise of this kind, and take it to define that 'other relationship' with reality at which Gödel hinted, and the circularity argument falls to the ground. It might be objected that a combination of Platonist ontology and teleological epistemology is even more question-begging than the original version of the theory. But, in fact, there is no logical circularity involved. It is the premises as such that are being objected to. The only grounds with which to justify such an objection are methodological ones. It can be said, for example, that a teleological picture is of little utility for purposes of research and inhibits the process of enquiry. We are, in other words, thrown back on the objection that such a view does not fit into current modes of scientific thinking. If, and only if, we use some such argument to block the resort to teleology can we declare that Wittgenstein's circularity objection disposes of Platonism as an account of mathematical practice.[7]

Where does this leave the issue of the right way to continue the number sequence, and follow the rule '+2'? It leaves it entirely dependent on instinct, training and convention. Wittgenstein makes this abundantly clear by painting a picture of what would happen if a pupil, being taught to add 2, repeated the sequence up to 1000 and then continued 1004, 1008, etc. When challenged we are to suppose that he declares that this *is* going on in the 'same' way. When we say that this is not going according to the rule he throws the objection back in our face: who says what 'accords' means here? We can coax and threaten; we can try to convey by gesture, precept and example what we want and what we mean by 'same'; but our reasons will soon give out. 'I have reached bedrock' says Wittgenstein, 'and my spade is turned' (*PI*, I,217).

Wittgenstein's rejection of Platonism is intimately connected with his finitism. The number series does not exist in advance of our use of it: its reality extends no further than our actual practice. The reason why it seems to pre-exist is because our use of the rule has become a mechanical routine. 'The rule can only seem to me to produce all its consequences in advance if I draw them as *a matter of course*' (*PI*, I,238). This has some interesting consequences. It means that every time we calculate a new decimal point, say in the expansion of π, we are being creative.[8] Wittgenstein does not hesitate to draw this conclusion. Because a number series does not exist in advance we cannot say, for example, that either there are, or there are not, four consecutive sevens in the decimal expansion of π. Intuitively, it seems obviously true that we can apply the law of the excluded middle in this way. After all, we can even get a calculating machine to churn out the expansion of π. If it printed out 7777 we would say that all along the sequence was there waiting to be discovered.

Wittgenstein's position is that we don't really know what we are saying when we glibly refer to the unknown and uncomputed parts of an infinite sequence of numbers of this kind. We are transferring intuitions derived from *finite* sequences of numbers, and are assuming that they apply without difficulty to the infinite case. If the machine printed out 7777 we would then know that a *finite* sequence contained the run of numbers. But the problem still remains of how we should talk about the case where it has not yet printed them out. Because Wittgenstein is being so boldly counterintuitive it is important that we appreciate the point he is trying to make. He is trying to remove or combat a certain picture that attaches to the remorselessness and inexorability of our mathematical practice. But, he says, what is in question

> is of course not merely the case of the expansion of a real number, or in general the production of mathematical signs, but every analogous process, whether it is a game, a dance, etc.
>
> (*RFM*, IV,9)

The point is that what we count as a continuation of the same process is not completely specifiable. As well as the mechanical repetition of the computations that are currently counted as 'generating the expansion' of π, there is always the possibility of entirely new techniques being introduced. These may radically alter our conception of what an infinite sequence actually is. This is why Wittgenstein asks what does 'the pattern . . . occurs' mean? (*RFM*, V,12).

Wittgenstein has a precedent in mind: the expansion of the concept of number to include complex numbers involving $i = \sqrt{-1}$. This is why he hints that these, as yet unknown, ways of looking at infinite series may involve us getting into a new 'dimension', where 'the mathematics of this further dimension has yet to be invented' (*RFM*, IV,11). This happened when complex numbers were introduced. We usually think of the real numbers as packed onto a line. Complex numbers can be represented as points on a plane. This is the other dimension. The complex number $a + ib$ refers to the point with co-ordinates (a, b) and can therefore be used to represent vectors, or directed lines, which connect a point of origin $(0, 0)$ with (a, b). By

> surrounding $\sqrt{-1}$ by talk about vectors, it sounds quite natural to talk of a thing whose square is -1. That which at first seemed out of the question, if you surround it by the right kind of intermediate cases, becomes the most natural thing possible.
>
> (*LFM*, p.226)[9]

Just as the nonsensical idea of the square root of a negative number can suddenly receive a clear meaning, so we may come to renegotiate the apparently self-evident assertion that either four consecutive sevens occur in π, or they don't. Our notion of what it is to follow the rule for generating π may change radically: 'If you read the newspapers and see how people get round pacts, you should not be surprised at this' (*LFM*, p.238).

The alternative to Platonism is some form of naturalism, and the most usual form of naturalistic theory of mathematics derives from empiricism. I shall now examine what Wittgenstein has to say about this approach.

5.2 'Doing drill with marbles'

Wittgenstein defines his relation to empiricist theories of mathematics by his account of the connection between calculations and experiments. Empiricists represent arithmetic as a set of simple but very general laws of nature. This approach has its virtues. It looks like obscurantism, says Wittgenstein, to deny that a calculation is a sort of experiment. But really these are two different language-games. They represent 'different modes of employment of words' (*RFM*, II,76). Suppose we put 2 apples on a table, make sure no one comes near or shakes the table, and then put on another 2 apples. If we count them the probability is that we will get the answer 4. Construed as an experiment about apples and human counting, nothing more needs to be said. We simply accept the result, as we would if the result were different. (If apples vanished of their own accord we would get different results, and this might show that apples were no good for teaching arithmetic.) Construed as a calculation, we don't simply accept the result. A certain result is deemed right and others wrong. The answer 4 acts as a base-line for describing what has happened, for example whether things have stayed the same or whether an apple has disappeared. It can be used to channel our descriptions, and it becomes part of the assumed background for conducting experiments. But, of course, the proper result of calculation is, nevertheless, 'connected with the facts of experience' (*RFM*, V,3). They are facts of experience that have, as he puts it elsewhere, become 'petrified' (*LFM*, P.98). Calculations are grounded in certain 'techniques' and 'the physical and psychological facts that make the technique *possible*'. But calculations don't express or state these conditions; they take them for granted (*RFM*, V,1).

What are these 'techniques'? Wittgenstein's examples show that he is referring to conventional routines for manipulating objects, including symbols. To forget the vital significance of conventions makes it look as if we have a direct apprehension of mathematical truth. Wittgenstein imagines someone saying: 'You need only look at the figure

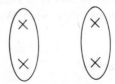

Figure 5.1

to see that 2 + 2 are 4.' The claim is that we can directly apprehend the mathematical significance of the figure without the need for accepted techniques for analysing it, and without any agreed conventions for manipulating its parts or synthesising the information it is meant to convey. Wittgenstein deftly demolishes that error: in that case, he says, 'I only need look at the figure

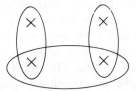

Figure 5.2

to see that 2 + 2 + 2 are 4' (*RFM*, I,38).[10] The point is that the arithmetical truth has a complex relationship to the physical world, including the physical symbols used to represent it. If we believe we can see directly through Figure 5.1 to the mathematical essence it portrays this is because we are taking for granted all the habits and conventions that are involved. Without them the procedure of Figure 5.2 would be as legitimate a response.

Of all the indefinitely large number of techniques for manipulating objects that exist, we select those that provide useful patterns. If the technique of combining, or 'adding', shapes like this

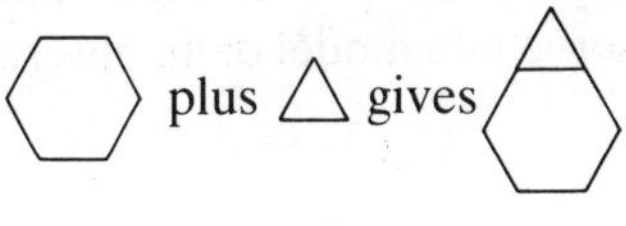

$$\bigcirc \text{ plus } \triangle \text{ gives } \bigcirc$$

Figure 5.3

were highly important in our daily life, then 'our ordinary concept of arithmetical addition would perhaps be different' (*RFM*, V,40). The operations and techniques that are fastened upon, and which become memorable patterns, are the ones that become central to the training given to children.

> What I am saying comes to this, that mathematics is *normative* ... Mathematics forms a network of norms.
>
> (*RFM*, V,41 and V,46)[11]

Wittgenstein carefully explains that 'norm' does not mean the same as 'ideal'. In other words, the compelling force of mathematical procedures does not derive from their being transcendent, but from their being accepted and used by a group of people. The procedures are not accepted because they are correct, or correspond to an ideal; they are deemed correct because they are accepted. Mathematical truth, said Wittgenstein, isn't established by agreement, as if we were all 'witnesses of it'. It is *because* we agree that 'we lay it down as a rule, and put it in the archives' (*LFM*, p.107). The basis and cause of these agreements are not matters to be settled by *a priori* reflection. They must be investigated empirically: 'One might give an ethnological account of this human institution' (*RFM*, V,2). The first step towards such an account, however, is to be clear about the general character of the norms or techniques involved.

What our mathematical techniques for manipulating objects and symbols do is to produce one structure out of another. We use them as paradigms of identity – complicated definitions of identity – but their 'experimental character disappears when one looks at the process simply as a memorable picture' (*RFM*, I,80). We use them to define the 'essential' features of a change and see them as yielding relations which are not merely contingent:

> We regard the calculation as demonstrating an *internal property* (a property of the *essence*). But what does that mean? The following might serve as a model of an 'internal property':

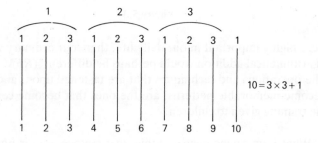

$$10 = 3 \times 3 + 1$$

(*RFM*, I,99)

There seems to be something inexorable and undeniable about this (though we know from the little example of the four crosses in Figures 5.1 and 5.2 that this is not so). In fact it is just a picture until it is given a use and incorporated into a technique (*RFM*, I,62). If we forget this we will think of the picture as dictating its own use, as if it possessed 'action at a distance', but that mysterious property really resides in the fact that we apply the scheme in a definite way (*RFM*, I,65).

Wittgenstein is here proceeding along typically Durkheimean lines. The claim is that the belief in mathematical essences is a reified perception of social processes. The conventional aspects of our techniques become transmuted in our consciousness into something mysterious. How can we explain the inherent activity, the action at a distance, that seems to reside in mathematical structures, making them appear fundamentally different from empirical happenings? Wittgenstein's reply is that it is the form taken in our consciousness by the social discipline imposed upon their use. It is as if the work that society puts into sustaining a technique returns to its users in the phenomenological form of an essence. Thus:

> if you talk about *essence* –, you are merely noting a convention. But here one would like to retort: there is no greater difference than that between a proposition about the depth of the essence and one about – a mere convention. But what if I reply: to the *depth* that we see in the essence there corresponds the *deep* need for a convention.

> (*RFM*, I,75)

This helps to explain the attractions of Platonism, despite all its circularities and obscurities. It also helps to explain both the strengths and the weaknesses of the usual arguments used to reject empiricist theories of mathematics. J. S. Mill tried to account for arithmetic in terms of manipulating groups of pebbles and treated numbers as the characteristics of these groups. This never convinced Russell – it felt wrong.[12] For Frege it was a contemptible theory that totally failed to explain the objective and impersonal character of mathematics.[13] Wittgenstein addresses precisely this issue. He considers a set of manipulations imposed on 100 marbles. We number them 1 to 100, make a gap after every ten, then take the sets of ten and put them below one another; then we number the rows 1 to 10. 'We have, so to speak, done drill with the marbles' (*RFM*, I,36). Wittgenstein wants to know what is the mathematically significant core of the procedure. If we filmed the movements of the marbles, so we just saw dots rearranging themselves, what would be conveyed? How can we ever show something other than the fact that *these* marbles can be moved in *these* ways? Why isn't our procedure just a proof about their physical properties?

Wittgenstein's answer is that this unfolding of the properties of a row of marbles becomes the unfolding of the properties of the number 100, when it is used to 'impress a procedure' (*RFM*, I,39). It is a mathematical rather than a physical demonstration in as far as it displays in a memorable form 'the *role* which "100" plays in our calculating system' (*RFM*, I,81). So the emergence of the mathematical out of the physical occurs when the empirical manipulations are put to a certain use; when they become taken up in a certain language-game; when they become part of a certain technique, and when they become subject to certain conventions and norms. This would not satisfy Frege; he would not recognise the objectivity of mathematics as something that lay in things of this kind. But if Wittgenstein is right, this is its true character, and this is what J. S. Mill's psychological and individualistic bias left out of account.[14]

Wittgenstein's sociological approach allows him to avoid both the obscurity of Platonism and the inadequacy of empiricism. To say that mathematical propositions refer to a special mathematical reality may be, Wittgenstein says, a 'natural tendency' (*LFM*, p.140). But the reality behind our mathematical techniques is quite different from the ethereal imaginings of the Platonists. As Wittgenstein says: 'there *is* a reality corresponding to this, but it is of an *entirely* different sort'. The reality is that we have a use for certain techniques: 'it's an ethnological fact – it's something to do with the way we live' (*LFM*, pp.244, 249).

5.3   Analogies and proof-procedures

So far I have examined what Wittgenstein has said about a few elementary processes of arithmetical calculation. I now want to

look at how he extends his ideas to cope with a broader range of
mathematical activity. The central concept here is analogy. Starting from the idea of a calculation as a kind of experiment that
becomes frozen into a criterion of identity, we may imagine a
gradual widening of the range of experimental procedures so
treated. Beginning with techniques derived from the ordering and
sorting of discrete objects, like Mill's pebbles, we may introduce
other empirical procedures such as rotation, translation, stretching, cutting and balancing. The range of models that might be
taken up from experience, and turned into paradigms of identity,
has no known limits. What can be said, however, is that available
models are exploited by assimilating novelties and problematic
cases to them. Models are made applicable to new cases by creating analogies between them. Wittgenstein puts it like this:

> A proof goes in fact step by step by means of analogy – by the
> help of a paradigm . . . Mathematical conviction might be put in
> the form, 'I recognise this as analogous to that.'

(LFM, pp.62–3)

The word 'recognise', here, does not mean acknowledging a pre-
existing fact: it indicates 'the acceptance of a convention' (*LFM*,
p.63). We need examples to illustrate these, and other, important
features of Wittgenstein's analysis. I shall take some elementary
material from Boyer's *History of the Calculus*. [15]

The seventeenth-century mathematician Roberval revived the
ancient doctrine that lines are made up of points, and surfaces are
made up of lines, and solids are made up of surfaces. This idea
allowed Roberval to create an analogy between magnitudes and
numbers. Consider, for example, a right-angled, isosceles triangle
OAB such as that in Figure 5.4a. Roberval pictured it as made up

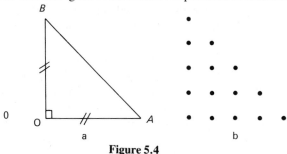

Figure 5.4

of many points. If we imagine looking at the vertex *B* through a super-magnifying glass, then according to Roberval's theory it ought to look like Figure 5.4b. Guided by this analogy Roberval considered the number of points in triangles with successively longer sides. The triangle whose sides (starting from *B*) are made up of, say, 4 points, contains a total of 10 points. The triangle with sides of 5 points, has a total of 15 points. That of side 6 has 21 points, and so on. (This can be verified by inspecting the Figure.) Roberval then noticed that this sequence of numbers can be expressed in the following orderly way:

$$10 = \tfrac{1}{2}(4)^2 + \tfrac{1}{2}(4)$$
$$15 = \tfrac{1}{2}(5)^2 + \tfrac{1}{2}(5)$$
$$21 = \tfrac{1}{2}(6)^2 + \tfrac{1}{2}(6)$$
etc.

This way of breaking down the numbers 10, 15, 21, etc. may look arbitrary and unreavealing, but it is neither. It follows from thinking about the structure of triangles. Take the easy case of the triangle whose sides are made up of 4 points. We can imagine creating this triangle by drawing the diagonal of a *square* with sides made up of 4 points, thus:

Figure 5.5

The square obviously has 16 points in it, but of course the triangle created by drawing the diagonal does not have simply half this number, as Figure 5.5 shows. It has 10, not 8 points. The excess of the triangle over half the square, that is, the extra 2 points, is equal to half the number of points in the sides of the triangle. That is why the number 10 was broken down into half the square of 4, plus half of 4. The same rule applies to the next triangle, with sides of 5 points, and so on. As the number of points in the sides of the triangle increases, the significance of the second term in the breakdown grows less and less by comparison with the first term. When we reach the number of points in any real triangle, whose sides will be made up of countless dots, the significance of the second term will be vanishingly small. As Roberval put it: 'it does not enter into consideration'.[16] In this way we have produced a proof of the result that the area of an isosceles triangle is half times the square of either of its two equal sides.

This might seem like a very small result for a large expenditure of effort and ingenuity. The reason why this is not so is because this approach can be applied to a whole variety of other, more complicated cases. The reason it interests us to learn such techniques, said Wittgenstein, is 'that it is so easy to reproduce them again and again in different objects' (*RFM*, I,79). Let us see how we can generate other structures by Roberval's method and how, when we have proved further results, the proof 'exhibits the generation of one from others' (*RFM*, II,29). We may picture a square pyramid as being made up of layers of squares, where each square is in turn made up of dots. See Figure 5.6.

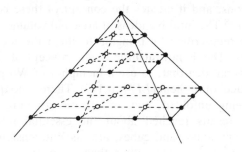

Figure 5.6

The pyramid with 4 points down each of its edges will be constructed out of a total of 30 points, i. $1^2 + 2^2 + 3^2 + 4^2$. This may be expressed, by analogy with the previous case, as:

$$\tfrac{1}{3}(4)^3 + \tfrac{1}{2}(4)^2 + \tfrac{1}{6}(4)$$

Proceeding in a similar way to before, and neglecting the last two terms, which will be very small compared with the first, Roberval was able to conclude that the volume of a square pyramid was one-third of the volume of a cube of sides of the same length. The overall pattern that then emerged from yet further applications of this technique was that if, as above, the sum of the squares is given by one-third of the cube, then the sum of the cubes is given by one-quarter of the fourth power, the sum of the fourth powers by one-fifth of the fifth power, and so on.[17] This sequence of results could be, and later was, rendered in the notation of the integral calculus as:

$$\int_{o}^{a} x^{n} \, dx = \frac{1}{n+1} a^{n+1}$$

The result with the triangle is a special case. There are grave dangers in recasting an old result in modern notation, and more will have to be said on that topic, but for present purposes it may at least serve to show that Roberval's technique was non-trivial. It helped to build up a pattern of results that laid down guidelines for the techniques of the calculus.

This example allows us to give real substance to Wittgenstein's important claim that 'the proof . . . changes our concepts. It makes new connexions, and it creates the concept of these connexions (*RFM*, II,31).[18] The intuitive ideas of area and volume are reconstructed and redescribed by bringing to them the technique of counting dots. This is not intrinsic to the concept of triangle or pyramid. It is an idea that, to use a metaphor of Wittgenstein's, had to be 'glued' onto them (*LFM*, p.119). There is no question of a concept being unfolded, and its intrinsic structure being revealed. The results reached about the essential relationships between say, pyramids and cubes, are, as Wittgenstein's finitist approach requires, created rather than discovered: a sentence asserting an internal relation between two objects, such as a mathematical sentence, is not describing objects but constructing concepts' (*LFM*, p.73). We do not have to accept the invitation to look at the figures in the way suggested by Roberval, and we do not have to accept his conventions about the inconsequential character of the neglected terms. But if we do we are enabled to recognise one thing as analogous to another. As Wittgenstein said: 'Do not look at the proof as a procedure that *compels* you, but as one that *guides* you' (*RFM*, III,30).

In describing Roberval's procedure I deliberately expressed myself in a boldly metaphysical manner: a real triangle is made up of countlessly large numbers of dots; if we could really see the vertex *B* of the triangle *OBA* then it would look like this, etc. But, of course, this creates an air of mystery that tells us that a mistake has been made. It sounds as if Roberval was intimate with the ways of infinitely large numbers of infinitely small entities. We must beware, said Wittgenstein, of inflated or 'puffed-up proofs', that is, proofs that seem to prove more than they do (*RFM*, II,3). Really, nothing infinitely large or infinitely small entered into the proof. We will not have understood the real character of the mathematician's activity until we can see through the misleading picture to the matter-of-fact practices beneath it. The mysterious points that make up the essence of geometrical figures seem like very fundamental, and eternal things: 'not subject to wind and weather like physical things' (*RFM*, I,102). But they are unassailable in the way shadows are unassailable. They are shadows cast by the conventions of our language-game.

5.4   Is a proof not also part of an institution?

Wittgenstein sometimes referred to what he called the 'point' of a word. The point shows itself in use, but 'the kinds of use we feel to be the "point" are connected with the role that such-and-such a use has in our whole life' (*RFM*, I,16). Elsewhere he indicated that when it comes to defining the point of a language-game 'what is regarded by one person as essential may be regarded by another as inessential' (*LFM*, p.205). I shall now illustrate these ideas by developing an example that Wittgenstein touched upon in another connection. He drew attention to the boundary between geometry and physics. It is natural for us, he said, to regard it as a geo-metrical rather than a physical fact that we can fold a square piece of paper into various shapes, say, that of a boat or hat. The geometry of the shape is what makes it possible.

> But is not geometry, so understood, part of physics? No; we split geometry off from physics. The geometrical possibility from the physical one. But what if we left them together?

> (*RFM*, V,40)

This is a good question and it is a pity that Wittgenstein simply posed it without trying to answer it. There was an extensive debate on this very question in Britain in the latter half of the nineteenth century in connection with the work of a brilliant Cambridge mathematician, W. K. Clifford. Clifford followed Helmholtz and Riemann in *not* separating geometry from physics. He was emphatically of the opinion that geometry is an empirical science. The reasons for this opinion, and the technical and other issues at stake, bear directly on Wittgenstein's claim that the point of a language-game, even in mathematics, can implicate our 'whole life'.[19]

In 1873 Clifford translated an important paper on non-Euclidean geometry by Riemann.[20] Non-Euclidean geometries are the result of modifying the axioms laid down by Euclid. The controversy over their status and meaning became inextricably tangled with a broader controversy that was also taking place at that time. This was the dispute about the status of science itself. On the one side there was a group that has been called the scientific naturalists. These were centred around T. H. Huxley the biologist, John Tyndall the physicist, and W. K. Clifford. On the other side there was the Church and more orthodox members of the scientific community. The scientific naturalists can be looked upon as the advanced guard of the newly emerging scientific profession. They presented uncompromising arguments designed to show that science was the only form of knowledge, and scientists the only men of knowledge. Experiment and experience were our only guides. Hence science should be freed from any subordination to other alleged sources of knowledge. The profession must be answerable to no higher authorities or institutions. While a Whewell, a Maxwell, a Tait or a Jevons wanted to make a compromise between their science and their religion, Huxley, Tyndall and Clifford wanted to separate them entirely. Rather than compromise they wanted to invade territory formerly occupied by the Church.[21]

Geometry had a special role to play in all this. In its Euclidean form it represented a paradigm of secure knowledge about reality. In fact, it was this and more. It became charged with ethical and social significance. As the eminent mathematician J. J. Sylvester humorously observed: 'there are some who rank Euclid as second in sacredness to the Bible alone, and as one of the advanced outposts of the British Constitution'.[22] The reason was that Euclid proved that deep truths could be known, and known in a way that overleaped the bounds of anything that could be derived from mere experiment or observation. As Whewell, the influential Cambridge mathematician and philosopher put it in 1845: 'The peculiar character of mathematical truth is that it is necessarily and inevitably true; and one of the most important lessons we learn . . . [is] that there are such truths, and a familiarity with their form and character.'[23] Whewell emphasised, as a fact about its form and character, that geometry was more than a set of arbitrary definitions. Its import and certainty were not purely verbal. Its 'real foundation' and reference, he said, is the Idea of Space. This is something implanted permanently in our minds, and is neither invented by us nor derived from our experience.

Clifford seized on the work of Riemann and Helmholtz and used the new, non-Euclidean geometry to attack these ideas. A link was forged between non-Euclidean geometry and the empiricist philosophy of the scientific naturalists. Non-Euclidean geometry took on a meaning that derived from a particular view of the role of scientists in society. It became a proof that we do not have access to transcendental truths. It became a vehicle for the message that experience reigns supreme after all. It established that science provides no legitimation for theology or other *a priori* and non-experimental forms of knowledge. So science does not point beyond itself: it is the be-all and end-all of knowledge.

Helmholtz's work was particularly useful for this purpose. It helped overcome one of the main arguments used to separate geometry from merely experimental results. This was the claim that we can conceive of experimental results being different, but we cannot conceive of the truths of geometry being different. Oh yes we can, said Helmholtz, and proceeded to describe the sequence of experiences that we would have if we lived in a non-Euclidean world. We can infer from the 'known laws of our sensible impressions', he wrote in 1876, 'the series of sensible impressions that a spherical or pseudo-spherical world would give us, if it existed'.[24] We can represent the look of it without meeting any impossibility or inconsistency, so it is purely for experience to decide what the actual geometry of the world really is. Hence, he concluded, with a stab at thinkers like Whewell, 'it cannot be allowed that the axioms of our geometry depend on the native forms of our perceptive faculty'.

The naturalists were not, however, wholly representative. Other mathematicians argued that Riemann's paper was not really about space at all. The mathematical starting-point of his work, they said, was merely a general idea of magnitude. Helmholtz's argument, based on the conceivability of non-Euclidean space, was more worrying. It relativised the Idea of Space itself. The critics of the naturalists therefore tried to find some other property that made Euclid a special case. Some other way must be found to prove that Euclid still embodies our most basic apprehension of what space really is. The logician Jevons replied to Helmholtz in 1871 by pointing out that the inhabitants of non-Euclidean worlds would find that their books of Euclid contained theorems that still applied to small areas. So, claimed Jevons, they would, after all, be able to see that Euclid was true and hence translate their strange experience into Euclidean terms.[25] The great geometer Cayley made a similar case. Even dwellers in a spherical space, he said, could come to know of Euclidean space. The mere fact that it is impractical for them to use does not, he claimed, detract from its transcendent truth.[26]

Cayley had a second, and more important argument. He showed how a non-Euclidean geometry could be constructed by imagining that the length of a ruler systematically changed with its position and orientation. It was this reading of non-Euclidean geometry that forged the connection with projective geometry, and it was into projective geometry that late nineteenth-century British mathematicians poured their energy. It provided a way of understanding what happens when distance-measures change. We need only think of how the shadow of an object is cast on a screen, or of how a map-maker projects a globe onto a flat surface. The systematic changes in distance-measures which generate the various forms of non-Euclidean geometry are nothing more than different projections. All we need do is to reconstruct, in ordinary Euclidean space, the various processes of projection and we have shown what these anomalous non-Euclidean geometries really amount to. By thinking about the behaviour of lines and points under projection in three dimensional space we can, in Cayley's words, 'without any modification at all of our notion of space... arrive at a system of non-Euclidean (plane or two dimensional) geometry'.[27] Our notion of space emerges intact; the anomaly has been rendered harmless. New analogies have been created and a new programme of research founded. What is more, the social meaning of non-Euclidean geometry has been neutralised. As another mathematician put it, in an address to the London Mathematical Society in 1882, we can now accept the work of the non-Euclidean geometers 'without pomp and blow of trumpet as a signal victory for the empirical school'.[28]

So Wittgenstein was right. The kinds of use that are found for a concept, the 'point' of a specific language-game, can indeed connect with our 'whole life'. And what some people see as essential others don't. They may put an opposite construction on it. The example also shows that we cannot afford to assume that we know what the point of a language-game is, just because we can see similarities with language-games with which we happen to be familiar. We might recognise a certain language-game as geometry, say, but it doesn't follow that its players are giving it the same point as we give it. A twentieth-century mathematician would not, in all probability, attach the same significance to non-Euclidean geometry as either party to the nineteenth-century dispute. (He might assume that Helmholtz's concern with building models of non-Euclidean experience was an attempt to provide consistency proofs, rather than being part of the differently motivated debate over conceivability.) We can only find out what is at stake in a language-game by looking and seeing.[29]

5.5   An allusion to something extra-mathematical

The proof of a mathematical proposition, claims Wittgenstein, enriches and therefore changes its sense.[30] How, then, can there be two different proofs of the same proposition? Each proof would endow it with a special sense, so there will be two different propositions where before there was only one. Wittgenstein dismisses this objection. It depends, he says, on 'what we choose to say settles its sense'. If both proofs demonstrate that the proposition is a 'suitable instrument for some purpose', then we can say they prove the same proposition. He explains his meaning by analogy. Imagine two proofs of the same proposition but 'without the organism of applications which envelops and connects the two of them'. They would be like 'two bones separated from the surrounding manifold context of the organism in which we are accustomed to think of them'. It is the surroundings, the applications, the 'allusion to something extra-mathematical' (*RFM*, V,7) that determines whether we say we have the same or different mathematical propositions before us.

Consider the equation for the three-dimensional, bell-like shape that is called the correlation surface or the bivariate normal distribution. This is often written:

$$h(xy) = \frac{1}{2\pi\sigma_1\sigma_2\sqrt{1-r^2}} \exp\left\{ -\frac{1}{2(1-r^2)} \left[\frac{x^2}{\sigma_1^2} - \frac{2rxy}{\sigma_1\sigma_2} + \frac{y^2}{\sigma_2^2} \right] \right\} \quad (1)$$

The surface is determined by three parameters, σ_1, σ_2, and r. The σ_1 and σ_2 are measures of how broad or narrow the bell-shape is in cross-section along the x and y axes, while the symbol r measures the degree of connection or correlation between the distribution of the x and y values. The history of this equation is of interest because it is very difficult to decide who first wrote it down. The difficulty is not because the fact is lost in the mists of time, but because there are problems of principle in deciding on the identity of an equation. Thus in the 1890s the eminent mathematician Karl Pearson, who was one of the pioneers in the study of the bivariate normal surface, identified equation (1), or its equivalent, in the work of an earlier mathematician. Thirty years later, going over the same ground, he concluded that it wasn't there at all. We shall find that what was at issue was precisely the organism of applications which enveloped and connected these equations with their surroundings. It was the allusion to the extra-mathematical.

In order to understand more fully what was at issue it will be useful to draw attention to a few of the formal properties of equation (1). The bivariate normal surface is a three-dimensional generalisation of the much more familiar, two-dimensional, bell-shaped curve now known as the normal curve. If we write down the equation for two such normal curves, one along the x-axis, and one along the y-axis, we have:

$$f(x) = \frac{1}{\sqrt{2\pi}\,\sigma_1} \exp\left\{ -\frac{1}{2} \frac{x^2}{\sigma_1^2} \right\} \quad (2)$$

$$g(y) = \frac{1}{\sqrt{2\pi}\,\sigma_2} \exp\left\{ -\frac{1}{2} \frac{y^2}{\sigma_2^2} \right\} \quad (3)$$

Just by inspecting the equations we can see their similarity to (1), except of course for the mysterious parameter r and the terms involving it. In order to see what its role is let us compare (1) with the result of simply multiplying (2) and (3). This multiplication will also produce a three-dimensional bell-shaped curve, but it will be the product of two quite independent normal distributions. Multiplying (2) and (3) gives:

$$f(x)\, g(y) = \frac{1}{2\pi\sigma_1\sigma_2} \exp\left\{-\frac{1}{2}\left(\frac{x^2}{\sigma_1^2} + \frac{y^2}{\sigma_2^2}\right)\right\} \qquad (4)$$

Comparing (1) and (4) shows us that (4) contains no terms involving the product xy. We also see that (4) could be obtained from (1) by putting $r = 0$. So the product of two independent normal distributions is a special case of (1). The complicated equation is a more general case in which two normal distributions that are not independent of one another are multiplied together.[31] The parameter r is called the coefficient of correlation of the surface, and it indicates the degree to which the values of one variable depend on the values of the other.

In his 'Notes on the History of Correlation'[32] Pearson explains that there were two routes by which mathematicians approached the idea of correlation and the bivariate normal surface. One was via the statistical distribution of errors of measurement. This is why the 'normal curve' was originally called the 'law of error'. It was, of course, of importance in surveying, gunnery, and astronomy. Mathematical work on this subject stemmed from Laplace and Gauss, and it was an error-theorist called Bravais to whom Pearson first ascribed the discovery of the idea of correlation and the discovery of equation (1).

The other line of approach was through the study of inheritance and its laws. Here the pioneer was Darwin's cousin, Francis Galton. Galton's work was taken up by Pearson and became the foundation for much of the modern theory of statistics. When Pearson revised his opinion it was in order to say that Galton, not Bravais, had discovered the concept of correlation and the correlation surface.

Let us look first at a simplified form of Bravais's argument. He was concerned with the problem of specifying a point in space as it might be needed for the practice of surveying or artillery. Suppose we wanted to specify a point (x, y) on a plane. If we could first measure the x co-ordinate and then the y co-ordinate, the overall pattern of error would be given by simply multiplying the two independent laws of error, that is, equation (4) above. Bravais, however, addressed the more difficult case where the same series of elementary measurements $(m, n, p, \ldots)$ is used in the calculation of both the x and y co-ordinates. In other words, $x = \Phi(m, n, p, \ldots)$ and $y = \Psi(m, n, p, \ldots)$ where Φ and Ψ are, say, trigonometric methods of calculation. Proceeding on the assumption that the equations relating x and y to $m, n, p, \ldots$ are linear, and that his basic observations are all independent and obey the law of error, Bravais was able to deduce a joint law of error of the form

$$\frac{k}{\pi} \exp \left\{ - (ax^2 + 2exy + by^2) \right\} \qquad (5)$$

where k, a, b, e are constants to the evaluated. If we compare Bravais's equation with the modern equation (1) we can see how close they are. We may translate one into the other by writing

$$k = \frac{1}{2\sigma_1\sigma_2 \sqrt{1-r^2}}$$

and finding similar expressions for a, b and e.[33] In particular we can see that Bravais's equation contains the crucial product term in xy. This is what would be missing if he had not treated his variables x and y as being in some way connected. We can also see why it is tempting to say that the concept of correlation is present in the equations of the error-theorists. Nothing but a process of symbolic manipulation and regrouping seems to stand between the equations of Bravais and the normal surface expressed by means of the concept of correlation. No wonder that Pearson had once said, 'The fundamental theorems of correlation were for the first time and almost exhaustively discussed by Bravais.'[34]

But if Bravais had possessed the concept of correlation, if he had been concerned with the correlation of his variables, he would have evaluated his constants k, a, e, b, in those terms. As Pearson was to stress later, 'this is precisely what Bravais does *not* do'.[35] Instead of exhibiting the dependence of x on y, he merely evaluates the constants in terms of the probable errors of his basic observations, $m, n, p \ldots$ and the equations Φ and Ψ by means of which the values of x and y are computed. The precise nature of the relation between x and y was of no special interest to him, nor was the product term in his equation singled out for examination. The reason, Pearson explains, is that Bravais was following Gauss, and his approach was in many respects the direct opposite of that of the modern student of correlation.

> For him the *observed* variables are independent [because they are the results of independent acts of measurement], for us the observed variables are associated or correlated. For him the non-observed variables are correlated owing to their known geometrical relations with observed variables; for us the unobservable variables may be supposed to be uncorrelated causes, and to be connected by unknown functional relations with the correlated variables.[36]

In short, Bravais was 'occupied with an entirely different problem' to that which led to an awareness of the idea of correlation.[37]

What, then, was the new problem that interested Galton and that separated his work from that of the error-theorists? Galton was trying to understand and manipulate the relations between parent and offspring generations. He was a eugenist. Whereas the error-theorists wanted to get rid of, or correct for, the presence of variation, this was the very thing Galton wanted to understand, preserve and exploit. When Galton reflected on the normal distribution of some characteristic, say height or intelligence, in the parent and offspring generations, his attention was focused on the connection between the two distributions. This connection had a physical meaning: it was the pattern of inheritance. The underlying causes may be complicated or obscure, but there were patterns that emerged on the level of observable and measurable effects. It became apparent through Galton's experiments that offspring 'reverted' to the norm. The extent of this reversion, and the simple law that it obeyed, were then discovered. Here was the empirical prototype of the statistical concept of regression. When Galton's mathematical helper set about to write down the equation of the joint distribution of offspring and parents for some measurable feature, the coefficient of reversion had a prominent place in it. First you write the equation for the parent generation; then you write the conditional equation saying that, for given parents, such-and-such an offspring distribution will be produced via the relation of reversion. Multiplying these yields the joint distribution. In other words: a form of equation (1).[38]

The idea of regression is only half the story of correlation. Galton had to take further steps to turn his biologically based idea into a general relationship with pleasing formal features, but here too he was guided by biological ideas. The significance of these can be exhibited at each step in Galton's reasoning.[39] The result was that although Bravais and Galton wrote down very similar equations, they were parts of quite different patterns of reasoning. Their goals were different and their background analogies and models were different. The superficial similarity of the symbolism obscured the different techniques and transformations that gave them life and meaning. In Wittgenstein's vivid metaphor, we could say the equations were like two bones. They might look similar but in fact they belong to two different species of organism. Put them back in context and their differences become apparent. Here were two different equations lurking under similar symbolic forms.[40]

For our purposes, however, more needs to be said. Wittgenstein's theory does not commit us to saying that Galton's equation was in fact different from Bravais's. Rather, it is a theory about when the two will be deemed the same or different. The point, really, is that 'what we choose to say settles its sense', that is, the sense of the equation. And what we choose to say depends on what we are trying to do. The theory of language-games ought to explain the character of those games in which sameness of sense is imputed, as well as games in which difference of sense is celebrated. Let us, then, look at how and why we could say that Bravais *did* write down the bivariate normal equation, and *did* make reference to the concept of correlation.

To do this we need to create a sense of Bravais and Galton both talking about a single thing that exists independently of them – a thing that they both see and both describe with greater or lesser success. We need to construct an apparent reference for Bravais and then treat his preoccupation with error-theory as something that explains his partial access to it, his particular perspective on it, and his limited interest in it. For example, we could draw attention to the fact that equation (5) contains the term $ax^2 + 2exy + by^2$. If this is set equal to a constant it yields an ellipse. Thinking of him as making contact with a reality more fully described by Galton, we can say that he had stumbled across the elliptical, horizontal cross-

sections of the bell-shaped correlation surface. We can describe
Bravais's achievement, as one historian did, by saying that his
mind was hovering in the vicinity of a stupendous idea, and that
with one leap he could have pounced upon it.[41]

In many respects these ways of talking are part of our natural
attitude towards life and discourse. We unselfconsciously link up
fragments of talk by constructing a common reference for them.[42]
That this is a natural attitude is supported by the fact that Pearson
proceeded in this way when he first ran into Bravais's work.
Looking back, he declared himself puzzled as to how he could
have made the ascription. He says, I think revealingly, that he was
far too excited by the new field to stop and ponder such questions:
'I wanted to reach new results and apply them.'[43] So he looked not
only beyond the symbolism itself, but also beyond the intentions of
its author and took for granted that he knew the reality to which it
referred. Later, when the new field was established, and it became
more important to decide who had really founded it and who
should be honoured, the natural attitude would give way to more
circumspection. Of course this is just as natural, in its own way,
but it subserves a different set of 'needs'. Of *both* of these attitudes
equally Wittgenstein says: 'I want to say: it *looks* as if a ground for
the decision were already there; and it has yet to be invented'
(*RFM*, IV,9). We have to invent both continuities *and* discontinui-
ties. If we want to establish a sense of continuity we will naturally
use the language of realism to provide a common reference. If we
want to establish discontinuity, we will use that same language to
justify talking of essential differences. We will construct different
references for the two equations. A finitist theory of language-
games must describe both strategies.

5.6 The superposition of language-games

For the first time we are now genuinely in contact with the 'stream
of life' flowing through a language-game. Wittgenstein's hints
about needs, and his hints about the point of a language-game
connecting it with the 'whole of life', have now been illustrated
and expanded by empirical material. The fact that my historical
examples have been drawn from esoteric language-games involving mathematics is all to the good. This was the context in which

Wittgenstein introduced these ideas, and it also serves to show that there is nothing special about mathematics.

It is possible to draw from these examples a general principle for understanding the operation of language-games. This principle is at once simple and powerful and will prove important for opening out the theory of language-games and making it more amenable to empirical study. The principle is this: a language-game may serve more than one purpose at once. Two, or perhaps more, needs may be satisfied by a single move. Two, or more, purposes may be furthered simultaneously. I shall call this the principle of the superposition of language-games (by analogy with the superposition of waves in physics).

In the reception of non-Euclidean geometry both its supporters and critics were simultaneously participating in the enterprise of mathematics *and* exchanging important messages about professional autonomy. When Clifford said that geometry was an empirical science he was also saying that he would yield nothing to those influential institutions whose authority rested on claims to non-empirical sources of knowledge. The esoteric debates over non-Euclidean geometry and its relation to projective geometry constituted an oblique commentary on matters of social import. The same holds for Galton's technical innovation: the concept of correlation. This was at once an innovation in mathematics *and* in eugenics *and* in the social position of certain scientific experts. Correlation meant inheritance, and a law of inheritance gave these scientists special expertise in a field of human relationships that had hitherto been the preserve of the clergy or of lay competence. Galton, too, was a scientific naturalist. He was determined that a new priesthood – a 'scientific priesthood' – would impose its definition of the proper relations between man and woman and child and society.[44]

The final form in which a language-game is actually played can only be understood if one knows all of the factors that underlie each move. If we just look at technical problems confronting a thinker we will not understand why this rather than that is counted as a solution. If we just look at the social circumstances (conceived in a broad and superficial way), we will not discern their connection with the rest of thought. If we filter out certain patterns of relevance, and pick out only some of the contingencies that impinge on a particular piece of discourse or concept application, we will have failed in our descriptive enterprise. We will be lapsing into over-simplified models of language that it was Wittgenstein's aim to refute.

I shall return to the principle of superposition in a later chapter when I outline a general theory of language-games. The next step in the argument, however, is to face up to an objection that may be made against the material we have just examined. I have tried to illustrate some of Wittgenstein's ideas about mathematical thinking. It will have been noted that my material has all been drawn from more-or-less informal mathematical procedures. Although it has served to bring out the diversity of the special techniques involved, and the creative character of the thinking, it may be said that the really rigorous nature of proofs, especially modern, formal proof-procedures, has not yet been touched. What about steps in reasoning that are so tightly organised, and so abstractly formulated, that the steps compel us by the force of logic alone? This is the topic to which I shall now turn.

6
Compulsions, Conventions and Codifications

We often construct arguments in which we move deductively from premises to conclusions. Suppose we assert one proposition, call it '*p*', and then another to the effect that 'if *p*, then *q*'. From these we can deduce the proposition represented by '*q*'. The principle '*p*, if *p* then *q*, therefore *q*' is called *modus ponens*. What is the character of these deductive steps? Wittgenstein offers a purely naturalistic account: they are customs, set within a biological framework.[1]

6.1 The natural basis of deduction

What, asks Wittgenstein, does inferring consist in? He answers starkly, 'Surely in this: that in some language-game we utter, write down (etc.), the one proposition as an assertion after the other' (*RFM*, I,19). He sweeps aside the idea that such a sequence is only really an inference if it is accompanied by a mental process, 'as it were a brewing of the vapour out of which the deduction arises' (*RFM*, I,6). He then turns his attention to a more difficult objection: 'But still, I must only infer what really *follows*!' (*RFM*, I,8). Isn't 'following' the existence of a connection between two propositions which we follow up when we make an inference? This is Platonism again: the idea that logic refers to some kind of very abstract, very rigid framework of super-physical connections: the 'logical structure' of the world (*RFM*, I,8). In place of this he offers the thesis that logical inferences are simply those steps in a language-game that are not brought into question. The *must* of logic is a track laid down in language:

> Isn't it like this: so long as one thinks it can't be otherwise, one draws logical conclusions. This presumably means: as long as *such and such is not brought into question* at all. The steps which are not brought into question are logical inferences.
>
> (*RFM*, I,155)[2]

Without doubt, this is a species of conventionalism. When we use the words 'right' and 'wrong' to appraise an inference, what is the reality that 'right' accords with? Wittgenstein replies 'Presumably a *convention*, or a *use*, and perhaps our practical requirements' (*RFM*, I,9). The questions that must be faced are: what kind of conventionalism is Wittgenstein proposing? And: is his position defensible?

One form that conventionalism might take in logic is the so-called 'theory of analytic validity'. I shall show why it might look as if Wittgenstein subscribes to this theory, and then show that he does not do so. This is important because the theory is disastrously wrong. In fact Wittgenstein explains why the theory is wrong, but the response he makes to it is rather different from that of most logicians. I shall then go on to show that Wittgenstein's is the deeper, and ultimately the only, reply.

The theory of analytical validity says that the validity of a formal, deductive inference is grounded in the meanings of the logical words used in the argument, words such as 'and', 'all', 'if . . then . .', etc. In as far as the meanings of these words are specified by clear conventions, which are then adhered to, these meanings determine whether the inference is valid. To take a trivial example, logicians usually say that the inference from '*p* and *q*' to '*p*' is valid. Why? On this theory it is valid because of the meaning of the word 'and'. This meaning is given by two rules. First, from any pair of propositions '*p*' and '*q*', we can infer '*p*-and-*q*'. This is called the 'conjunction' of *p* and *q*. Second, from any conjunctive statement '*p* and *q*' we can infer either conjunct. This, it is said, is why '*p* and *q*, therefore *p*' is valid.

The consequences of this theory of validity have been exposed by the logician A. N. Prior in a little paper called 'The Runabout Inference Ticket'.[3] He shows that on this theory any proposition would imply any other proposition. To prove this he introduces a specially contrived nonsense word, 'tonk'. Tonk is a new logical connective. Contonktive statements obey rules that are not wholly unlike those governing conjunctive statements. The first rule says that from any statement '*p*' one may infer the statement '*p*-tonk-*q*'. The second rule says that from any contonktive statement '*p*-tonk-*q*' one may infer '*q*'. By virtue of the transitivity of deduction this means that from any statement '*p*' we may validly infer '*q*'. At least, these are the rules that govern the meaning of the word 'tonk'. If the validity of an inference flows from the meaning of the logical words involved, then the inference is valid. Of course, Prior's purpose was not to defend 'tonk' but to attack the theory of analytical validity. The lesson to be learned is that we must not try to justify the validity of an inference by appeal to meanings and rules. Validity must reside elsewhere. There must be a higher court of appeal – higher than the meanings of the logical words and the rules and conventions governing them. Something must judge the rules.

In a number of passages Wittgenstein looks as if he is embracing the theory of analytical validity as Prior defines it. At one point in the *Remarks on the Foundations of Mathematics* he considers the inference: if all objects have the property 'f', then this object has the property 'f'. He symbolises this is as the move from '$(x)fx$' to 'fa'. Doesn't this *have* to follow if '$(x)fx$' is meant the way we mean it? And don't we learn the meaning of 'all' by learning, among other things, that 'fa' follows from '$(x)fx$'? Later he asks: what would be wrong if we said that 'p' should always follow from 'not p'? (The negation of 'p' is represented by ' $\sim p$') Surely, he says, we don't have to say it is wrong. We could just say that 'such and such a rule would not give the signs " $\sim p$" and "p" their usual meaning' (*RFM*, V, 23). This certainly looks like the theory in question: the meaning of a word is given by the inferences it permits, and the inferences are justified because they follow from the meaning. He even seems to embrace the consequences of the theory: 'the rules of inference are involved in the determination of the meaning of the signs. In this sense rules of inference cannot be right or wrong' (*RFM*, V,23). It seems to follow that the rules for conjunction must have the same status as the rules for Prior's 'contonktion'.

Why, then, do we not play language-games with Prior's 'tonk' in them? 'After all, I can presumably go as I choose!' (*RFM*, I,113). Wittgenstein explicitly confronts the critic who declares that on his theory he could infer anyhow. He poses the question that has been raised by all those who have been provoked by Prior's paper: is logical inference correct when it is made according to rules, or only when it is made according to *correct* rules? (*RFM*, V,23).[4] The answer he gives is interesting. He does indeed erect a court of appeal which is separate from the meanings of the logical words and the conventions that govern their use. He says:

thinking and inferring (like counting) is of course bounded for us, not by an arbitrary definition, but by natural limits corresponding to the body of what can be called the role of thinking and inferring in our life.

$$(RFM, I,116)$$

So the reason why we do not play tonk-like language-games is because they fall outside the bounds of what would pass as thinking and inferring. Wittgenstein does not think that these bounds are sharply defined (*RFM*, I,116). Nevertheless, from this naturalistic perspective we can see what is wrong with 'tonk' as a mode of thinking and inferring. It is tantamount to thinking by free-association. All coherence and discrimination are lost. From what he says of similar cases, it is clear that Wittgenstein would sympathise if we reacted to a tonk-like logical howler by saying of its perpetrator: 'while he may indeed *say* it, still he can't *think* it'. What we would be saying, explains Wittgenstein, is that we 'can't fill it with personal content . . . can't really *go along with it* – personally', with our intelligence (*RFM*, I,116). Our reaction is, so to speak, one of natural repugnance.

I shall now compare this theory of Wittgenstein's with a logician's response to Prior's 'tonk'. It might be expected that much more powerful methods can be used to discriminate between legitimate and illegitimate modes of inference than something that, in the end, amounts to an appeal to our natural intelligence and its place in our life. What, for example, about the theories of deduction developed by Gentzen? These have been used by Belnap to try to correct the theory of analytic validity and reveal what, on Prior's formulation, had been left out.[5] We shall find, however, that these arguments are really weaker than Wittgenstein's. They stop where he starts.

Belnap claims that whenever we define a logical word, like 'and' or 'if .. then ..', we are working within an 'antecedently given context of deducibility'.[6] (This is really conceding Prior's point. Validity does not reside in rules, but in something to which the rules are answerable.) Belnap then defines these antecedent 'assumptions'. Using the symbol '⊢' for deducibility, he says that our entire notion of deducibility can be characterised by four rules:

1.   THE RULE OF WEAKENING
   from $p, \ldots, p_n \vdash r$ to infer
       $p, \ldots, p_n, q \vdash r$

2.   THE RULE OF PERMUTATION
      from $p, \ldots, p_i, p_{i+1}, \ldots, p_n \vdash r$ to infer
          $p, \ldots, p_{i+1}, p_i, \ldots, p_n \vdash r$
3.   THE RULE OF CONTRACTION
      from $p, \ldots, p_n, p_n \vdash q$ to infer
          $p, \ldots, p_n \vdash q$
4.   THE RULE OF TRANSITIVITY
      from $p, \ldots, p_m \vdash q$,
      and $r, \ldots, r_n, q \vdash s$ to infer
          $p, \ldots, p_m, r, \ldots, r_n \vdash s$.

Belnap says that these rules show that there is no such connective as 'tonk', while allowing that there is such a connective as 'and'. The reason is that 'tonk' would lead to inferences, such as '$p \vdash q$', not involving 'tonk' itself, which could not be reached by any of the four rules at our disposal. This would be inconsistent with the assumption that the rules defined all the valid deducibility statements not involving any special connectives. This conclusion, is, of course, entirely relative to the antecedent characterisation of deducibility. Belnap is explicit on this. If different structural rules had been stated, then 'tonk' might have been permitted. (This would be the case if '$p \vdash q$', for arbitrary 'p' and 'q', had itself been a rule or, for example, if the rule of transitivity had been omitted.) So the question is: why these four rules? Why this picture of deducibility? Belnap's paper provides no answer.

Wittgenstein, however, does have an answer. He does not try to justify the rules but says that, if they are to be more than arbitrary definitions, they must correspond to the body of thinking and inferring in our life. The rules must describe the general structural features of our intelligence. It is not difficult to see them in this way. I have remarked that, psychologically, 'tonk' amounts to a form of free-association. By contrast, Belnap's four structural rules make much more psychological sense. When psychologists build their learning-theories they tend to assume that organisms have brains that obey rules rather like these.

The rule of weakening answers to the requirement that secure and well-reinforced patterns of behaviour ought not to be disrupted by new and irrelevant information. An organism pre-programmed in this way would be better at learning than one where established associations fell apart under the impact of new information. The rule of permutation says that (for some purposes) an appropriate response will still be produced if the relevant stimuli are received in a different order. The rule of contraction indicates that an organism can shed redundant information and does not have its performance disrupted by repetition of stimuli. Finally, and most important of all, the rule of transitivity indicates the capacity of an organism to combine information.

It is significant that transitivity was a rule whose absence would immediately permit the 'tonk' connective to enter the language-game of deduction. Unlike the other rules, which express principles for preserving or simplifying information, this is the one that permits combination and construction. It is a principle for selectively combining information. It therefore stands at the opposite pole to the unprincipled, unselective, free-association that is the psychological meaning of 'tonk'.[7]

This psychological rendering of the structural laws of deducibility will not recommend itself to philosophers. The idea that logic can be seen as a theory of mind has had little support since the disciplines of logic and psychology became differentiated in the nineteenth century. Wittgenstein, however, did not swim with the tide. He reverted to the old idea:

> The laws of logic are indeed the expression of 'thinking habits' but also of the habit of *thinking*. That is to say they can be said to shew: how human beings think, and also *what* human beings call 'thinking'.

> (*RFM*, I,131)

This is just what the four structural rules show.

One thing that a naturalistic reading of the laws of deducibility will *not* do is to justify them. To treat them as thinking habits will not prove that they are habits of right-thinking, at least, not in any stronger sense than showing that they are pragmatically effective. In the next section I will examine the attempt to go one better than Wittgenstein and justify our deductive tendencies. There is, of course, a very obvious snag in this enterprise. If we try to use deductive arguments in the course of justifying deduction, we will have argued in a circle. We will have helped ourselves to the very principles whose status was in question. On the other hand, if we confine ourselves to an inductive justification it will be too weak.

A variety of arguments have been produced which are designed to circumvent these facts. All of them fail. Seen in this dismal light, Wittgenstein's naturalistic and non-justificatory theory might seem worthy of more respect than it has been given.

6.2   The codification of deductive practices

When logicians formulate explicit principles, such as *modus ponens*, they are codifying our intuitive deductive practices. Some philosophers think that this process of codification can provide us with a justification of deduction. Nelson Goodman is aware that a deductive justification of deduction is circular, but he says that it is a virtuous, not a vicious, circle.

> The process of justification is the delicate one of making mutual adjustments between rules and accepted inferences; and in the agreement achieved lies the only justification needed for either.[8]

So codification is its own justification. Our practices justify the rules that codify them; and the rules justify the practices that accord with them. Richard Rudner explains the position more fully. He asks us to imagine a logical law-giver who finds a people with certain deductive practices and discriminations but no explicit or general principles. The law-giver, referred to as 'Aristotle', eventually comes forward with a codification. Using Aristotle's codification, says Rudner:

> people are enabled to make explicit their reasons for discriminating valid from invalid deductions by referring to the explicit rules which Aristotle has placed conveniently at hand. Of course no one would have paid any attention at all to these rules if they did not, with fair accuracy, reflect established practice – this is indeed what constitutes their validity as a set of rules.[9]

These arguments are painfully inadequate. To see why, all we need do is to substitute for Aristotle (or the imagined Aristotle of Rudner's example) another figure who helped to codify a body of practices and discriminations in another field of human endeavour. Consider, for example, Adolf Hitler. Finding anti-semitic practices and discriminations, he came forward with a codification. These were called the Nuremberg Laws. Using these laws people were enabled to make explicit their reasons for discriminating Jewish from non-Jewish persons by referring to the rules that Hitler had placed conveniently at hand. Of course, no one would have paid any attention to these rules if they had not reflected certain established practices. But this, the argument goes, is just what constitutes their validity as a set of rules.

Obviously this example is not meant to be accurate history, any more than Rudner's was. In both cases the story is meant to bring out issues of principle. But would we really allow anti-semitic prejudices to justify the Nuremberg Laws, and the laws to justify the practices? No matter how 'delicate' the mutual adjustments might be, would we want to say that this was the 'only justification needed for either'? I think not. As an exercise in justification the mutual-adjustment model of codification is bankrupt.[10] If it were correct, any and every process of codification would be justified. This position is just a superficial form of relativism. That is why it works as well for Hitler as for Aristotle. It would only work as a justification if it were capable of raising some conceptual schemes above others in terms of their validity. Of course, as a pure description with no evaluative overtones, the implicit relativism of the mutual-adjustment model is no drawback. There is surely some plausibility in the idea that practices and codifications lend one another support. Practices can be used to give (local) credibility to laws, and laws can be used to give (local) legitimacy to practices. But if the problem of justification is not to be handled in an entirely self-serving fashion, it must be addressed to *both* parties in this interaction. If this cannot be done, then we should content ourselves with description. And, of course, wholesale but non-circular justifications of this kind are not available. Justification, as Wittgenstein put it, must end somewhere: 'The danger here, I believe, is one of giving a justification of our procedure where there is no such thing as a justification and we ought simply to have said: *that's how we do it*' (*RFM*, II,74).

6.3 Do conventions have remote consequences?

I have said that Wittgenstein was a conventionalist, while denying that he subscribed to the kind of conventionalism involved in the theory of analytic validity. That is: he does not try to ground validity in verbalised rules that govern the use of logical connectives. There is no problem here provided we use the word 'convention', in connection with Wittgenstein, to refer to non-verbal and pre-verbal patterns of behaviour. The kind of conventionalism in logic that fails, as the theory of analytic validity fails, treats conventions as verbalised rules. Treating conventions as unverbalised habits is a better and deeper idea. This follows from the fact that the use of a rule is itself conventional, but cannot (in the last analysis) be governed by verbally formulated rules. That Wittgenstein's conventionalism is of this non-verbal kind is clear from the fact that he always stresses the consensus of *action* rather than the consensus of opinion or belief as the basis of knowledge.[11]

The main difficulty with conventionalism is that it seems to be caught between the devil and the deep blue sea. If we adopt a convention then we are presumably committed to its consequences. But how is a conventionalist to analyse the remote consequences of conventions? If he allows that these consequences are whatever follows logically from the convention, he is depending on an idea of logical consequence and logical compulsion of the very kind that the idea of convention was meant to explain. This is a half-hearted doctrine of no interest. If, on the other hand, the conventionalist says that the consequences of a convention are themselves matters of convention, he seems to be denying obvious facts and destroying the very idea of logical compulsion. It suggests that each logical consequence has to be legislated for separately, and that we could freely choose to accept or reject it.

Sensing Wittgenstein's preference for extreme rather than half-hearted solutions, Dummett does not hesitate to present him as a full-blooded conventionalist of the second kind: 'for him the logical necessity of any statement is always the *direct* expression of a linguistic convention. That a given statement is necessary consists always in our having expressly decided to treat that very statement as unassailable'.[12] This, says Dummett, is difficult to accept. We normally think of a proof driving us along willy-nilly. If we have clearly formulated our premises, then we will have so specified our concepts that 'there is no room for any further determination'.[13] We cannot lay down that a given form of words is necessary without regard to their existing meaning: 'we have a responsibility to the sense we have already given the words of which the statement is composed'.[14] So Wittgenstein's finitist picture, and his full-blooded conventionalism, seem to fragment meanings into a sequence of express decisions.

Although nothing of importance hangs on matters of terminology, it is worth noticing that Wittgenstein is not in fact happy with the idea of a sequence of decisions. See, for example, how he responded to the intuitionists, like Brouwer, who said that each application of a rule, or each step in a calculation required an 'intuition'. Wittgenstein remarks that we might as well say that what we need is not an intuition but a decision. Then he adds: 'Actually there is neither. You don't make a decision: you simply do a certain thing. It is a question of a certain practice' (*LFM*, p.237). So the preferred category is not that of 'decision', with its overtones of explicitness and self-consciousness, but 'practice' with its suggestion of routine and lack of questioning. One thing is certain. Wittgenstein accepts that there is indeed a connection between our application of a concept now and our past practices. He even uses the same word as Dummett who was criticising him. Dummett opposed Wittgenstein's (alleged) decisionism by the idea that we have a 'responsibility' to the sense we have already given a word. Wittgenstein says: 'one is responsible to certain things. The new meaning must be such that we who have had a certain training will find it useful in certain ways' (*LFM*, p.66). But notice the subtle difference between how Wittgenstein and his critic construe that responsibility. For Dummett we have responsibility to the *sense* of existing concepts. For Wittgenstein this ultimately reduces to a responsibility to the *users* of the concept. The responsibility is to 'we who have had a certain training'. So something does answer to the idea of logical constraint. It is the requirement that we can continue to play the language-game, and this means being able to sustain our interactions with people who have certain dispositions and behavioural tendencies. What, in the realm of language and ideas, we refer to as logical relations, and logical constraints, are really the constraints imposed upon us by other people. Logical necessity is a moral and social relation. Wittgenstein is quite explicit on the point. Of course the laws of logic can be said to compel us, he says, 'in the same sense, that is to say, as other laws in human society'. A clerk who made idiosyncratic calculations and inferences would be punished. If we don't draw the same conclusions as other people, then we get into conflict, 'e.g. with society; and also with other practical consequences' (*RFM*, I,116).

When Dummett referred to our responsibility to existing meanings he meant that we ought not to contradict ourselves. Logical relations are conceived of as prior to, or more basic than, acts of usage. How does Wittgenstein handle the phenomenon that we call contradiction? Here, surely, is the point at which logic itself exerts its force upon us and requires us to acknowledge the implications of our past propositions. Wittgenstein, of course, gives us a naturalistic analysis. Just as the constraints of a concept's meaning were decoded into the constraints of its users, so our picture of contradiction must be replaced by an awareness of the socio-psychological phenomena that underlie it.

A contradictory order like 'Sit down and don't sit down' is nonsense unless it is given a special meaning. To explain this we often assume, said Wittgenstein, that as well as the words there are also meanings, and it is these meanings that are, so to speak, jamming together (*LFM*, pp.184,187,190). In the general case of '*p* and not *p*' it is the meaning of the word 'not' that causes the jamming. We use this picture as an explanation of the properties of contradictions and the reason why they cause trouble. But for Wittgenstein this is the wrong way round. We should not explain the lack of use of '*p* and not *p*', when conjoined, by appeal to the meaning of negation. The meaning of negation does not determine the use; the use determines its meaning (*LFM*, p.182).

What, then, does underlie our response to contradiction, and hence give it its peculiar role? It is, says Wittgenstein, our sense of the 'naturalness' of a given continuation of past practices (*LFM*, p.186). 'The phenomenon of jamming *consists* in the fact that we say it jams' (*LFM*, p.191). And we say this just because we don't, in fact, know how to handle the signals we are receiving. So the 'action at a distance' of our conventions resides in training and our natural responses to it. It extends as far as our habits take us without running into conflict with other people. Again, it is habit that links practices at different times. The practical difficulties that surround the utterance of contradictions are not to be explained by logic. Rather, their logical properties are to be grounded in these practical problems:

What I am driving at is that we can't say, 'So-and-so is the logical reason why the contradiction doesn't work'. Rather: *that* we exclude the contradiction and don't normally give it a meaning, is characteristic of our whole use of language.

(*LFM*, p.179)

So conflict and exclusion in the realm of meaning must be understood as a problem in the organisation of coherent patterns of behaviour.

The upshot is that a conventionalist doctrine, of the kind that Wittgenstein adopted, does not have to appeal to the idea of the non-conventional consequences of conventions. The remote consequences of conventions can themselves be explained naturalistically as habits: by our drawing them 'as a *matter of course*' (*PI*, I,238). Nor does this view have to pay the price by offering an implausible picture of human behaviour as a sequence of disconnected decisions. Habit and practice remove the need for express decisions at every point. These problems only attend conventionalism if it is given a superficial form, in which conventions are verbal maxims.

The position so far is that Wittgenstein's descriptive and naturalistic conventionalism has shown itself free from the defects that are usually imputed to it. Furthermore, we have seen that it is an approach to the nature of logic that seems to go as deep as it is possible to go. To consolidate these claims we badly need an example, so let us scrutinise an interesting piece of formal logical reasoning from a descriptive and naturalistic point of view. This will help pinpoint the role played by social processes.

6.4 Intuitions of validity

There will be no unique codification of our natural reasoning propensities, any more than there will be a unique set of conventions for structuring our other basic urges. It is the variety of these conventionalised expressions that provides the sociology of knowledge with its subject-matter. The plurality of logical systems that this entails will come as no surprise to the logician. This is because there is a current bias in favour of pluralism. Nevertheless, the idea of logical pluralism should not be dismissed as obvious. No community of reasoners *has* to accept it as legitimate or desirable. It is perfectly possible to defend the idea of one, true system in logic just as it is in, say, morality. The point that needs to be addressed by the sociologist is why either position might seem obvious and justifiable.

It is a truism, but an important truism, that the formal codification of our reasoning practices is itself the outcome of reasoning. Since our concern now is description and explanation, rather than justification, it is not a source of embarrassment to acknowledge that these basic thought processes cannot be justified. Even the activity of seeing whether an instance is in conformity to a rule involves the use of informal processes of judgement. The creation and manipulation of any system of symbols depends on an underlying body of skills. The very act of casting arguments into the stereotyped arrangements that are said to reveal their logical form is something that has to be learned. We reason when we separate out the major and the minor premises of a syllogism; or when we discern the need for a hidden premise to be made explicit; or when we see that an ambiguity must be resolved. In order to illustrate these points I shall examine a controversy that has dogged formal logic for over half a century. It concerns the validity of two theorems in the propositional calculus. This will take us into an area that is impossible to better in terms of formal rigour, and yet is at the same time extremely simple to grasp. It is therefore ideal material to use for illustrative purposes.

The story might be said to begin in 1906 with the notion of implication that Russell used in his *Principles of Mathematics*.[15] Russell said that the notion of logical implication is indefinable, but he treated '*p* implies *q*' as equivalent to: 'not (*p* and not *q*)'. In other words, the proposition '*p*' implies the proposition '*q*', for any *p* and *q*, provided only that we avoid the case where '*p*' is true and '*q*' is false. This working definition of implication fitted neatly into the symbolic system that Russell built up to provide a foundation for mathematics. Two counter-intuitive results follow immediately. The first is that a false proposition implies any proposition. The second is that a true proposition is implied by any other proposition. Both claims can be made because they avoid the one forbidden condition of having a true antecedent and a false consequence. In principle a number of responses can be made to these results. We might treat them as evidence that the logical system that generates them must be fundamentally wrong; or that our informal understanding of implication is unsatisfactory and should be modified; or that the word 'implies' simply means something different in logic and ordinary discourse.

A combination of these responses lay behind the position developed in 1912 by Lewis.[16] He noted the divergence between the technical and the intuitive notion of implication and tried to close the gap by modifying Russell's logical system. He did not declare Russell's calculus worthless, but he did pronounce it 'untrue' in a certain sense. Lewis wanted a more 'useful' definition of implication because, he declared, logic should be a subject that has application to 'practical human endeavour'. He drew an analogy with geometry. Writing on the assumption that, for all practical purposes, space is really Euclidean, he said:

> The present calculus of propositions is untrue in the sense in which non-Euclidean geometry is untrue; and we may reproach the logician who disregards our needs as the ancients might have reproached Euclid had he busied himself too exclusively with the consequences of a different parallel postulate.[17]

In place of Russell's idea of implication, which is called 'material implication', Lewis introduced the idea of 'strict implication'. This made use of notions of possibility and necessity. These notions are intuitively available to us, but they had not been extensively exploited or explicated in the original logical calculus. A proposition '*p*' strictly implies '*q*' when it is impossible for '*p*' to be true and '*q*' to be false. Most of the technical consequences of this idea do not concern us, but Lewis observed that when the idea was made precise it revealed 'certain ambiguities and confusions which exist even in what ordinarily passes as reasoning'.[18] Nevertheless, its 'advantage over any present system lies in the fact that its meaning of implication is precisely that of ordinary inference and proof'.[19] So it is sanctioned by its almost complete harmony with our deductive intuitions, and where the two diverge it is our intuitions that are wrong.

Unfortunately, the 'startling theorems', as Lewis called them, which had been the focus of the initial worry about material implication, had equally startling counterparts in the system of strict implication. (Or to be more precise, the system of strict implication left intact some theorems in the old system that were, if anything, more worrying than those that had occasioned the new work.) Rather than a false proposition (materially) implying any proposition, we now have the result that any impossible or contradictory proposition (strictly) implies any proposition. Again, rather than any proposition implying any true proposition, we have the theorem that any proposition implied any necessary or tautological proposition.

Consider the first Lewis theorem. Stated informally it seems to say that 'It is raining and it is not raining' implies, say, that 'Grass is green' or 'God exists', or what you will. Stated formally we have 'p and not p implies q', for arbitrary p and q. We will concentrate on the formal statement and begin by listing the assumptions on which the proof of it depends. These assumptions may look trivial or obvious, but that only makes the fact that they issue in a peculiar result all the more interesting. The assumptions are:

(a) p and q implies p
(b) p and q implies q
(c) p implies p or q
(d) p or q, and not p, implies q

The last assumption is called the disjunctive syllogism. To prove the first Lewis theorem let us begin with any impossible proposition, call it 'p and not p'. From this we prove that it implies 'q' by the following steps:

		(1) p and not p	premise
(1) implies		(2) p	by (a)
(1) implies		(3) not p	by (b)
(2) implies		(4) p or q	by (c)
(3) and	(4) imply	(5) q	by (d)

Now let us see how the theorem and proof might be challenged. I shall take my argument mainly from the work of Belnap and Anderson.[20] The result clashes with our intuitive sense of validity for the simple reason that the conclusion has nothing whatsoever to do with the premises. It seems reasonable to demand that the premises and conclusions of a valid inference should be connected together by the meaning of the ideas and terms that occur in them. Anything that amounts to a complete break in the relevance of one to the other surely violates the requirements of sound reasoning.

So the charge against the Lewis theorem is that it commits a fallacy of relevance.[21]

The layman's logical intuitions would, I suspect, incline him to support this doubt about the Lewis theorem. Asked what follows from an impossible assumption (or a contradiction) the impulsive answer of 'nothing' seems more likely than the logician's reply of 'everything'. The fact that we have a carefully formalised proof of the result, however, means that we need to say which elementary assumptions used in it are wrong. If the theorem really is wrong the error must have crept in at some definite point, and the critic must pinpoint the trouble. Let us therefore give our logical intuition free reign and scan the various assumptions behind the proof.

Can we doubt the principle that 'p and q implies p': that a conjunction implies one of its conjuncts? That depends on what we mean by conjunction. Does a true conjunction simply say that 'p' is true and that 'q' is true, or does a conjunction amount to a new entity that functions as a whole? When we say that 'p and q' implies 'p', it is clear that only one side of the conjunction is doing the work of implying. The 'and' has no role. It isn't 'p-and-q' taken together that is implying 'p'. On these grounds we could perhaps object to the first two assumptions in the proof.[22] We can also doubt the third and fourth assumptions. Does 'p' really imply 'p or q'? Where did that irrelevant 'q' spring from? Can we trust the disjunctive syllogism? What sort of things are the disjunctive facts symbolised by 'p or q'? Is the negation or absence of one component really enough for asserting the presence of the other?

Our intuitions will not, of course, always lead us to doubt steps in the proof. They might provide support for them. In some respects our intuitions speak in favour of the disjunctive syllogism. If a dog knows two routes home, say, R_1 and R_2, and finds route R_1 blocked, then won't he go by route R_2? So there we are: R_1 or R_2, not R_1, therefore R_2. Since Wittgenstein makes appeal to our instincts this would seem to give the disjunctive syllogism a place in his theory.[23]

It is possible to turn these intuitive responses into clear policies and work out their consequences for the propositional calculus. If we reject the move from 'p' to 'p or q' we could impose on the formulae of the calculus the requirement that every propositional symbol occurring in the consequence of an inference must occur in the premises. This would break the proof of the Lewis theorem. It also provides one way of expressing our intuitions about relevance. Such a restriction would preserve typical axioms like '*p* and *q* implies *p*', but would not allow us to apply our intuition that we ought to be able to turn this inference round and say 'not *p*' implies 'not (*p* and *q*)'.[24] We could of course follow out the policy of denying that '*p* and *q* implies *p*', but as one authority put it, this would make our logical system useless except where 'the user has sufficient control over the premises to be able to put them in a suitable shape (e.g. by dissolving conjunctions) before the official development is begun'.[25]

The most interesting objections to the Lewis proof, however, focus on the disjunctive syllogism. This is where Belnap and Anderson have made their attack on what they call Lewis's 'self-evidently preposterous' argument.[26] They claim that the Lewis theorem rests on an ambiguity in its treatment of the logical word 'or'. Consider the word 'or' as it occurs in the move: 'not *p*, *p* or *q*, therefore *q*'. The claim of the critics is that this inference depends for its validity on '*p*' and '*q*' being genuinely relevant to one another. We need to know that '*p*-or-*q*' really means that there is a choice to be made between them, so that rejecting the one commits us to the other. Anderson and Belnap refer to this as the 'intensional' sense of 'or'. These requirements are not satisfied if the disjunction is concocted simply by putting the word 'or' between any two arbitrary propositions. So the condition for the validity of the last step in the proof of Lewis's theorem (that is, the disjunctive syllogism) is violated by a previous step where, from the proposition '*p*', we infer '*p* or *q*' for arbitrary '*q*'. Anderson and Belnap refer to the sense of 'or' on which this previous step depended, as the 'extensional' sense. So if we survey the list of assumptions on which the Lewis proof is based we can argue that assumptions (c) and (d) cannot both be true at once in the same sense. Their co-presence depends on an ambiguity in the notion of disjunction. This is passed over in silence by those who find the proof compelling. Remove the ambiguity in the word 'or' and the proof fails.

The point that Belnap and Anderson are making about the conditions for a valid disjunctive syllogism belong to a venerable tradition. They can be found, for example in the logic texts of Bradley and Bosanquet. (The idealists might be called the original relevance logicians.) Bosanquet said that

By true disjunction I mean a judgement in which alternatives falling under a single identity are enumerated, and are known in virtue of some pervading principle to be reciprocally exclusive, and to be exhaustive.[27]

Applying this to the Lewis proof the point is that the move from '*p*' to '*p* or *q*' does not create a 'true disjunction'. There is no 'pervading principle' or overarching identity relating its parts. This, of course, is what is then assumed when the disjunction is later made a premise of the disjunctive syllogism.

Bradley said that a disjunction needs a 'ground'. It must be formulated on the basis of an 'assumption' about the 'sphere within which the disjunction is affirmed'.[28] Psychologically, he said, the 'or' answers to a process of choice made within this sphere of relevance.[29] It is worth noting that, when our intuitions spoke in favour of the disjunctive syllogism, they did so in exactly the way that Bradley stated: with an assumption of relevance between the conjuncts. This was the case, for instance, in the imaginary example of the dog who reasoned disjunctively. Bradley developed these ideas in a very interesting way. He said that the subject of the judgements we make in real life do not usually appear explicitly in our verbal formulations. For instance, when we say 'b or c' we do so against an unstated background and with a reference and an interest that is taken for granted. The real subject is

> that which is 'understood' for the purposes in hand, which limited purpose, not being made explicit, is easily ignored or forgotten. Thus in 'A is b or c', the A which we *mean* is A qualified and limited by our special object and interest. It is of and within this qualified A that our 'b or c' holds.[30]

What Belnap and Anderson express in terms of relevance, Bradley and Bosanquet express in terms of pervading principles, grounds, identities, and what can be understood given our taken-for-granted purposes. So the Lewis proof ignores the contextual character of some of the inferences on which it depends. Another way of stating this is to say that the proof is bedevilled by the fact that not all the conditions involved in the inference had been fully stated. Not all the premises had been made explicit. There were hidden premises; so in logician's terms, the argument was an enthymeme. This is exactly how Anderson and Belnap attack the second Lewis theorem – the one that said that each necessary proposition is entailed by every proposition. Let us now examine this proof. The second Lewis theorem can be proved as follows:

(1) q
(1) implies (2) (q and p) or (q and not p)
(2) implies (3) q and (p or not p)
(3) implies (4) p or not p

Informally, this means that we start with any proposition 'q' and then say that if 'q' is true, then either: 'q *and* p' must be true; or, 'q and *not* p' must be true. We then rearrange the terms by grouping together the two parts of the tautology, 'p or not p'. Finally, on the basis that a conjunction implies either of its conjuncts we detach the tautology to give the last line of the proof. So any proposition whatever, implies any necessary or tautologous proposition: from 'q' we can arrive at 'p or not p', for any 'p' and 'q'.

Anderson and Belnap challenge the move from (1) to (2) on the grounds that it is an enthymeme. They deny that 'q' implies '(q and p) or (q and not p)'. The latter proposition, they say, cannot be validly inferred from 'q' alone. It is only implied by something of the form 'q and (p or not p)'. In other words, they do not allow that the 'p's and 'not p's can spring from nowhere. They insist that they must be present from the beginning and should have been stated in the first premise. If they appear to spring from nowhere this is because they were, in Bradley's language, 'understood'. Once this tacit understanding is made explicit then we can see that the tautology with which the argument ends has not really been implied by the arbitrary premise at all: it was sitting there all the time alongside it.

There is much more that could be said about the debate over the Lewis theorems, but we now have enough information to draw some conclusions and to relate the example to important themes in Wittgenstein's work. Logical inferences, he said, are the steps that are not brought into question. So long as we think it can't be otherwise, we draw logical conclusions. This is the doctrine that lies at the heart of the very special kind of conventionalism that Wittgenstein advocates. The example of the Lewis proofs supports this doctrine. Here are proofs in formal logic that could in principle be challenged but, for most purposes, are not. Despite their rigorous formal character they rest on a taken-for-granted basis. For example: the assumption that the word 'or' is being used in a univocal sense throughout the proof. As long as this is not brought into question everything appears perfectly mechanical and absolutely compelling.

The idea that logical inferences are the taken-for-granted moves in a language-game looks, at first, as if it is merely an account of what *passes* for inference. It sounds as if it is merely a comment about the inferences that are allowed to pass muster when, perhaps, they really ought to be questioned and rejected. On this reading, the only really logical inferences are the steps in a language-game that would or should survive all criticism. We may then suppose that the reasoning of our best logicians or mathematicians would have this unique character. This sequence of thoughts leads to an inversion of Wittgenstein's picture and the conclusion that logic does not depend on our language-game. Rather, our language-game is the way it is because it is designed to conform to the requirements of logic. At least, we may feel that this is how it is for the language-games played by logicians.

The example of the Lewis theorem does not prove this wrong, but it should shake our confidence. Here is a prize candidate for absolute rigour that can be shown to depend on convention and habit. Rather than having reached any logical rock-bottom we are merely led by the logician along paths that are worn smooth by custom and use. The radical reading of this example sees it as typical of all formal proofs. The non-radical reading is to say *either* that the proof is perfectly valid and the critics wrong; *or* that the theorem fails and should be replaced by other results which really are theorems. Logicians, whether defenders or critics, tend to take one of these two positions. Wittgenstein's position does not place him either on the side of the critics of the Lewis proofs, or on the side of the defenders. He would say that if the Lewis proofs are deemed valid it is because they represent a stable language-game. If they are deemed invalid it is because we are wanting to replace one language-game by another. To a defender of the Lewis theorem who says that surely '*q*' *must* follow from '*p* and not *p*' Wittgenstein would reply: 'No, it is not true that it *must* – but it *does* follow: we *perform* this transition' (*RFM*, I,12). The point is that the Lewis system, just like Russell's original system, 'is a game that has to be learnt' (*RFM*, I,18). But like any game, including the rival relevance logics, there is no ultimate, necessary stopping-point for criticism. We can always make trouble, discover ambiguity, or turn accepted steps into enthymemes. Any stopping-point that happens to be accepted, therefore, is a matter of convention.

6.5 A three-part model

In the dispute over the Lewis theorems two things are being set against one another. On the one side are our intuitions about deductive validity; on the other are the existing achievements of the formal logician – symbolic systems that we have become used to operating and which therefore seem to possess machine-like rigour. Each can be used as a measure with which to assess the other. If we take for granted the virtues of some formal logical system then we can make our intuitions look capricious. No definition of entailment, we may say, 'can satisfy all the demands that we unreflectingly make of it because these are inconsistent'. In a long-suffering tone we find logicians patiently explaining the requirements of 'serious logical work'. The trouble with intuitions of relevance is that 'p' can be relevant to 'q', 'q' relevant to 'r' while 'p' is *not* relevant to 'r'. Logic, however, needs 'unrestrained transitivity' and 'for intensive logical work we already possess a satisfactory entailment-relation', namely the classical two-valued logic that gave rise to the Lewis theorems.[31] On the other hand, if we take for granted the virtues of intuition we can immediately deny that the existing idea of entailment and implication *is* satisfying. We can argue that 'intensive logical work' should concentrate on removing the crudities of material and strict implication with their unfortunate offsprings, the Lewis theorems. We must willingly abandon these invalid and spurious achievements, and penetrate more deeply into the issues involved.

It is interesting to see how readily Lewis appealed to intuition and commonsense practices to criticse Russell and, later, how Belnap and Anderson did the same thing in order to criticse Lewis. It is even more interesting to see how attentive Lewis was to the voice of intuition when it provided a justification for his formal innovations, while later he would fail to hear it when others announced that it spoke out against his results.

Given the existence of these two great polemical resources that can be played off against one another, the issue resolves itself into that of deciding whether our formal systems provide a full and adequate expression of whatever is valid to our intuitions. A positive answer to this question may be expected from those who have a prior commitment to some formal system. (Perhaps they invented it, or have gained a reputation through refining and extending it.) A negative answer will be expected from those who would benefit in some way from its demise. Here we come to the third great factor in the story. First there is intuition; second there are the existing formal systems; third there are the interests that relate to the exploitation of these two things.

There is more than one cause that might be served, and therefore more than one reason, for using an appeal to intuition to criticise a given codification of logical principles. There will be those who, in a thoroughly anti-scientific spirit, wish to oppose or minimise the achievements of formalisation as such. Their aim will be to increase respect for other modes of knowledge. To do this they will treat our informal reasoning skills as intuitively immediate and as possessing an awe-inspiring subtlety that will never be captured by rigid and abstract systems of symbols. One example would be Thomas Carlyle's characteristically Scottish attack on the new methods of mathematical analysis. Analysis, he said, had become a mindless 'arithmetical mill', mechanically grinding out results without the simple clarity of the older, geometrically based methods. Bradley's attack on formal logic had a similar character,[32] and so, later, did Wittgenstein's criticisms of Russell's work on symbolic logic. For Wittgenstein, mathematical logic had 'completely deformed the thinking of mathematicians and philosophers, by setting up a superficial interpretation of the forms of our everyday language' (*RFM*, IV,48). It is no coincidence that in both form and content Wittgenstein's *Remarks on the Foundations of Mathematics* is more akin to Bradley's *Principles of Logic* than to Russell's *Principles of Mathematics*.

As well as a root-and-branch opposition to formalisation, an appeal to intuition can also be expedient for those who merely want to modify existing codifications. The informal practices of natural language then become something positive for the formal logician to exploit. It is like new territory to be conquered. It holds out promises of new discoveries and new laws.[33] From this point of view a criticism of existing work in formal logic simply makes more room for innovation. It means that previous workers have not solved all the problems. There are still prizes to be won and reputations to be made.

It is perhaps not surprising that the defenders of an existing system of logical codification sometimes fail to discriminate between these two lines of attack. After all, they both appeal to intuition, and they both represent a threat. To criticise the propositional calculus is, therefore, to risk being seen as unscientific. To their evident displeasure even the dauntingly formal relevance logicians have been the butt of this kind of objection. One orthodox logician put objectors to the Lewis theorems on a par with those who simply refuse to believe theorems about transfinite numbers in mathematics because they conflict with intuitions derived entirely from finite numbers. The objections, he said, are 'in the same anti-scientific spirit'.[34]

The problem confronting the participants in debates of this kind is how to attach credibility to the positions that they take up. Somehow they must mobilise support, and to do this they must appeal to something that commands our allegiances. Appeals to intuition; appeals to existing codifications that are already there as established institutions; appeals to the 'costs' of making alterations in the logical system – all these are publicly available sources of credibility. Whatever their private motives, whatever the idiosyncratic, autobiographical origins of their preferences, the resources for justifying them and giving them credibility are not things that are within the heads of individual thinkers. For this reason the analysis that has just been given of the structure of the debate over the Lewis theorem is, in fact, a sociological one.

It would be a mistake to suppose that issues of credibility can be separated from the 'real content' of the dispute. They are its very substance because what is at issue is the credibility of the claim that certain formal steps in reasoning are valid steps. Arguments of this kind are, by their very nature, informal, and we would be failing in our duty to analyse them if we simply offered our own estimate of their strength. That would be to take sides. It would be to respond to their credibility without enquiring into its real nature. Consider, for example, the most prominent kind of argument in the debate. This concerns the utility or cost of a proposed line of action, for example some proposed modification or restriction on the propositional calculus. If we block the Lewis theorem we weaken or complicate the propositional calculus. Sometimes the residue has pleasing formal properties of its own, but mostly this is not so.[35] Arguments of this kind are clear appeals to expediency. They touch the interests that certain sub-groups have in preserving certain cultural achievements. Their credibility is as local as the group on whose practices and reputations the modifications would impinge. On the other hand it must be admitted that appeals to the scientific spirit, which also feature in the debates, are principled enough. The trouble here is that their application in any given case is highly problematic.

Even where the argument becomes technical, the ultimate points at issue remain informal. Thus a defender of the Lewis theorem might justify the use of the disjunctive syllogism by pointing out that in the propositional calculus, if 'not p' is a theorem, and 'p or q' is a theorem, then 'q' is a theorem. The critic of the Lewis theorem can grant this but still argue that there is no generally valid inference of the form 'not p,p or q, therefore q'. He would say that the issue is the relation between a valid inference and the formally similar patterns within the two-valued propositional calculus. The problem is the meaning of the formal machinery of the calculus. This takes us straight back to the realm of informal reasoning: to the problem of setting up a formal language-game and institutionalising its techniques and practices.[36]

The three factors that have featured in this analysis may be represented as in Figure 6.1.

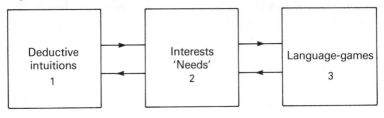

Figure 6.1
Three-part model codification

The investigation of box 1 belongs to the psychologist. It refers to our natural reasoning propensities and the patterns that are built up by contact with simple features of the empirical world: the patterns that become petrified into basic laws of logic and arithmetic.[37] But if our logical intuitions themselves are presented by box 1, any claims that we make about them, or any verbal principles that we formulate in order to capture them, belong in another place in the scheme. We are now in the realm of language-games, and these I have put in box 3. Box 1 is non-verbal, and pre-verbal; box 3 is verbal. The connection between our implicit skills and our explicit language-games is a mediated one. This is where the items referred to by Wittgenstein as 'needs' enter the scene. They are represented in box 2. In the light of the discussion of the Lewis theorems, and bearing in mind the examples from the previous chapter about Clifford and Galton, I am right in grouping these under the heading of social interests. My claim is that a pursuit of the causes that make us deploy our intuitions one way rather than another, leads straight to social variables of this kind. This is why we are prompted to develop our language-games in the way that we do, taking our stance for or against existing bodies of knowledge and the achievements of the past. It is the items grouped into box 2 that gives a language-game its point. Omit this and we have omitted a significant part of what Wittgenstein called 'the complex nature and variety of human contingencies' that provide the 'natural foundation' for our concepts (*RPP*, vol.II,614). This is the mistake in the theory of codification given by Goodman and others. Their picture has just two parts: our informal practices and our codified rules. But how rules relate to practices, and why our practices receive a particular codification, is different under different circumstances. They have left out a whole class of variables. They tell us about box 1 and box 3, and forget box 2. This is why their account fails, not only as a justification, but as a description too.

7

The Systematic Study of Language-Games

We have now seen Wittgenstein's ideas applied across the whole spectrum of our culture, from psychology to logic. Furthermore we have seen him expose the myths that have so often been used to justify a lack of naturalistic curiosity: myths about mental images and acts, myths like Platonism and the belief in a special force of logical compulsion. Having fought the battle for a social theory of knowledge in these, the hardest cases, there is no need to make concessions elsewhere. There can no longer be any excuse for offering the meaning of an actor's beliefs as an explanation of his behaviour, or of his future beliefs. Verbalised principles, rules and values must be seen as endlessly problematic in their interpretation, and in the implications that are imputed to them. They are the phenomena to be explained. They are dependent, not independent, variables. The independent variable is the substratum of conventional behaviour that underlies meaning and implication. As Wittgenstein put it: 'What has to be accepted, the given, is – so one could say – *forms of life*' (*PI*,II,xi).

Wittgenstein leaves us in no doubt about the dimensions along which forms of life and language-games will vary. Criteria, family-resemblance groupings, analogies, needs and purposes, will differ from game to game. But neither he, nor his followers, have ever given us a comparative framework within which this variation can be understood and its causes and laws traced. The nearest thing that we have seen to a classificatory scheme is a dichotomy between the language-games of science and the language-games of everyday, social interaction. Even that was formulated with dubious accuracy and had little more than polemical significance. It is high time this deficit was repaired. My aim in this chapter will be to describe a simple, comparative theory of language-games. In order to do this it will first be necessary to sketch a typology of forms of life. We must hit upon a few, significant variables and then describe the machinery linking these variables to the cultural forms and patterns of verbal exchange that they generate. The most important single component of this machinery has already been introduced: it is the principle of superposition.

Wittgenstein enjoins his readers to look and see rather than think abstractly about the employment of concepts. He wants to encourage respect for the particular case. Unfortunately he did not follow his own advice. For this reason the present chapter will have a distinctly un-Wittgensteinean tone. Exposition is going to give way to development. Analysis will give way to synthesis and theoretical construction. For a while Wittgenstein will have to take a back seat so that other figures may come to the fore. I want to survey some of the important themes that are now emerging from the researches of anthropologists, historians and sociologists that bear directly on our concerns. By the end of the chapter it should be evident that the discontinuity of tone masks an underlying continuity of substance.

7.1   Strangers and anomalies

Properly understood, the family-resemblance theory means that the world will always harbour things that might be used to confound our classificatory efforts. How, then, do we keep the conventions of a language-game intact? At one point Wittgenstein suggested that our concepts are bound to have a certain looseness about them. 'If a concept depends on a pattern of life', he says, 'then there must be some indefiniteness in it' (*RPP*, vol.II,652). He then immediately made a much more interesting suggestion:

> Thus can there be definiteness only where life flows quite regularly? But what do they do when they come across an irregular case? Maybe they just shrug their shoulders.

> (*RPP*, vol.II,653)

I take 'definiteness' to be a reference to the sharpness of conceptual boundaries and the tolerance of borderline cases. What we have, then, is a guess about the relation between patterns of life and the response to anomaly. This is a theme worth pursuing, but we have to turn to other writers to find the idea put to work.

The anthropologist Mary Douglas has pointed out that there are only a small number of different ways in which we can respond to anomaly. We can see the connection with patterns of life, she suggests, by noticing the similarities between responses to anomaly and responses to strangers. We can ignore strangers and be indifferent to them. We can exclude them and reject them as a threat. We can assimilate them with due respect into our existing social categories, or perhaps expand our categories to accommodate them. Finally we can embrace strangers with enthusiasm for the opportunities they may bring; and drop them as quickly if no advantages follow. So indifference, exclusion, accommodation and opportunism define a space of possibilities.[1]

The idea that there are only a small number of basic strategies for responding to anomaly receives support from Lakatos's work in the history of mathematics. In his *Proofs and Refutations* he studied a debate that lasted for one hundred and fifty years.[2] It concerned the validity of Euler's theorem about the law connecting the number of vertices (V), edges (E) and faces (F) of a polyhedron. The theorem said that $V - E + F = 2$, but critics kept producing figures that were alleged to be polyhedra but which did not fit the law. (For example, two tetrahedra joined at a vertex.) Lakatos shows that only about four or five different strategies of response were used during the entire course of the debate. He gave them amusing but revealing names. For instance, what he calls 'monster-barring' corresponds to the strategy of excluding strangers. It amounts to the claim that the anomalous figures are not really polyhedra at all. This involves building up ever more complicated definitions to exclude them. Then there is 'monster adjustment' and 'exception barring'. These are both strategies of accommodation. The first involves showing that the difficult cases can be understood in a way that makes them fit the theorem after all, say, by discovering 'hidden edges' in the figure. If ingenuity fails we can always make the second of these moves and say that there are different *kinds* of polyhedra. The theorem is then said to be true, but its truth only has a certain scope. Then there is 'primitive exception barring'. This is just indifference to counterexamples: it is Wittgenstein's shoulder-shrugging response. Finally there is what Lakatos calls the 'dialectical' strategy. This was the one that he favoured. It corresponds to opportunism. Anomalies and irregularities are welcomed and seen as the justification for new approaches, new concepts and new methods.

Response to anomaly satisfies the main condition for a useful classification of language-games. We only want a small number of basic categories in our classification because this increases our chances of spotting law-like regularities. If there are only about four different ways of responding to anomaly, and if this is a deep property of a belief system, then there ought to be about four basic kinds of language-game. Just as a consistent policy of responding to strangers would create a recognisable social style, so a consistent policy of responding to anomaly will stamp a characteristic physiognomy on a language-game. The policy cannot, of course, be cited as the cause of the language-game having the form that it does. The policy *is* the language-game. What we can do, however, is to ask *why* a given policy is being pursued: why is the game played in this way? What gives it credibility? This is where Douglas's work comes into its own. While neither Wittgenstein nor, for that matter, Lakatos has anything to offer on this question, Douglas has a theory about the social causes that are at work.[3]

7.2   A typology of language-games

What Wittgenstein called a 'pattern of life' or a 'form of life' can be thought of as a pattern of socially sustained boundaries. Consider, for example, the boundaries around a group that separate insiders from outsiders and the boundaries that separate different roles, ranks, stations and duties within a group. Douglas calls these respectively, 'group' boundaries and 'grid' boundaries. Clearly, they can vary in strength and degree of definiteness. If, for simplicity, we treat variations in these two general classes of boundary as if they were independent then we can easily generate a typology. We can represent variation in the strength of group boundaries along a horizontal line and variation in the grid strength along a vertical line, in each case putting weak definition and low strength near the common origin. This gives four idealised 'patterns of life' that can be linked with our four strategies for responding to anomaly: see Figure 7.1.

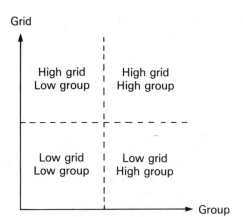

Figure 7.1
A typology of forms of life (from Douglas)

Consider the bottom right-hand quadrant called 'low grid, high group'. This refers to social structures that have a strong group boundary separating insiders from outsiders, while at the same time having a low degree of internal organisation. The sociologist might sometimes identify this form in the ghetto, while the anthropologist might recognise it in certain isolated African villages. The historian may see an analogy with the exclusive academies of bickering savants in eighteenth-century France or the closed, collegiate Prussian universities before the reforms of 1812.[4] These, says Douglas, are the pollution-conscious societies which hate anomalies. They are usually small, often surrounded by enemies, and have to maintain order through the threat of expulsion. Their circumstances encourage a strong sense of a good inside and a bad outside, and yet they are rent with discord. Internal strife is understood in terms of the penetration of evil from the outside, and much attention is devoted to maintaining internal purity and detecting weak points in the external defences. The human body will frequently be used as a symbol of social integrity and its orifices as symbols of socially vulnerable exits and entrances. Poison will be a fear, and scapegoating and witch-hunting will be ever-present temptations. Dietary restrictions will be a common practice, and distinctions between the clean and the unclean will provide potent symbols of group membership.[5] Because of its simplicity this form of social life will not be able to support a diversified view of the world. The same themes will be reiterated and the same ideas applied time after time. Accepted pieces of culture will become surrounded by a high wall of protective definitions and secondary elaborations. The result will be that all parts of the cosmology of such groups will resemble all other parts, resonating with one another and reinforcing the sense of unity.

It is easy to see how these circumstances call forth hostile responses to strangers and 'monster-barring' responses to anomaly. Both are symbols of external threat and internal disorder. They are abominations, to be cast out or kept at a distance. Anomalies, for example, might be seized upon by enemies, malcontents and traitors, and used to justify an attack on both the social and the cognitive order. In these circumstances the threat of expulsion is all that can be used to sustain the culture. If the group boundary is indeed strong, if there is nowhere else for the dissidents to go, then the threat of expulsion is a powerful one. Of course, the revolutionaries might win and sweep away the old guard. They will proclaim a wonderful new beginning and, for a while, all will be well. Then the whole pattern will repeat itself.

These processes can sometimes be seen in scientific revolutions, or what Kuhn calls 'paradigm changes'.[6] Frankel's vivid account of the political manoeuvring in the Paris Academy during the revolutionary change from the orthodox corpuscular theory of light to the new wave theory, is a case in point. It was a power-struggle between the supporters and the opponents of Laplace that precipitated the crisis and sealed the fate of the old theory.[7] Rationalist critics of Kuhn sometimes ask how, on his account, scientific revolutions are possible at all. If a group are committed to an existing paradigm, why don't they elaborate and defend it forever? Kuhn treats the eventual downfall of a paradigm as a quasi-inevitable consequence of the accumulation of anomalies. His critics don't see why, if commitment and dogmatism are present, they shouldn't in the end prove triumphant.[8] The point is a good one, but the correct answer will not be welcome to them. They have put their finger on a point where Kuhn is not being sufficiently sociological. A potential anomaly can only create a crisis and precipitate a revolution if somebody makes it do so, hence the whole process depends on the balance of power in the relevant group. Revolutionary discontinuity will only occur in something akin to a low-grid, high-group arrangement. Elsewhere in the space of social structures the pattern of cultural continuity and change will have to be different.[9]

We need only complicate this pattern of life a little to see how dependent the 'monster-barring' strategy is on its social surroundings. Suppose we modify the high-group, low-grid case by introducing a single internal boundary. Suppose, for example, that we have two independent academies of savants, two learned interests groups, rather than one. This hardly moves us up the grid axis at all, but already a new response to anomaly is necessary. If we have the defenders of a theory in one place, and the defenders of the counter-example in the other, the threat of expulsion becomes empty. The imageless-thought controversy had something of this character. No matter how much Wundt denounced the followers of Külpe, the threats he issued from Leipzig could not touch those who sheltered at Würzburg. Külpe and Bühler violated the boundary that Wundt had drawn between his newly founded scientific laboratory and everyday life. They had polluted his theory and practice, but they could not be silenced by expulsion. Because psychologists were divided into two camps, expulsion from one simply pushed the traitors into the other. Conversely, as long as the Wundtean position had able defenders and loyal pupils like Titchener, there could be no thorough-going revolution: only trench warfare.[10]

Suppose, however, that there are no pressures forcing our two groups to struggle with one another, nor yet other pressures (like common enemies) inclining them to co-operate. If they can each go their own way, and disregard the other, then we have not only moved up the grid axis, but also down the group axis. On this supposition the boundary encompassing the two sub-groups is weak. These are the circumstances pictured in the top left quadrant: high grid, low group. Here the exponents of theory and counter-example, belief and counter-belief live side by side, indifferent and apathetic. The overall picture is one of fragmentation and alienation. This is the home of the strategy of 'primitive exception barring' and shoulder-shrugging. On the other hand, if there are pressures making our groups come together to strike bargains and co-operate for mutual benefit, then an explicit compromise formula must be found. There will be a need to regularise the relation between theory and anomaly. This moves us towards the circumstances pictured in the upper right quadrant: high grid and high group. The increased interaction increases the extent to which the sub-groups are bound together to form a larger social entity.

High-grid, high-group societies have extended gradations of rank with varying rights and duties associated with them. The army, or a bureaucracy, is high grid. Here we are dealing with stable patterns. Many interests will have been accommodated and complex relations will have emerged between the different segments of society. Correspondingly complex conceptual accommodations are needed to justify them and render them intelligible. Anxiety about pollution will be lowered because there is no simple social dichotomy for it to symbolise. It will be the internal structure of boundaries that will be the focus of concern. The salient feature of such a society will be the automatic response to those who disturb its complex equilibrium. The efficacy of received forms will be the main preoccupation; ritual rather than pollution the keynote.

A social form of this kind will need an extensive repertoire of methods for responding to anomaly. Subtlety in reclassification will be a valued skill. Complicated rites of atonement, promotions and demotions, special exceptions, distinctions, assimilations and legal fictions will abound. Pervading the use of all these expedients will be a diffuse sense of overriding unity. This, says Douglas, is the home of scholastic subtlety, elaborate theologies and metaphysical systems. And, of course, it is also the home of 'monster adjustment' and 'exception barring'. As we saw with the example of the projective geometers outflanking and neutralising non-Euclidean geometry, these are techniques to justify the co-existence, and even the co-operation, of those who uphold a classificatory scheme and those who begin to exploit an anomaly. It gives them both a role and a measure of respect. Reality is parcelled out between them. So here is a way of preserving stability through growth and complexity, rather than through anxious exclusion.[11]

What of the final quadrant, called low grid, low group? Because of the lack of a boundary separating insiders from outsiders this is a social form which makes it difficult to apply pressure by appeal to group loyalty or the threat of exclusion. Because of the lack of clearly demarcated roles it will also be difficult to pressure people by appeal to their stations and duties. The whole system is characterised by movement and fluidity. There is nothing to inhibit the

pursuit of any advantage that is believed to follow from trans-
actions across the boundaries of accepted, classificatory schemes.
This puts anomalies in a new light. Like strangers they must be
scanned for the opportunities that they may bring. Discontinuity
and irregularity cannot be viewed with indifference or hostility,
but will be more highly prized than regularity. Boundary-violating
phenomena and hybrids will not be abominated. As Caneva neatly
expressed it, summing up his detailed historical studies of the
reception of the strange new hybrid effect of electro-magnetism:
these are 'monster-embracing' societies.[12]

Groups of this kind are individualistic, pluralistic, competitive
and pragmatic. If, as Durkheim suggests, the sense of a divine
presence is really a sense of group cohesion, then these societies
will be secular. The successful individual, those with an extra
endowment of luck, skill or wealth, will be the nearest to something that is held sacred. The only social bonds are the abstract
rules of the competitive game. A secular, pragmatic cosmology is
not, of course, the prerogative of modern capitalism or of techno-
logically sophisticated societies. There are primitive, secular and
individualistic societies as well. It would also be wrong to treat low
grid and low group as if it meant a slackening of social pressures. It
only means a change in its focus. There may be little need to be
anxious about pollution or about ritual, but the reality of social
pressure reveals itself in what has been ruthlessly discarded. Stable
meaning has gone; there are no fixed essences; the years do not
bring wisdom and respect. The great fear is failure: being left
behind by age or incapacity.[13]

7.3 Use theories versus reflection theories

We now have a workable typology of language-games and forms of
life. Although it would be wrong to impose too heavy a burden on
a scheme of this kind, it is remarkable how much information it
codifies. It has already proven its utility in the organisation of
empirical material and in alerting investigators to unsuspected
patterns in their data.[14] As a simple framework within which to
pursue a comparative study of language-games it has, I believe, no
serious rival.

There is an important feature of the approach that must not be overlooked. I have not presented a typology of language-games (or responses to anomaly) and a typology of forms of life and then postulated an arbitrary correlation between them. Nor have I appealed to their structural characteristics and assumed that social patterns will be passively reflected on the cognitive plane. The thesis is much more specific and the mechanism joining the social and the cognitive much more intelligible. The point is that a given response to anomaly can only be sustained if the conditions are right for mobilising support for it. Thus in a low-grid, low-group social structure it would be quite impossible to sustain a monster-barring strategy. The players of a language-game would be forced to exploit anomalies and compete with others in the race to innovate. Naturally, every position in the space of social structures will find people *voicing* sentiments, and trying to encourage responses to anomaly, that do not belong there according to the theory. I illustrated this in the case of Wundt. The theory is not, however, about the responses that will be voiced; it is about the responses that will be viable. Because people are active creatures there will always be those who are trying to push or pull the social pattern in a direction that they believe will be more favourable to them. Those who have risen to the top of a competitive ladder will see the virtues of securing a monopoly. Those who are trapped by others in a grid of obligations, traditions, rules and precedents will reach out for the benefits of a more open, competitive structure, or yearn for the warmth of a small enclosed community. But the theory does not try to predict what an individual will think, nor how the pattern of collective life may change, carrying its members from one part of social space to another. What it illuminates are the conditions under which a given kind of language-game will in fact mediate the activity of an organised group of people, and have a genuine not a fantasy function in the organisation of their behaviour.

The point may be illustrated by Malcolm's treatment of the categories of sleeping and waking. We have seen that he wants to maintain a deep division between them in order to block inferences from the waking state to the mental processes that might, analogously, make up our dreams. What, then, does he do with cases that straddle this division and fail to satisfy the criteria for proper sleep-behaviour? Nightmares, talking in sleep and restless sleep are all anomalies in his scheme. The answer is that he treats these category-violating cases like the ancient Israelites treated the pig. The pig cleaves the hoof but does not chew the cud. It does not satisfy the criteria for proper class-membership laid down in the Pentateuch. It pollutes God's categories, so it is an abomination and must be kept from the table.[15] Likewise, nightmares pollute Malcolm's scheme. He does not treat them as revealing or interesting. He does not even respect them as uncanny and mysterious. He turns his back on them, and bids us do the same. They are abominations: the 'unclear' has become the 'unclean'.

Does this mean that the author of *Dreaming* must be a member of an isolated and quarrelsome little group huddled in the bottom right-hand quadrant of the grid-group diagram? No; but what his rhetorical methods show is that, after a fashion, he is trying to get to such a location. In telling us that dreams are one thing, while what the psychologist studies is quite another, he is inviting us to draw a boundary round our everyday life and cut ourselves off from science, keeping our practices pure, simple and stable. What the theory predicts is that it is only under the conditions defined by high group and low grid that Malcolm's rhetorical strategies could ever win acceptance. These are the only circumstances in which his claims could have credibility. In reality, of course, scientists won't conveniently go away. Nothing can stop them exploiting the anomalous cases and using them as an inductive bridge between sleeping and waking. Science does not, however, prove Malcolm wrong: even its most enthusiastic proponents have had to admit this. The point is that its presence robs Malcolm of credibility. Properly understood, a glance at the grid-group diagram shows why so few people will believe Malcolm's claims: his language-game does not fit our form of life.

In talking about anomaly I have also touched on broader features of culture. We have been catching glimpses of world-views and cosmologies: pollution fears, and witchcraft; ritualism; secular pragmatism; and alienation. This overlap has been unavoidable because responses to anomaly are made against a taken-for-granted background. As Wittgenstein says: 'What belongs to a language-game is a whole of a culture' (*LCA*, p.8). When signals pass back and forth in a language-game they often embody definite pictures of the world and seem to trigger responses in a highly mediated fashion. We need to know more about this process. Where do these large-scale cosmologies come from, and how do they work? What we are really looking for here is a theory of the *a priori* parts of knowledge. We need to be able to relate these to the variables in the grid-group figure. Douglas advances the following claim:

> Apprehending a general pattern of what is right and necessary in social relations is the basis of society: this apprehension generates whatever *a priori* or set of necessary causes is going to be found in nature.[16]

Once again it is to be stressed that the process of generation referred to is not one of passive reflection. Something more active and interesting is involved. Consider, for example, the material quoted by Douglas from a study of the Cheyenne Indians. The Cheyenne depended for their survival on hunting bison. One part of their accepted system of belief was that if a tribesman killed another member of the tribe, the corpse would give off a special smell that would be detected by the bison and would frighten them away. Killing a member of another tribe had no such consequences and left their vital food source undisturbed. So here is a causal principle, imputed to nature, which links things together in such a way that natural boundaries are neatly aligned with the social boundaries around the group. This doctrine not only serves to inform tribesmen about the ways of bison, it also serves as a powerful device for securing group loyalty.

Cultural mechanisms of this kind have been called 'social uses of nature'. They represent the most important instances of the general principle that a language-game can serve more than one need at once. The world is understood in such a way that it becomes a resource for upholding the social order. It is this social use that explains why some beliefs have a privileged and fixed status within a system of empirical knowledge. Social life itself revolves around them and holds them in place.[17] Obviously the same mechanism can work in reverse: nature can be understood in such a way that it can be used to criticise the accepted social order. Rival groups will construct rival conceptions of reality; nature is open to both a radical and a conservative employment. Recalling the grid-group diagram we can see that the Cheyenne example is not only a conservative use, it is also focused on the group boundary. Other uses, and other examples, will show the social use of nature focused on the internal structure of a group, or the grid boundaries. One typical arrangement of the internal boundaries of a group is in the form of a hierarchical structure of rank and status. Nature can be made morally significant by making it reproduce this hierarchy. Analogies could be drawn between a series of social levels and a series of ontological levels in the real world. Constructing such an alignment could help to render the social hierarchy 'natural', just as the Indians made their group boundary 'natural'. Conversely, a rejection of the social hierarchy could be signalised by claiming that nature did not have a hierarchical structure. So language-games can be scrutinised to see how their users are manipulating symbols of hierarchy. These themes have proved to be extremely important in the history of thought, and in the next section I shall investigate this family of cases.

7.4   Games with spirit and matter

At first sight the speculative systems built by metaphysicians do not appear to be language-games that could be analysed in terms of their social use. Take for example the lofty and complex systems of the German Idealists that began to attract the attention of British thinkers in the mid and late nineteenth century. Why should some people have begun to find them preferable to the native tradition of empiricism? It was influential men of letters such as Coleridge and Carlyle who first set them forth and explained their significance.[18] Carlyle, for example, said:

> The reader would err widely who supposed that this Transcendental system of Metaphysics was a mere intellectual card-castle, or logical hocus-pocus, contrived from sheer idleness and for sheer idleness, being without any bearing on the practical interests of men. On the contrary . . . it is the most serious in its purport of all Philosophies.[19]

Carlyle then went on to explain exactly how these ideas had a bearing on the practical interests of men. What they did was to provide a picture of the relative standing of the man of science within the social hierarchy. According to the Idealists the laws of the mind were constitutive of nature and this meant that 'all inductive conclusions, all conclusions of the Understanding, have only a relative truth'. They are, as Carlyle put it, only true for us, and true if some other thing is true. This follows because the Understanding is only one of our mental faculties. There is a higher faculty, ignored by empiricists, which transcends the Understanding and gives us contact with non-relative sources of knowledge.

> We allude to the recognition, by these Transcendentalists, of a higher faculty in man than Understanding; of Reason (*Vernunft*), the pure, ultimate light of our nature; wherein, as they assert, lies the foundation of all Poetry, Virtue, Religion; things which are properly beyond the province of the Understanding.[20]

So the social significance of Idealism for Carlyle was that it would ensure what he called the 'Magesty of Reason'. In a burst of social metaphor he tells us that Reason should 'everywhere reduce its vassal, Understanding, into fealty, the right and only useful relation for it'.[21] Reflecting on this forceful rhetoric we see how Carlyle mapped science onto one mental faculty, religion and morality onto another faculty, and then set these provinces of the mind into a hierarchical relationship. He defined the relation between Reason and Understanding in a terminology that refers directly to the hierarchies defined by the grid axis of our typology. Since the mind is constitutive of reality this literally builds these status differences into the nature of things.

There is nothing isolated or idiosyncratic about this case. While the utilitarians and philosophical radicals deployed the empiricist tradition to justify reform and the uninhibited operations of the market, Tory propagandists like Coleridge had already used Idealism as a vehicle for a rival theory of society.[22] In opposition to the atomising individualism of contemporary capitalism Coleridge offered a vision of society stably structured and balanced by different, large-scale interests: the landed interests, the manufacturing interests, and the clerisy. The clerisy were the guardians of our spiritual and cultural tradition. They had the role of mediating and synthesising the forces of stability and the forces of change. While the philosophical radicals developed a hedonistic psychology tailored to the requirements of economic calculation, Coleridge proceeded, like Carlyle, to give the mind a structure with a different social meaning: 'the understanding or experiential faculty, unirradiated by reason and the spirit, has no appropriate object but the material world in relation to our worldly interests'.[23] These worldly interests, as Coleridge makes clear, were commercial interests. The penalty of letting them run rampant, uncontrolled by anything higher, would be anarchy and revolution.[24]

These examples show clearly how institutional boundaries and relations are turned into boundaries and relations between the powers and parts of nature. In this case the nature that is being used to uphold a social pattern happens to be the mental structure of human nature, but the technique is widely diffused through a whole range of different language-games. For example, the doctrines of Coleridge and Carlyle were eagerly and explicitly taken up by the brilliant nineteenth-century Irish mathematician Sir William Rowan Hamilton.[25] They can be traced in his reflections on the nature of algebra and may even have influenced his technical innovations. Hamilton had deeply conservative commitments and deplored what he saw as the crassly utilitarian character of much of the science of his time. He tried to interpret his own subject, mathematics, so that it could be seen to be, in Coleridge's words, irradiated by spirit. Algebra, declared Hamilton, was the science of pure time. The fundamental concepts of mathematics, such as number and the operations of addition and subtraction, were built up in our minds, not through our experience of the outer world, but through an innate capacity to make and remember sequences of mental acts. Through their connection with the *a priori* apparatus of the mind he sought to display mathematical concepts in their connection with even higher and more spiritual preoccupations. As an advocate of such views he was naturally opposed to the quite different account of algebra developed at that time by the influential school of symbolical algebra at Cambridge. If Hamilton was an intuitionist, they were formalists. Algebra for them was a purely formal language; a set of symbols obeying strict, but ultimately arbitrary, rules. The Cambridge school's conception of mathematics differed from Hamilton's because they deliberately narrowed down its meaning, stripping it of all significance beyond that which was under the control of the mathematical specialist. For Hamilton this demeaned the science, reducing its symbols to 'an affair of pothooks and hangers' – a characterisation nicely chosen to convey all the associations of materiality and low-status.[26]

Without question the most detailed case studies dealing with these themes come from the history of matter theory. An issue that has long been debated by natural philosophers is whether matter is active or passive. The varying answers that have been given to this question have implicated fundamental issues such as the nature of force, the proper formulation of the laws of motion and the role and status of the ether (that is, the medium that was thought to underlie phenomena such as light). It has proved impossible to trace the full history of these debates without taking into account the extent to which appeals to the passivity of matter have been determined by its social use.[27]

Wittgenstein, like many other thinkers, appreciated the extent to which our scientific theories constitute a connected system of propositions. Our understanding of the world, and our response to experimental results, depend on certain propositions being held stable, directing our doubts into other parts of the system: as it were, the 'hinges on which those turn' (*OC*,341).[28] Suppose we take a very well-known phenomenon like the rise in the level of water in a straw when the air is sucked out. Whatever language-game we play when we come to put this experience into words it is going to turn upon some taken-for-granted principle. Up to the seventeenth century the proposition that was widely employed to make the behaviour of the water intelligible was the principle that nature abhorred a vacuum. It was central to the corpuscular philosophy, developed by Robert Boyle in the late 1640s, that a new description was to be given and a new language-game developed which would hinge upon a different principle. Boyle's principle was the passivity of matter. Matter, he declared, was brute and inanimate. Nature could not therefore abhor anything. He treated it as self-evident that matter could neither move nor organise itself. As well as rejecting the Aristotelean theory of the *horror vacui* he also criticised the ancient atomists for treating their atoms as eternal and self-moving. It was plain, he said, 'that motion is no way necessary to the essence of matter . . . Nor has any man, that I know, satisfactorily made out how matter can move itself.' All motion comes from outside matter, from the laws of motion laid down by God and directly sustained by his will.

For Boyle and his contemporaries, the social significance of these ideas was not something that was implicit or covert: it was explicitly acknowledged and used in assessing their truth. As Boyle put it, nature was a book that was to be read for the moral instruction it contains: 'For each page of the great volume of nature is full of real hieroglyphicks, where (by an inverted way of expression), things stand for words, and their qualities for letters.'[29] To see why Boyle insisted on playing the language-game of matter theory in the way he did, we need to know what message he wanted the world to convey, and at the same time we must decode the hieroglyphick in the rival theory which made matter active rather than passive. Boyle, we must remember, wrote during, and in the aftermath of, a civil war, and in a period of continuing constitutional crisis. The machinery of social control was in continual danger of collapse. An important symptom of this collapse was the uncontrolled upsurge of the politically and theologically radical protestant sects: Levellers, Diggers, Ranters and Familiasts. In the famous phrase of the time, they threatened to 'turn the world upside down'.[30] The sectaries were one of the main targets of Boyle's writings. When we see what they were saying about the workings of nature we will appreciate the importance that Boyle attached to the passivity of matter. The sectaries were making a bid for autonomy. They were trying to throw off the control of the church. They refused to pay church tithes, demanded the redistribution of property and social equality. They instituted the important right of lay preaching, and acted out their own definitions of marriage and morality. Their theological justification was that God spoke directly to them: their beliefs were the result of immediate revelation. By making God immediately present to themselves in their experience, by bringing God down to earth, they at once collapsed the hierarchical structure of the cosmos and the hierarchical structure of society. For, of course, this was to so arrange things that it left no role to be played by priestly intermediaries and external sources of authority and guidance. In particular, this collapse of the cosmic hierarchy removed the distinction between creator and creature. As the sectaries said, God is nothing outside his creation. So God becomes the soul of the world, and nature itself becomes divine. If nature is divine, then it will contain within itself the very motor of things. It becomes active and animate, self-moving and self-organising.

The crisis of 1679-81 generated by the failure to exclude the future James II from the throne, and the possibility that, as a political manoeuvre, the king would grant general toleration to Catholics and Dissenters alike, prompted the publication of Boyle's *Free Enquiry into the Vulgarly Received Views of Nature*. Here he wrote:

> there is lately sprung up a sect of men, as well professing Christianity, as pretending to Philosophy, who ... do very much symbolize with the antient Heathens, and talk much of God, but mean such a one, as is not really distinct from the animated and intelligent universe.[31]

It was in the place of this animated and intelligent universe that Boyle put his corpuscular philosophy with its inert and irrational matter. In this way Boyle was able to reassert the threatened distinction between matter and some higher organising principles, and then read from the book of nature the appropriate moral message about similar distinctions and hierarchies in society. The dependence of brute matter on external God-given laws made nature prefigure the dependence of civil society on the Anglican Church. God controlled material motion; the Church controlled social motion. So the themes that were being debated through rival theories of matter were the great questions of autonomy and dependence. The grid of social categories and relations was being upheld or collapsed by upholding or collapsing the relations imputed to matter and spirit.

The concern with the passivity of matter did not, of course, stop with Boyle. In his will Boyle made provision for a series of lectures which were to be the vehicle for propagating his doctrines and relating them to changing circumstances. This has enabled historians to trace the doctrine of passivity, and examine its uses, in the writings of the English Newtonians and, indeed, in the technical core of Newton's own work. Much of the complexity of Newton's scientific thinking derives from the fact that he was trying to marry together matter and force, where the first was conceived as a principle of pure passivity, while the second was conceived as a principle of pure activity. Despite the difficulties that he encountered he would not let go of the passivity of matter. A recent study, devoted to tracing the shifting subtleties of Newton's writings on matter and force, identified this as his basic commitment:

'he sought one means after another to avoid attributing activity and agency to matter'.[32] If we ask why this was so, then the social use of nature can provide a key to what would otherwise be a profound interpretive puzzle. Newton was under no technical compulsion to say that matter was passive. Indeed, some contemporaries, like many later readers of his work, concluded that his theory was in fact based on the idea that matter could move itself. But Newton frequently and publicly said that this was not his position.[33] His determination not to be seen to grant this point is intelligible when we appreciate the continuity between Boyle's preoccupations and those of Newton and the Newtonians. Like Boyle, Newton insisted that God was the Lord of Creation, not, as the sectaries said, the Soul of the World.[34] We know of Newton's involvement in low-church politics, his concern for the Whig cause and his role in coaching the Boyle Lecturers. As he said to a protégé who was preparing to give one of the Boyle lectures: he was 'delighted' to see his work put to such a use: 'when I wrote my treatise upon our system I had my eye on such principles'.[35]

7.5 The problem of insulation

Tracing the social uses of the idea that matter is passive rather than active is an exercise with wide ramifications. Wynne, for example, has shown how similar themes recur at the very end of the Newtonian tradition among the physicists of late-Victorian Cambridge. Their postulate of an all-pervading, non-material ether had similar technical and social uses to the old active principles and non-material forces of the corpuscular philosophy.[36] There are also obvious parallels in the biological sciences. Here the question 'can matter move itself?' finds its counterpart in the question 'can matter generate life?'. The detailed studies of Farley and Geison have placed the debates and the experiments on this question in their scientific and social context. Even in the work of Pasteur they have revealed the wide range of interests that have borne in upon this issue.[37] Nevertheless, the question must be posed: is science like that now? Surely, it will be objected, the language-games of contemporary science must be seen in a different light. A point that may be readily agreed is that since the days of Boyle and Newton there has been a decline in the extent to which questions of political and theological orthodoxy are routinely assumed to be relevant when assessing the work of a scientist. The whole process referred to as the 'professionalisation of science' stands between us and a Boyle or a Newton. There are, of course, cases where the narrow concerns of the professional have been brought into contact with broader political questions, but these tend to be viewed as pathological phenomena and are usually cited as cautionary tales, and as explanations of error and distortion.[38] As an image with which to capture this change we may think in terms of an 'insulating barrier' drawn around science which seals it off from society at large. Clearly this barrier is itself a convention, and a social accomplishment. The problem is correctly to describe its workings and assess its significance for the theory of language-games.

One theory that has some currency amongst critics of the sociology of knowledge is as follows. The professionalisation of science means the disinterested pursuit of knowledge, so the insulating boundary is to be thought of as a social decision to allow reality itself to control our theorising. The barrier holds back society and insulates scientists from all the processes of the kind that might interest a sociologist. It allows the vision of the scientist to be socially undisturbed. By removing the factors that distort our knowledge it opens up a window on the world. So, despite Wittgenstein's instruction to the sociologist to refrain from making judgements about progress, it will be the progress of knowledge itself that will put the sociologist of knowledge out of business.[39]

This view of the matter must be wrong because it ignores the requirements that underlie any plausible theory of meaning. By going back to the first principles of Wittgenstein's work we can see that if any concepts are to be used within the bounded territory of a specialist discipline, it can only be in virtue of a set of local conventions. Exposure to the world does not itself yield concepts, or explain their use. There is no meaning without language-games; and no language-games without forms of life. Wittgenstein's discussion of training made it clear that a culture cannot be sustained unless we have the power to control behaviour while we are transmitting information. However esoteric the culture, and however unremitting its focus on the natural world, the two processes are inseparable. So whatever the mode or subject of cognition, it cannot lose its essentially social character.

For the student of behaviour this means that insulation and professionalisation changes nothing but the size of the tribe. Commitment for or against a mode of community life is replaced by commitment for or against a pattern of disciplinary conduct. Issues of power and authority in society at large are replaced by issues of power and authority in the profession. Broad social interests are replaced by narrow professional interests. Once a theory has been invented and found to have some application there will spring up an interest in its preservation and extension. Its survival means the continued recognition of the achievements of those responsible for its development. In return for support and patronage, newcomers may form an alliance with existing authorities; or they may play for higher stakes by challenging established practices. Again, it is routine for scientists to try to expand the scope of their special methods and this frequently gives rise to border clashes and demarcation disputes within the profession. The professional boundary that insulates a subculture from its surroundings merely requires an 'internal' sociology to supplement the 'external' sociology of knowledge. We caught a glimpse of these processes, and saw how significant they can be, when looking at some of the disputes in formal logic. There are now a host of detailed empirical studies dealing with what may be called 'professional vested interests', and these provide solid support for the general conclusions that can be derived from Wittgenstein's social theory of knowledge.[40]

One simple way to approach the problem of insulation is to see it as a case of the division of labour. It is plausible to suppose that nature is most energetically put to social use when it is difficult to mobilise other means of social control. Where policemen, bureaucrats, factory time-tables and market forces are firmly in control then the student of nature, and hence nature, are relieved of some of their social obligations. Nevertheless, we cannot just see this process as one of progressive simplification which allows things to fall back into their naturally separate classes. It is something that has to be actively kept in play. We must not forget the stream of life flowing through the language-games of specialist subcultures.

Consider, for example, what happened within the insulating boundaries of professional science when they were in the processes of being erected. When the scientific naturalists of the nineteenth century made their bid for autonomy they put themselves in a position very similar to that of the seventeenth-century sectaries. They were, of course, respectable middle-class Victorian gentlemen, not itinerant tradesmen or the remnants of Cromwell's army, but they too wanted to usurp the authority of the church, preach their own subversive sermons, and take over the right to define the proper relations of man to woman. We need only recall Galton's call for a 'new priesthood' of scientific experts, Huxley's *Lay Sermons*, Tyndall's notorious attack on the church in his Belfast Address to the British Association for the Advancement of Science, and the important rise of the eugenics movement.[41] Here too were men who would turn the world upside down, only this time they were better equipped, more sophisticated, and more successful. When we look at their cosmology, what do we find? They too collapsed the spirit-matter hierarchy and made matter active and self-moving. In the place of the immediate revelation of the sectaries we find the analogous doctrine of immediate experience. The world is directly apprehended by our sense-organs: it just is what we experience, and the laws of nature are just the laws of succession and correlation of sense-data. And what of the distinction between passive matter and active force, pressed so hard by the early Newtonians? Theologically orthodox members of the scientific community, who wanted to compromise with the church, tried to retain it, or some analogue of it. The more aggressive naturalists rejected the distinction. They either made force a property of matter itself, or they abolished it altogether. To say that force is a cause of motion, they jeered, is like invoking a tree-god as the cause of a tree's growth. The tree just grows; matter just moves. Newtonian mechanics was duly re-formulated so that force was eliminated. Force was reduced to the level of a mathematical symbol: it was simply a shorthand representation of the mutual acceleration of whatever elements made up the experienced world.[42] Once again the cosmos was made into a symbol of autonomy.

Discovering recurrent patterns such as these shows that investing effort in the construction of a modest theoretical apparatus soon begins to pay dividends. By tying the idea of a form of life to social structural variables I have been able to present a simple typology, and using the response to anomaly as a starting point, I was then able to show how we can place language-games in this comparative framework. Perhaps most important of all, I have brought Wittgenstein's theoretical concepts into contact with a range of social processes that have, for too long, been kept at a distance from them. The idea of the social use of nature, of making nature carry a moral message, of manipulating symbols of hierarchy and group membership, not to mention the conflict of interests and the division of labour, are all important devices for giving an inner structure to the idea of language-games. They give it real substance and help us explore its different dimensions in a systematic fashion.

Having now shown how Wittgenstein's idea of language-games can be enriched by empirical material, and opened out by simple theoretical models, I shall return to the task of exposition. I cannot draw my account of Wittgenstein to a close without saying something about the morality and the world-view that is so vigorously expressed in his writings.

8
Positivism and Cultural Pessimism

Wittgenstein is sometimes said to be remarkable for the novelty of his work and for the fact that he cannot be classified with an established school of thinkers.[1] This is not true. Wittgenstein was a 'conservative thinker' in the sense given to these words by Karl Mannheim.[2] This link was made implicitly by W. H. Walsh when he drew attention to the similarities between Wittgenstein and Edmund Burke.[3] The accuracy of this comparison has recently received strong support from the work of J. C. Nyiri, who has exhibited numerous affinities and links between Wittgenstein and the conservative tradition.[4] My interest in this connection is not biographical or historical: rather, I want to bring out a structural feature of his thought. This will enable me to confront the 'anti-positivist' Wittgenstein and the standard, method-oriented readings of his work that I mentioned in the first chapter.

8.1 Conservative thought

The idea of a conservative style of thought does not refer to a cast of mind – a mere resistance to change – but to a cultural product with a definite historical origin. It began as a counter-ideology with which to challenge the doctrines of the Enlightenment and the French Revolution. Because it has been articulated in diverse ways it has the character of one of Wittgenstein's family-resemblance groupings. At one extreme it gave rise to systematic, metaphysical theories, and at the other to fragmented expressions of a despairing irrationalism. Nevertheless there are recurrent themes that can be identified, and these are intelligible in the light of the interests that this tradition served.[5] Where the spokesmen of the Enlightenment asserted their belief in progress, conservatives appealed to history. In opposition to the appeal to the individual reason, conservatives appealed to the wisdom of tradition. In opposition to the rights of the individual, conservatives stressed our dependence on culture, nation and institution. The progressivist desire to clarify, simplify and reform was opposed by asserting the complexity of social reality. Cosmopolitan appeals to the universal requirements of mankind were met by a stress on the variability of our needs and the importance of local interests.

To outflank the rationalist critic of society and the over-eager reformer, conservatives encouraged us to cherish what we normally take for granted. They did this by investing our routines and familiar ways with dignity and mystery. A quotation from the romantic poet Novalis will illustrate this technique. Novalis speaks of the soul as made up of a series of levels, but urges us to understand the lower-self in terms of the higher-self. Generalising this, he declared that the world must be 'romanticised', and explains that:

> Romanticising means nothing but raising to a higher level of quality ... giving a noble meaning to the vulgar, a mysterious appearance to the common place, the dignity of the unknown to the known, the semblance of infinity to the finite.[6]

It would be wrong to think of the conservative style of thought as inherently complacent. Conservative thinkers are often critics of society and have a sharp nose for decay and, sometimes, an acute sense of crisis. The point is that when they are critics their criticism has to be immanent rather than transcendent. They deplore any movement away from the order and organic unity that they value. Mannheim sums up all these facts of the conservative style in philosophical categories by saying that conservatives accord priority to the Concrete over the Abstract, Life over Reason, and Practice over Norms. Of course, 'reason' here refers to an abstract discursive mode of understanding, and 'norms' to verbalised rules. Stated in the most general terms possible we can say that conservatives give Being priority over Thought.

Wittgenstein's texts show how, time and again, he develops the characteristic themes of conservative thinkers. Take, for example, the notion of Life. My life, says Wittgenstein, shows what I know and what I am certain about (*OC*,7). 'My *life* consists in my being content to accept many things', he tells us elsewhere (*OC*,344). A language-game, we are reminded, is not something reasonable or unreasonable: 'It is there – like our life' (*OC*,559). Closely connected with the category of Life is that of Action. Goethe is quoted: 'Im Anfang war die Tat' – in the beginning was the deed (*OC*,402). Justification must come to an end somewhere, says Wittgenstein, but it does not end in a state of intellectual doubt or in the apprehension of self-evident truths. It ends in 'an ungrounded way of acting' (*OC*,110). The difficult thing to grasp, we are told, is the groundlessness of our beliefs (*OC*,166,253,477). Language rests on consensus, but a consensus of action, not belief (*LFM*, p.184). We are introduced to this by training which rests on an innate trust by the child for adults and accepted authorities (*OC*,150,263,493,509). The result is that we inherit a system of belief whose certainty derives from the fact that 'we belong to a community' (*OC*,94,140–1,298). Doubting is parasitic: an acquired skill for directing attention at limited areas of belief (*OC*,283, 310–17). So there we have it. The entire categorical framework of conservative thought: authority, faith, community – all woven together to show the priority of Life over Reason, Practice over Norms, and Being over Thought.

Perhaps the most explicit link with the conservative tradition comes from Wittgenstein's use of the doctrines and sentiments he found in Oswald Spengler's *Decline of the West*.[7] This book was published in Germany shortly after the military collapse in 1918. Its pessimistic Life-Philosophy represented a massively influential expression of the conservative style of thought. Not only was Wittgenstein influenced by Spengler but, as G. H. von Wright puts it, "he *lived* the "*Untergang des Abendlandes*" '.[8] We also have Wittgenstein's word on the question of influence. Spengler's name is explicitly mentioned on one of the rare occasions when Wittgenstein made an acknowledgement of his intellectual debts.[9] It is therefore appropriate to take a brief look at Spengler's doctrines.

8.2   Wittgenstein and Spengler

The *Decline of the West* tells the story of the rise and fall of great cultures. This, says Spengler, is the reality of history because mankind, as such, is a mere abstraction. Each culture stamps its material, its mankind, 'in *its own* image; each having *its own* idea, *its own* passions, *its own* life, will and feeling'.[10] Cultures, like people, have life-cycles with a vigorous youth, a stable middle age, and an inevitable death. So every period of high culture must give way to a period of decline, a period that Spengler calls 'civilisation'. Because cultures embody a unique spirit or world-view they cannot be understood by the rigid categories of cause and law. They grow, says Spengler, 'with the same superb aimlessness as the flowers of the field'. Like plants and animals they belong 'to the living Nature of Goethe, and not to the dead Nature of Newton'.[11] So Spengler calls for a new 'physiognomic' knowledge in contrast to the 'systematic', causal knowledge of science. Scientific experience is contrasted with 'vital' experience.[12] Historical understanding, for example, becomes for Spengler 'the art of portraiture transferred to the spiritual domain'.[13] If we appreciate each culture in its individuality we will realise that the 'unshakeable' truths and convictions of its members are but 'expressions of one specific existence and one only'.[14] Spengler was even prepared to apply this to mathematics. Mathematics is not a universal thing: there is not, and cannot be, number as such. There are different 'number-worlds', and the character of a piece of mathematics 'depends wholly on the Culture in which it is rooted, the sort of mankind it is that ponders it'.[15]

The reasons for the enormous success of Spengler's book are not far to seek. It gave world-historical significance to the plight of German-speaking Europe. Their military, economic and political crises could be read as crises in Western culture as a whole. In this way defeat could be turned into victory. Spengler identifies the lineaments of youth and age in each epoch. He argues that our civilisation – the remnants of Faustian Culture – shows the signs of coming to its end. The real victims of history will therefore be the very forces that brought about defeat: the shopkeeper-civilisation of Britain, the shallow rationalism of France, and the alarming mass-movements of the proletariat. All of them are symptoms of decadence. Perhaps the most interesting of the symptoms that Spengler identified was our dependence on the concept of causality. Spengler's book became the vehicle for the massive, anti-scientific reaction of the post-war years in Germany and Austria. Hence the crisis of culture came to be symbolised by a crisis in causality.[16]

Now listen to Wittgenstein and hear the same themes. In 1930 he wrote that his work was alien to the spirit 'of the main current of European and American civilization'. We are not living at a time of 'high culture', he went on, indeed we are without culture at all (*CV*, p.6). Instead we have a shallow commitment to what we think of as 'progress':

> Our civilisation is characterised by the word 'progress'. Progress is its form rather than making progress being one of its features. Typically it constructs. It is occupied with building an ever more complicated structure.
>
> (*CV*, p.7)

But mere technical complexity is without soul, 'spirit plays no part' (*CV*, p.3). This is why Wittgenstein declared himself indifferent to whether 'the typical western scientist' understands his work: 'he will not in any case understand the spirit in which I write' (*CV*, p.7). Wittgenstein's goal was not to innovate or to construct, but to understand the here and now. He wanted to open our eyes to what he called the problem 'of the intellectual world of the West' (*CV*, p.9). This, he explained, is the problem of experiencing and describing our culture 'as an epic'. It involves seeing it as a whole and giving it meaning. But Wittgenstein was pessimistic about reaching his goal: it is too late. An epic description could only be produced by a culture's greatest figures, and these are the products of its youth. When the end comes there will be no one who can capture it in art or philosophy, just as a man cannot experience his own death. Our age

> just no longer is an epic, or is so only for someone looking at it from outside, which is perhaps what Beethoven did with prevision (as Spengler hints somewhere).
>
> (*CV*, p.9)

This is pure *Lebensphilosophie*, with its tone of pessimism, the heroic role of the artist-seer, the strict distinction between culture and mere civilisation. And on top of this, of course, we have the thesis of cultural relativism applied to mathematics and the fashionable rejection of causality. Wittgenstein's *Remarks on the Foundations of Mathematics* must be one of the few attempts that have ever been made to put Spengler's bold but diffuse ideas on a firm footing. As for causality, Wittgenstein was all too eager to abandon the idea that orderly behaviour must depend on an orderly substratum of causal connections in the brain:

> Why should there not be a psychological regularity to which *no* physiological regularity corresponds? If this upsets our concept of causality then it is high time it was upset.
>
> (Z,610)

Wittgenstein was not, however, an uncritical reader of Spengler. He is reported to have said that Spengler might have written a great book if he had had the courage to write a small book.[17] Again, we need only recall Wittgenstein's use of family-resemblance groupings in preference to Spengler's postulate of a cultural 'soul'. It is also clear that the world-historical proportions of Spengler's vision are lost. In the place of heroic cultures we have small-scale language-games. In view of the highly speculative character of the former this is, perhaps, to be welcomed; but there is no denying that Spengler's vision of cultural unity has been eroded by a sense of fragmentation and alienation. One thing that is retained is the 'superb aimlessness' with which cultures or language-games are said to 'spring up'. This became Wittgenstein's unfortunate doctrine of 'spontaneity'.

8.3   The meeting of extremes

I now want to probe beneath this rhetoric to the structural properties of conservative thought in general and Wittgenstein's version of it in particular. In the last chapter I introduced the idea of language-games that were structured around artful manipulations of the spirit-matter hierarchy. Clearly these themes are again at work. The particular meanings attached to the ideas of matter and spirit, and their various relations and combinations, can of course only be discovered by looking at their precise context of use.[18] Nevertheless there are some general observations that can be made about the more extreme employments of this scheme of representation. At one extreme there is the strategy of completely spiritualising matter; at the other extreme is the strategy of com-

pletely materialising spirit. If we represent the spirit-matter hierarchy as a vertical line, with passive matter at the bottom, and
active spirit at the top, then it is clear that we can collapse the
hierarchy in two ways, either upward or downward. The various
possibilities of unifying or separating matter and spirit move
between two poles. At the top is the equation 'matter = spirit'; at
the bottom 'spirit = matter'. So the dualistic theories that exploit
the distance between the top and bottom of the line are bounded
by limiting cases which have an important common feature: they
are both monistic. The old philosophical quip that idealism and
materialism are the same (except that good men believe in idealism and bad men believe in materialism) may be feeble, but it is
not without its point. See Figure 8.1.

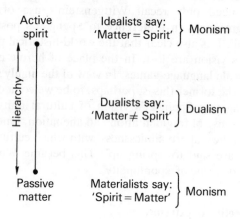

Figure 8.1
The spirit-matter hierarchy

When conservative thinkers try to endow our routines with
spiritual significance, and raise them to a higher level of quality,
then they are, so to speak, trying to raise the floor up to the
ceiling. As a strategy this makes good sense because it helps to
reinforce their claim that the critic cannot rise above society and
judge it from some superior standpoint. It gives the critic no room.
But, of course, a similar meaning can be given to the opposite
strategy: the reductionist moves of positivists, empiricists and
materialists. They lower the ceiling until it touches the floor. Once
again the critic has no room for manoeuvre, and we have a picture
that can be used to convey the idea that a detached, critical,

reflective consciousness is a sham. The brutal collapsing of the spirit-matter hierarchy in a downward direction suggests that genuinely disinterested thought is impossible. In both cases we can say that Being has been given priority over (abstract) Thought.

The same meeting of extremes can be detected in the characterisation of nature and natural laws. Notice, for example, that Spengler's 'living nature' is an animated and intelligent world. The 'dead nature of Newton' is just a cultural artefact. Dispense with the restrictions of a culture in the grip of a rigid, causal principle and we get the strange, self-organising reality hinted at by Wittgenstein. Here, order causelessly emerges from chaos. This is oddly similar to the self-moving, active matter that was central to the world-view of the scientific naturalists.

An important, special case of this affinity lies in the fact that Wittgenstein can easily be read as a behaviourist. He implies that he is not a behaviourist, but some of his critics don't believe him.[19] From what we now know about the structure of the spirit-matter hierarchy both the origin and the solution of this interpretative problem should be clear. First its origin. By turning references to mind into references to patterns of behaviour or dispositions to behave, the behaviourist is offering us a monistic theory. It is, of course, a scientific monism, an exercise in reductionism, which collapses the spirit-matter hierarchy in a downward direction. Wittgenstein's rejection of mentalistic and dualistic theories is, likewise, a form of monism. Nevertheless it belongs to a different tradition whose advocates reject reductionism:

> Am I saying something like, 'and the soul itself is merely something about the body'? No. (I am not that hard up for categories.)
>
> (*RPP*, vol.II,690)

Wittgenstein does not consider himself to have turned soul into body because he has not let go of the categories at the top of the spirit-matter hierarchy. He has not repudiated them because he is implicitly collapsing the hierarchy upwards, not downwards. Now we can see why the imputation of behaviourism is plausible, why it can be illuminating, and why it can be rejected in good faith.

My analysis of the structure of conservative thought explains why it is so easy to connect Wittgenstein's ideas to work that belongs to a tradition that is, in other respects, so totally opposed. The strategies used by conservatives and positivists represents a meeting of extremes. This is why the products of the one tradition can often by juxtaposed with the products of the other, and an affinity detected between them. This is why, quite independently and approaching the problem from opposite directions, Skinner and Wittgenstein both reached the same conclusions about the limits of introspection and the impossibility of private languages. In the same way, it should now be clear why Durkheim, the arch-representative of sociological positivism, could develop a social theory of knowledge so close to Wittgenstein's. Generalising Wittgenstein's idea of language-games by appeal to grid-group theory – an exercise squarely in the Durkheimean tradition – is therefore, not merely a possible line of development, but an eminently natural one.

8.4   Does Winch compromise Wittgenstein?

To say that there is a natural continuity between the Wittgensteinean and positivist traditions is to reject the received opinion. For example, it contrasts sharply with the impression given in Peter Winch's book *The Idea of a Social Science*.[20] With minor reservations both supporters and critics alike see this as a faithful development of Wittgensteinean thought. Ernest Gellner, for example, tells us that Wittgenstein's mature philosophy (WM) implies the doctrines of Winch's book (ISS). So confident is he of this connection that he is prepared to refute Wittgenstein on the basis of it.[21] Gellner sets out his argument like this:

$$WM \rightarrow ISS$$
but ISS is absurd

therefore WM is absurd

The absurdity that is imputed to Winch is, for instance, the move from the truth that concepts are institutions, to the falsehood that institutions are (merely) concepts. We shall see that the charge is a plausible one. What worries me is not this, but Gellner's first premise – that Wittgenstein points inexorably to Winch. I shall now put my identification of Wittgenstein as a conservative thinker to work in assessing this important claim.

Winch is a writer who is, in many ways, admirably responsive to the conservative tradition. A significant part of his book is an appreciation and assessment of the doctrines of Michael Oakeshott, perhaps the leading contemporary academic spokesman of conservatism in Britain.[22] Thus, Winch agrees that human intelligence must not be construed 'rationalistically', that is, as something that comes to behaviour 'from without'.[23] He also says that he does not think that behaviour can be completely summed up in a set of precepts. But despite these areas of apparent agreement Winch wants to put distance between himself and conservatives like Oakeshott. As we shall see, this means that he also puts distance between himself and Wittgenstein. Winch says that conservatives begin to go wrong when they argue that human behaviour can be accounted for 'in terms of the notion of *habit* or *custom* and that neither the notion of a rule nor that of reflectiveness is essential to it'.[24] The reasons for his reservations are clear: habit and custom are too mechanical and causal for his liking. They suggest that human behaviour might be assimilated to non-human, animal behaviour. For Winch, animals differ qualitatively, not merely quantitatively, from humans whose conduct is characterised by interpretation and reflection. These endow it with meaning because they involve principles and rules. It is clear that Winch understands principles and rules to have an essentially verbal form. They are maxims. Like a good conservative Winch insists that principles arise in the course of conduct, but he is always careful to add the qualification that

> equally, the nature of the conduct out of which they arise can only be grasped as an embodiment of those principles. The notion of a principle (or maxim) of conduct and the notion of meaningful action are *interwoven*.[25]

At this point Winch has to meet the objection that he is over-intellectualising our behaviour. He allows that not all conduct seems to 'express discursive ideas', but then insists on the continuity between that which does and that which does not. Behaviour which does not express discursive ideas 'is sufficiently like that which does to make it necessary to regard it as analogous to the other'.[26] At first sight this looks like a classic conservative move: approaching the lower-self via the higher-self and elevating the former. The point to notice, however, is that in Winch's hands it becomes a device for sustaining the spirit-matter hierarchy, not for collapsing it. Social relations between men, he says, 'exist only in and through their ideas'.[27] Since the relations of ideas are to be understood 'internally', that is via their meanings and logical connections, then social relations must be a species of internal relation too. In other words, society is to be approached *via* meaning, not meaning *via* society. This inverts the conservative priority of Being to Thought, and yields a theory in which Thought has priority to Being.[28]

In order to appreciate just how far Winch has shifted away from Wittgenstein, contrast the following two quotations. Winch says:

> the dog has been *conditioned* to respond in a certain way, whereas I *know* the right way to go *on the basis* of what I have been taught.[29]

Wittgenstein might have been replying to this when he said:

> Giving grounds . . . comes to an end; – but the end is not certain presuppositions' striking us immediately as true, i.e. it is not a kind of *seeing* on our part; it is our *acting*, which lies at the bottom of the language-game.
>
> (*OC*,204)

For all Winch's insistence that rules arise out of social interactions, his conception of that process of arising is always based on a kind of 'seeing'. This is particularly clear in his handling of logical inference. In discussing the nature of logical compulsion he concludes that the process of drawing a logical inference cannot be fully represented by logical formulae. Inferring is an activity that we learn. But he immediately gives this a gloss which invokes a kind of logical seeing: 'a sufficient justification for inferring a conclusion', he says, 'is to see that the conclusion does in fact follow'.[30] Wittgenstein never argued in this empty fashion. He classified the experience of certainty as something 'that lies beyond being justified or unjustified; as it were, as something animal'. (*OC*,359).[31]

Exactly the same trend in Winch's argument shows itself in his discussion of legal reasoning. He begins by reminding us of the distinction between case-law and statute-law. Statute-law has sometimes been said to amount to little more than the faithful and mechanical application of rules. Case-law, on the other hand, calls for a less formal judgement based on the analogies between the case in hand and previous cases or precedents. On this basis it is sometimes said to involve 'intuition'. Consider how a conservative might arrange these two kinds of law along our vertical dimension: the 'higher' activity would be the one involved in case-law. Something that calls for informal, concrete, particular acts of judgement is more expressive of life and activity than the mechanical application of rules. Of course a conservative thinker who was pressing his insights to the limit would say that even the mechanical application of rules really depends on a tacit set of informal, analogical and intuitive steps. (We can recognise Wittgenstein's conception of rule-following as being of this kind.) Winch, however, goes in the opposite direction. Rather than saying that the application of rules really involves the use of precedents, he insists that the appeal to precedents actually involves the application of rules. Relevance between cases and precedents, he says, can only be mediated by rules.[32] His picture is one in which rules and maxims have the superior status, and precedents the lower status. Arguments from precedent are seen as things that are in grave danger of becoming reflex expressions of our base urges and instincts. He quotes with approval a lofty declaration by a legal authority to the effect that a principle 'raises the judicial act beyond the realm of sheer expediency' – as if principles weren't the playthings of expediency too.

Enough has now been said to establish the systematic divergence between Winch and Wittgenstein. By realising that Wittgenstein is a conservative thinker we become more sensitive to the categorical structure of his argument. It then becomes easy to see that Winch has actually inverted it at crucial points. We can therefore no longer proceed in the widely held assumption that therefore no longer proceed on the widely held assumption that *The Idea of a Social Science*. Gellner's premise is wrong. Consequently, the shortcomings in Winch's position cannot be read straight back into Wittgenstein. It is always necessary to check the argument for its bearing on the relation of Being to Thought.

Where the shortcomings in Winch derive from his estimate of the role played by discursive ideas, principles, maxims and rules, then we certainly cannot blame Wittgenstein for the same fault.

8.5 The problem of participation

From a naturalistic standpoint our social life and higher mental processes are the outgrowth of simpler patterns of animal interaction and response. Any satisfactory theory must do justice to the new orders of fact that emerge without losing sight of the matrix of connections and continuities. The dialectical strategies and pitfalls that can be involved are best approached by looking at specific arguments. One thing that is very clear is that Wittgenstein's strong sense of continuity contrasts sharply with Winch's determination to put all the weight on discontinuity. Winch is always trying to draw boundaries around our social behaviour, where Wittgenstein's stance always reminds us of intermediate cases:

> I can easily imagine that a particular primitive behaviour might later develop into a doubt. There is, e.g. a kind of *primitive* investigation. (An ape who tears apart a cigarette, for example. We don't see an intelligent dog do such things.) The mere act of turning an object all round and looking it over is a primitive root of doubt. But there is doubt only when the typical antecedents and consequences of doubt are present.
>
> (*RPP*, vol.II,345)[33]

There are no puzzled apes in Winch's world. Dogs are taken as representative, and dogs, it is claimed, have no conception of what they are about nor any alternative to their stimulus-bound responses.[34] By contrast human behaviour is flexible and adaptable:

> Whereas Oakeshott maintains that . . . change and adaptability . . . occurs independently of any reflective principles, I want to say that *the possibility* of reflection is essential to that kind of adaptability.[35]

It is apparent that Winch thinks that we are adaptive *because* we are reflective. But isn't it more plausible to invert this and say that we are reflective because we are adaptive? Organisms whose brains are complex enough to formulate reflective principles will be those whose behaviour already shows flexibility. Both will be the product of the same cause: the large capacity of the brain. We can, indeed, say that the possibility of reflection is essential for flexibility, but that is only because the preconditions for the former are the same as those for the latter.

Psychologists have long been alert to these problems in their theories about the relation of language and learning. Animals, such as monkeys, can learn to release themselves from a cage by undoing a number of catches, but they find it difficult to solve the same problem if they have to undo the catches in a definite order. The extra burden defeats them, whereas it does not defeat humans. The old-fashioned explanation of this was similar to Winch's appeal to reflective principles: it was that humans could solve this problem by mastering the rule of the sequence. For example, they might say the sequence to themselves. The psychologist Donald Broadbent points out in his important book *Perception and Communication*, that this puts the cart before the horse.[36] Humans don't solve the problem because they can formulate the rule; they can formulate the rule because they can solve the problem. Language and reflection are the result of the capacity to process information, not its cause. While Winch gives priority to abstract thought, that is, rules and maxims, it will now be no surprise to find modern, experimental psychologists at one with conservative thinkers like Wittgenstein in their desire to ground what is verbal and abstract in something non-verbal.

Winch's other argument to prove that there is a qualitative break between the social sciences and the rest of the scientific enterprise concerns the different patterns of human participation that they involve.[37] The natural scientist, he says, orders his observations of the physical world on the basis of rules shared with, and acquired from, his fellow scientists. By participating in a tradition of theorising and enquiry he gains a sense of the meaning of his observations and experiments. The case of the social scientist, however, is different. His subject matter consists of people who already exist in a social world structured by rules. There are not one but two sets of rules to take into account. The social scientist does not simply participate in the culture of his fellow scientists; he must also participate in the culture of the people he is studying. So a whole new dimension enters into the structure of knowledge. See Figure 8.2:

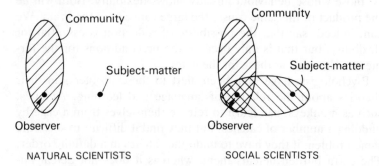

Figure 8.2
The problem of double participation

I think this argument is wrong. There are counter-examples to the idea that a qualitatively new methodological principle is at work in the social sciences. We can detect versions of the same two-rule structure in studies of animal behaviour. The double-participation problem is pre-figured at simpler levels. While it is often useful to insist that there are qualitative differences between animal and human social behaviour these are not, I shall argue, sufficient to justify the Winchean idea that their investigation must proceed by radically different methods. Consider, for example, a methodological principle that has been stressed in the study of animal behaviour at least since the time of Uexküll.[38] The claim is that to understand an organism it is necessary to take into account what is called the *Merkwelt* and the *Umwelt*: that is, the world of cues that are significant for it and that it notices. The reason is two-fold. First, different organisms have different sensory capacities. They filter their environment in ways congruent with their physical form, mode of navigation and response to predators. Second, the internal states of an organism undergo periodic changes, usually associated with nutrition and reproduction. Sometimes features of the environment take on a special significance: patterns of colour-ation or the shape associated with certain postures call forth in-stinctive patterns of behaviour. The ethologists' job is to explore and explain the structure of the world-as-noticed by an organism, and to detect and explain variations between species.

The similarity between what Winch says about culture and the ethologists' doctrine of the *Merkwelt* arises because they are both naturalised and relativised versions of Kant's theory of the mind. Kant can be read as a proto-psychologist who tells us about the innate structure of the mind and the organisation that it imposes on the data of experience.[39] There are then two ways in which his work can be generalised. First, the *a priori* structure of the mind can be turned into an historical and cultural variable. This was what both Spengler and Durkheim did in their different ways. Second, it can be treated as a biological variable. This created the tradition to which Uexküll belongs.[40] When Winch says that to understand human behaviour we must know how the world looks from the actor's point of view, the student of animal behaviour would immediately see the point, though to him it would sound like an elementary statement of scientific method, not a rejection of it. When Winch says that it is necessary to know what social actors count as the 'same' event, the ethologist would point out that much of his experimentation is designed to do just that for the organisms he is studying.[41] So there are two sets of rules, or rule-like phenomena, for the ethologist too. First there are the rules derived from the discipline of ethology itself; and second, the patterns of selection and significance used by the organism under study, the rules of the organism, so to speak. Here too the problem is one of interacting with the organism until the structure of its 'mind' is revealed, and this involves marrying the two sets of rules.

It is, of course, true that the *cues* to which an animal responds cannot be equated with the *concepts* that humans use. Nor are the *patterns* of animal behaviour the same as the *rules* of human societies. Nevertheless, by placing all the emphasis on the differences between human and non-human animals Winch flies in the face of Wittgenstein's quite proper sense of the biological basis of social life. Concepts and rules have their roots in a natural community of judgement. By failing to sustain this tension Winch generates intractable problems for himself. He tells us, for example, that to observe anything we must use concepts. But to have concepts, he says, means to have rules, and to have rules means participating in a culture. From this it follows that we cannot participate in a culture on the basis of observation. A relation to society is presupposed by observation, and so cannot be constituted by it. Winch is explicit in drawing this conclusion.[42]

The trouble is that this leaves the process of social learning shrouded in obscurity. How does social participation ever get started? The only way out of the impasse is to accept that there is a continuity between our untutored looking and educated observation, and between socially shared concepts and our innate sense of the groupings of things. That culture depends on such shared orientations to the world is what Wittgenstein assumed all along.[43]

8.6   Ideals of discourse: Wittgenstein and Habermas

Philosophical puzzlement, says Wittgenstein, is like a disease calling for therapy.[44] Problems arise when we do not know our way around an area of discourse. The cure is to recover our unselfconscious habits and make sure that our words are kept within their proper context. 'The confusions which occupy us', he said, 'arise when language is like an engine idling, not when it is doing work' (*PI*,I,132). And again: 'philosophical problems arise when language *goes on holiday*' (*PI*,I,38). The proper job of philosophy is 'to bring words back from their metaphysical to their everyday use' (*PI*,I,116). Nothing will be destroyed except 'houses of cards' (*PI*,I,118).

In Winch's writings this minimal conception of philosophy quietly gives way to something more expansive. Philosophy, it emerges, is to play a major role in our knowledge of society. Any 'worthwhile study of society', he tells us, 'must be philosophical in character'.[45] There is, declares Winch, a legitimate, *a priori* way of investigating social and natural reality because the 'concepts we have settle for us the form of the experience we have of the world'.[46] The significance of these claims emerges in Winch's discussion of Pareto. Pareto is a sociologist who advocates the 'logico-experimental method'. Far from seeing sociology as a philosophical enterprise, he sees it as part of science. A point that rightly catches Winch's attention is that for Pareto a scientific understanding of the world is itself quite unproblematic. It is to be used as a measure of the rationality of other cultures and is assumed to be the goal of all their cognitive striving. On this view magical practices, for example, are nothing but bungled attempts at the technological control of nature. Winch objects, with justice, that anyone who adopts this position is guilty 'of taking sides in just the sort of way which the application of the logico-experimental technique was supposed to preclude'.[47] We would expect a truly scientific stance to be impartial and detached. It transpires, however, that Winch believes that taking sides in this fashion is a fault inherent in the scientific approach:

> Science, unlike philosophy, is wrapped up in its own way of making things intelligible to the exclusion of all others. Or rather it applies its criteria unselfconsciously; for to be self-conscious about such matters *is* to be philosophical.[48]

The argument is this: there is a variety of different conceptions of the world, and science is just one form of culture alongside all the others. It is, therefore, one of the things that social scientists might investigate, and so it cannot act as the taken-for-granted basis from which to assess and explain everything else. What we need is a platform from which to view the whole array of cultural forms, science included. This, says Winch, is the role of philosophy: 'To take an uncommitted view of such competing conceptions is peculiarly the task of philosophy'.[49] Clearly, the activity called 'philosophy' must represent a breakthrough to a realm of intellectual freedom. It must be an activity unconstrained by its relation to existing cultural resources; a mode of discourse conducted with the highest degree of self-awareness. It would be difficult to imagine a more un-Wittgensteinean conception. Unfortunately Winch does not develop these themes and spell out the character of this activity. The rest of his book, of course, exemplifies the results of such practices. We are shown the conclusions that he draws from them, but not their ultimate ground or justification. Others have been much more forthcoming. Ricoeur, for example, takes Wittgenstein to task for confining himself to the pragmatic side of language and failing to do justice to our capacity to raise ourselves to a higher level of awareness: 'the philosopher', he says, 'is playing a game that is no longer a form of life'.[50] Perhaps the most determined effort in this direction, however, is Habermas's theory of the 'ideal speech situation'.[51]

Habermas distinguishes between the unselfconscious use of language, called 'communicative action', and a more theoretical mode called 'discourse'. He proceeds by imputing a complex set of presuppositions to the actors involved in any smoothly functioning language-game. These concern the sincerity of the parties in-

volved, the assumed truth of what they say, and their moral right
to say it. Common-or-garden breakdowns in communication can
be dealt with by appeal to whatever framework of norms are
shared by the speakers. Sometimes, however, trouble goes deeper
and this framework itself may be called into question. Then the
theoretical attitude takes over from the natural attitude. Discourse
takes over from communicative action by our putting aside all
motives except the desire to reach a 'rational consensus' about the
truth of the claims at issue, or the rightness of the rules under
question. Clearly not any consensus will do because people can
agree in an irrational way. The consensus, says Habermas, must be
achieved solely through the force of the better argument. Behaviour must be subordinated to the requirements of rationality. For
this we need an 'ideal speech situation' where all participants have
an equal chance to state their case and initiate or continue discussion. Everyone has an equal right to demand explanations or
justifications. Everyone can freely express his feelings and intentions. Domination and coercion are absent and all differences of
status and power are stripped away. Obviously, everyday communication is far from ideal in this sense. Nevertheless there is an
intimate connection: the ideal is said to be 'anticipated' in every
real instance of communcation:

> No matter how the intersubjectivity of mutual understanding
> may be deformed, the *design* of an ideal speech situation is
> necessarily implied in the structure of potential speech, since all
> speech, even of intentional deception, is oriented towards the
> idea of truth. This idea can only be analysed with regard to a
> consensus achieved in unrestrained and universal discourse.[52]

What Habermas has given us is his vision of total self-awareness,
and his account of the language-game of philosophy when we are
transported from mundane forms of life into the realm where
reason alone is our guide.[53] In short, we have a realisation of
philosophy as Winch has described it. I am not saying that this
would be Winch's realisation – I shall come to that shortly – but
here is a thinker putting content into the general plan that he laid
down. Look, now, at how the trick was done. Rationality has been
equated with one, very particular, definition of the good life.
Contentious ideals of freedom and justice have been insinuated

into the alleged structure of our verbal practices. Any conservative thinker would immediately see in Habermas's vision a piece of Enlightenment fantasy. Would unrestrained and universal discourse really lead to a rational consensus – or to anarchy? How would those who aspire to universal discourse avoid the fate meted out to the citizens of Babel, who also tried to reach heaven?[54] It represents a very special kind of faith to think that our intellectual life could survive once it has been robbed, as Habermas robs it, of all tradition, and all the authority and power needed to sustain it.

The ideal of philosophical self-awareness seems to be playing the same role as the ink-blot in the personality test. In itself it is an ill-defined thing, and we project our preoccupations and obsessions onto it. By seeing how we give it shape we reveal the mechanisms that we use to give our experience its meaning. In this case what we have found is that a definite and recognisable form of life has been projected onto the otherwise amorphous concept of rationality. If our typology of language-games is on the right lines then there ought to be just about four such ideals of discourse, because there are only four basic kinds of language-game available for projection.[55] Habermas's egalitarian and individualistic vision of rationality obviously represents a reference to the extremes of what have been called low grid and low group. But as well as this cosmopolitan, free-market ideal there are, of course, the range of social forms that would be projected by conservative thinkers. At one extreme there is the fragmented world of the powerless and alienated, with its diminished consciousness and pessimism, and, at the other extreme, the ideal of a traditional, authoritarian society. Here, convention and restraint, not freedom, make meaning possible. These are the themes that inform Wittgenstein's insights. What, then, is the implicit social form that gives structure to Winch's conception of rational discourse? Gellner makes an interesting suggestion. Translated into the language of our typology, he says that Winch's thinking is dominated by low-grid, high-group social patterns, that is by the image of small, highly bounded groups. Winch's strictures against positivist methodology, says Gallner, would make sense in 'a world populated by a set of fairly small tribes, discontinuous enough to have fairly little to do with each other and ... of roughly equal cognitive power'.[56] In this kind of world, with very strong group boundaries and static, homogeneous cultures within them, it would make sense to argue, along with Winch, that each tribe must be understood solely from the inside. Each group must be understood in its own terms with no regard for cross-cultural comparisons or laws of interaction and development. Here, and here alone, Gellner suggests, would Winch's position have some credibility. See Figure 8.3.

Even if these assessments are only approximately correct, it is clear that the idea of philosophical discourse taking us into a realm that is 'uncommitted', is remarkably naive. It would be closer to the truth to say that we have stepped into the realm of pure ideology where a limited number of social preferences vie with one another for the right to claim that they embody true reason.

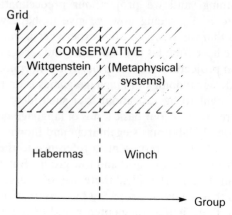

Figure 8.3
The social reference of ideals of philosophical discourse

Clearly, if science is just one piece of culture among others, the same applies to philosophy. If scientists are 'wrapped up' in their own special view of the world, then so are philosophers. If, for these reasons, the scientific stance inevitably leads to 'taking sides' (that is, to treating a part of culture as inherently unproblematic), then philosophical modes of enquiry into society will likewise result in taking sides.

In fact, while both science and philosophy are indeed in the same position, neither of them automatically commits the enquirer to taking sides. Furthermore, neither of them is, or contains, super-cultural elements that transcend our forms of life. The mistake is to think that 'taking sides' is the inevitable consequence of a sociologist using some accepted piece of culture as a resource in his investigation. Taking sides is a feature of *how* cultural resources are used, not the mere fact that they *are* used. (We must have *some* resources.) In principle we can start with any body of resources drawn from either science or common sense or from the writings of philosophers, provided that we use it to illuminate the entire spectrum of cultural forms. This was what Wittgenstein, at his best, did with his idea of language-games. It was a piece of descriptive and analytical apparatus that applied to concepts regardless of whether they were modern or primitive, esoteric or exoteric, secular or sacred. The ideal of scientific understanding has exactly the same formal symmetry. While Winch's charge against Pareto may have been justified, the practices that were singled out for criticism are surely abuses of scientific method rather than necessary features of it. If the goal is explanation by the location of causes and laws, then there is no need to use scientific beliefs as a measure of what is, or is not, in need of explanation. Furthermore, scientific bodies of knowledge can also be made the subject of scientific investigation, as the examples given in previous chapters will have demonstrated.

I do not, of course, think that the structural similarities and symmetries of the kind that I have been emphasising obliterate the differences between, say, positivistic and more descriptive work of the kind advocated by Winch and others who have appealed to Wittgenstein.[57] Drawing their resources from different parts of culture they will continue to approach knowledge from different directions. They will maintain their distinctive style and preferred methods. What I suggest, however, is that these differences do not have to be seen as deeply opposed metaphysical commitments. The depth and degree of opposition between different methodologies says more about their proponents than about the inherent relations of the ideas that are involved. In principle these methodological divergences could assume the status of procedural and technical preferences. They could cease to be the centre of attention and become nothing but different tactics for achieving the same strategic goals – goals common to Wittgenstein, and to many of the more empirically oriented students of culture.

9

The Heirs to the Subject that used to be called Philosophy

I have now carried through my plan to present a systematic account of the sociological and naturalistic themes in Wittgenstein's work. I have also indicated how his ideas can be developed by an empirical approach to the questions that he addressed – despite his own reluctance to do this. What I have tried to convey is a sense of the numerous points of contact between Wittgenstein's concerns and issues that are not only amenable to empirical study, but positively cry out for such an approach.[1] If we forge our picture of the world in the context of social interaction – and no one has demonstrated this in more detail than Wittgenstein – then we should be able to see why different groups produce different pictures. This is why I insisted on reconstructing the idea of language-games within a comparative framework. This was why Wittgenstein's cryptic references to 'needs' had to be filled out by giving them a social location and treating them as interests. With a theoretical framework to sharpen our vision we can see how his obscure talk of 'spontaneity' can be replaced by the thesis that the formation of language-games can be made law-like and intelligible. If I am right there are four main families of language-game that merit special attention. If this result is upheld it should help focus and simplify subsequent research. Even if particular empirical claims or theoretical constructs have to be modified, the vital point remains. We can now see how Wittgenstein's work can be taken up into the everyday practice of historical, anthropological and sociological enquiry. The fact that throughout my discussion I have been able to illustrate and justify my claims by case studies, shows that the systematic, empirical study of language-games is not a programme for the future: it is a well-established practice. Those who decline to inform themselves of its results diminish their capacity to understand Wittgenstein, and will progressively deny themselves the qualifications for assessing his achievements.

Wittgenstein referred to his work as one of 'the heirs to the subject which used to be called philosophy' (*BB*, p.28). My whole thesis could be summed up as the claim to have revealed the true identity of these heirs: they belong to the family of activities called the sociology of knowledge. Of course, not *any* form of sociological analysis will accord with the spirit and letter of his work, or be deepened by an appreciation of what he achieved. For instance, if we take his analysis of meaning, inference and rule following seriously, we will not be content with spelling out the norms or rules to which a group subscribes. Normative determinism, or the explanation of behaviour by reference to the rules, maxims or principles that it is said to embody, can never count as a satisfactory stopping-point for an analysis. Pseudo-explanations of this kind are never far below the surface of the numerous attempts to refer behaviour to 'value systems', 'methodologies' or bodies of 'rational principles'. What is left unexplained in these cases is not only where the rules come from, but what *counts* as following the rules in question: 'no course of action could be determined by a rule', said Wittgenstein, 'because every course of action could be made out to accord with the rule' (*PI*, I, 201). This is the real significance of his doctrine of finitism and the non-verbal form of conventionalism that informs his work. The point is that ' "obeying a rule" is a practice' (*PI*, I, 202).

If Wittgenstein's ideas are to make a continuing contribution to the sociology of culture we must take them more seriously than is customary. When he tells us that meaning equals use, we must stifle the pedantic instincts that immediately incline us to search out qualifications or refinements. Rather than responding on the plane of abstract reflection, it is better to take it quite literally. If meaning equals use, then it equals the whole use and nothing but the use. What then *is* the use? As Wittgenstein indicated, and as the examples in previous chapters have shown, this use will involve the whole culture. The stream of life in a language-game involves the whole, turbulent, cross-cutting stream of interests that we come across among men. There can be no *a priori* restriction on the contingencies that might be involved. If we are going to describe, then let us really describe, if we are going to look and see, then let us really look and see.[2]

I do not expect these conclusions to be received with much enthusiasm by philosophers. It would be understandable if they responded by drawing the boundaries of their discipline tightly around themselves. There would be little difficulty in defining the 'essence' of Wittgenstein's work, or in stipulating his 'real intentions', in such a way that disciplinary purity was maintained. All but the most commonplace of locally accepted facts could then be kept at a decent distance. The probability of such a response is high because delicate questions of ownership and territoriality are involved. If I am right, the competences that are needed to develop Wittgenstein's work do not belong solely, or even primarily, to philosophers. But it would be sad if philosophers were to conceive their professional interests in this narrow and unimaginative way. It would neither reflect well on them, nor would it help those who must now carry the main responsibility for exploiting Wittgenstein's intellectual legacy.

Notes and References

Chapter 1

1. L. Wittgenstein, *Tractatus Logico – Philosophicus*, London, Routledge & Kegan Paul, 1922. (First published in German in 1921.)
2. For biographical details, see N. Malcolm, *Ludwig Wittgenstein, A. Memoir*, London, Oxford University Press, 1958.
3. Useful comparisons and contrasts between the early and late work can be found in, for example: D. Pears, *Wittgenstein*, London, Fontana/Collins, 1971; P. Hacker, *Insight and Illusion*, London, Oxford University Press, 1972; A. Kenny, *Wittgenstein*, Harmondsworth, Penguin, 1973.
4. Two excellent treatments are to be found in: E. Specht, *The Foundations of Wittgenstein's Late Philosophy*, trans. D. E. Walford, Manchester, Manchester University Press, 1969, and V. Klenk, *Wittgenstein's Philosophy of Mathematics*, The Hague, Martinus Nijhoff, 1976. A useful collection of articles discussing the late philosophy is to be found in: G. Pitcher (ed.), *Wittgenstein: The 'Philosophical Investigations'*, London, Macmillan, 1968. As a measure of the intensity of Wittgensteinean scholarship there are now line-by-line analyses of much of the later philosophy, e.g. G. Hallett, *A Companion to Wittgenstein's 'Philosophical Investigations'*, Ithaca, Cornell University Press, 1977; G. Baker and P. Hacker, *Wittgenstein: Understanding and Meaning, An Analytical Commentary on the 'Philosophical Investigations'*, vol. 1, Oxford, Blackwell, 1980.
5. See, for example, P. Engelmann, *Letters from Ludwig Wittgenstein with a Memoir*, trans. L. Furtmüller, Oxford, Blackwell, 1967; A. Janik and S. Toulmin, *Wittgenstein's Vienna*, London, Weidenfeld & Nicolson, 1973; W. W. Bartley, *Wittgenstein*, London, Quartet Books, 1974. The cultural roots of Wittgenstein's work will be touched upon in Chapter 8.
6. Pears, for example, draws attention to what he calls Wittgenstein's 'linguistic naturalism' and to the 'anthropocentric' character of his later work; cf. Pears, *Wittgenstein*, pp.172, 184 and 140, 153, 168, 170. Strawson's review of *PI* emphasised the role given by Wittgenstein to 'customary practice' in rule-following, and Malcolm's review likewise drew attention to Wittgenstein's stress on the facts of 'human nature' and our natural propensity to extrapolate our training. Both reviews are reprinted in G. Pitcher (ed.), *Wittgenstein: The Philosophical Investigations*, Macmillan, London, 1968, cf. pp.37 and 71. One of the most explicit statements is P. Jones, 'Strains in Hume and Wittgenstein', in D. Livingston and J. King (eds), *Hume: A Re-evaluation*, New York, Fordham University Press, 1976, pp.191-209. The 'fundamental fact that man is a social animal', says Jones, 'is prominent in

the later work of Wittgenstein' (p.191). Jones argues, I think correctly, that a reassessment of the later philosophy is called for if we are to do justice to Wittgenstein's insistence on these social and naturalistic themes, (p.209). A recent, closely argued analysis of Wittgenstein's work which culminates in a clear acknowledgement of its social and naturalistic basis is S. Kripke, 'Wittgenstein on Rules and Private Languages', in I. Block (ed.), *Perspectives on the Philosophy of Wittgenstein*, Oxford, Blackwell, 1981, pp.238-312. My own, earlier, arguments to this effect can be found in D. Bloor, 'Wittgenstein and Mannheim on the Sociology of Mathematics', *Studies in History and Philosophy of Science*, vol.4, no. 2, 1973, pp.173-91.

7. See, for example, E. Durkheim, *The Elementary Forms of the Religious Life*, trans. J. W. Swain, New York, Collier, 1961 (first French ed. 1912) (the introduction and conclusion are particularly important); E. Durkheim, *Sociology and Philosophy*, trans. D. Pocock, New York, The Free Press, 1974 (this contains the important essay on 'Individual and Collective Representations' first published in 1898); E. Durkheim, *Essays on Sociology and Philosophy*, ed. K. Wolff, New York, Harper & Row, 1960 (this contains Durkheim's criticisms of pragmatism and his theory of the social origins of the dualism of human nature: both works date from 1914); E. Durkheim and M. Mauss, *Primitive Classification*, trans. R. Needham, London, Cohen & West, 1963 (first French ed. 1903). The closeness of Wittgenstein to Durkheim may be measured by the fact that some authorities treat Wittgenstein as someone who did little more than *rediscover* Durkheim's insights. See, for example, S. Lukes, *Emile Durkheim: His Life and Work*, London, Allen Lane, The Penguin Press, 1973, p.437; and E. Gellner, 'Concepts and Society', in *Cause and Meaning in the Social Sciences*, London, Routledge & Kegan Paul, 1973, ch.2, fn 3, 4.

8. See, for example, pp.486 and 493 of the *Elementary Forms*.

9. Hacker, for example, refers to the 'snippet-box method of composition of the later work', and calls for a 'comprehensive and systematic account' of topics that Wittgenstein 'delineated unsystematically and obscurely' (Hacker, *Insight and Illusion*, pp.141, 309). R. J. Fogelin, *Wittgenstein*, London, Routledge & Kegan Paul, 1976, complains in his preface about Wittgenstein's obscurity and lack of explicit argument. Malcolm in his review (*Ludwig Wittgenstein*) insists that beneath the puzzling collections of reflections there lies a true unity, but one that 'cannot be perceived without strenuous exertion', (p.65).

10. In what follows I shall use the word 'positivism' to refer to the methodological stance in the social sciences in which it is assumed, as Habermas puts it, that 'we can no longer understand science as *one* form of possible knowledge, but rather must identify knowledge with science': J. Habermas, *Knowledge and Human Interests*, trans. J. Shapiro, London, Heinemann, 1972, p.4. A useful survey of the relation of Wittgensteinean work to these various anti-positivist movements is to be found in R. Bernstein, *The Restructuring of Social and Political Theory*, Oxford, Blackwell, 1976.

11. P. Winch, *The Idea of a Social Science and its Relation to Philosophy*, London, Routledge & Kegan Paul, 1958.

Chapter 2

1. The classic denunciation of psychologism is, of course, Durkheim's principle that 'The determining cause of a social fact should be sought among the social facts preceding it and not among the states of the individual consciousness'. (E. Durkheim, *The Rules of Sociological Method*, trans. S. Soloway and J. Mueller, New York, The Free Press, 1938; see esp. ch.5, sect. II, p.110). For attacks on psychologism from the point of view of logic see G. Frege, *The Foundations of Arithmetic*, trans. J. Austin, Oxford, Blackwell, 1959; see esp. p.35. I have commented elsewhere on the similarities between Frege and Durkheim and the interesting consequences of bringing their theories together; cf. D. Bloor, *Knowledge and Social Imagery*, London, Routledge & Kegan Paul, 1976, ch.5. I show here that Frege's definition of objectivity is satisfied by social institutions.
2. The theory is much older than this. In 1690 John Locke wrote that 'words in their primary and immediate signification stand for nothing but the ideas in the mind of him that uses them'. (J. Locke, *An Essay Concerning Human Understanding*, ed. A. Pringle-Pattison, Oxford, Clarendon Press, 1924, bk III, ch II, p.225.
3. B. Russell, *The Analysis of Mind*, London, Allen & Unwin, 1921, p.201.
4. E. Titchener, *Lectures on the Experimental Psychology of the Thought-Processes*, New York, Macmillan, 1909, p.16.
5. Ibid, p.12.
6. See the accounts in: E. Titchener, *Systematic Psychology: Prolegomena*, Ithaca, Cornell University Press, 1972, esp. pp.194-201; and E. Boring, *A History of Experimental Psychology*, New York, Appleton-Century-Crofts, 1950, chas 17, 18, 19.
7. A. Schutz, *The Phenomenology of the Social World*, trans. G. Walsh and F. Lehnert, London, Heinemann, 1972, p.36
8. Ibid, pp.35-6.
9. Ibid, p.99. Schutz italicises the last words (cf. *PI*, I, 274).
10. Quoted by Titchener, *Lectures on the Experimental Psychology of the Thought-Processes*, p.66.
11. See E. Husserl, *Ideas: General Introduction to Phenomenology*, trans. W. Boyce Gibson, London, Collier-Macmillan, 1962, esp. the discussion of the 'sensile' and the 'intentional', pp.226-30.
12. Wittgenstein's classificatory game with the mystery word 'tove' proceeds in exactly the same way as the experiments on concept formation conducted by the Russian psychologist L. S. Vygotsky. There is much to be gained by reading Wittgenstein in conjunction with Vygotsky. It helps to show how easily Wittgenstein's concerns can be translated into a robust line of empirical research. See L. S. Vy-

gotsky, *Thought and Language*, ed. and trans. E. Hanfmann and E. Vakar, Cambridge, Mass: MIT Press, 1962. The book first appeared in Russian in 1934.

13. 'The student of psychology ... must still make his choice for the one or the other. There is no middle way between Brentano and Wundt'. E. Titchener, 'Brentano and Wundt: Empirical and Experimental Psychology', *American Journal of Psychology*, vol.32, 1921, pp.108-20, at p.108.

14. Quoted in Titchener, *Lectures*, p.5.

15. For a valuable and detailed discussion of the work of the Würzburg group and their idea of a *Bsl* see: G. Humphrey, *Thinking: An Introduction to its Experimental Psychology*, New York, Wiley, 1963, chs 3, 4.

16. For the complexities of the relationship of Külpe's work to Brentano and Wundt and Husserl see: A. Rancurello, *A Study of Franz Brentano, his Psychological Standpoint and his Significance in the History of Psychology*, New York, Academic Press, 1969, pp.104-8.

17. Quoted by Russell in his *Analysis of Mind*, p.224; Titchener is Russell's source.

18. Titchener, *Lectures*, p.235.

19. Bartley says, 'If any individual thinker can be said to have influenced Wittgenstein ... it must have been Karl Bühler.' He goes on to say that 'there are ... striking similarities between some of Bühler's leading ideas and those of the later Wittgenstein'. See W. W. Bartley, *Wittgenstein*, London, Quartet Books, 1974, pp. 104, 107, 108. Toulmin makes the same point, though perhaps in a slightly more guarded way. He says that it would be a remarkable coincidence if Wittgenstein arrived at the ideas of the *Philosophical Investigations* without a knowledge of the work of Bühler and his wife. He concludes an article on Wittgenstein by saying, 'To anyone interested in the historical origins of Wittgenstein's later ideas, I would therefore say "Don't overlook the Bühlers".' See S. Toulmin, 'Ludwig Wittgenstein', *Encounter*, January 1969, pp.58-71, at p.71.

20. These should be contrasted with Ach's reference to a 'lightening-like momentary illumination' (quoted in Humphrey, *Thinking*, p.49).

21. E. Durkheim, *The Elementary Forms of the Religious Life*, trans. J. Swain, New York, Collier-Macmillan, 1961.

Chapter 3

1. Strictly, what I have counted as different facets of the same game, Wittgenstein counts as different language-games.

2. The word 'finitism' has a variety of more-or-less technical meanings. My usage follows that of Hesse: M. Hesse, *The Structure of Scientific Inference*, London, Macmillan, 1974, ch.8.

3. Cf. also *Z*, 540-1.

4. 'If you use a rule to give a description, you yourself do not know more than you say. I.e. you yourself do not foresee the application that you will make of the rule in a particular case. If you say "and so on", you yourself do not know more than "and so on" ' (*RFM*, III, 8).

5. For a valuable discussion of the topics broached in this section see B. Barnes, 'On the Extension of Concepts and the Growth of Knowledge', *Sociological Review*, vol. 30, no. 1, 1982, pp.23-44.

6. In the *Blue and Brown Books* the idea of family-resemblance groupings is applied to psychological concepts like recognising, comparing, expecting, etc. The aim is to show that there is no single, characteristic experience that is referred to by these concepts; cf. *BB*, pp.87-8, 112.

7. L. S. Vygotsky, *Thought and Language*, ed. and trans. E. Hanfmann and E. Vakar, Cambridge, Massachusetts, MIT Press, 1962; e.g. pp. 61 and 62.

8. 'Don't look only for similarities in order to justify a concept, but also for connexions. The father transmits his name to the son even if the latter is quite unlike him' (*RPP*, vol.I, 923).

9. Opinions have divided sharply on the status and scope of family-resemblance theory. The majority opinion seems to be that its scope is limited. An important exception to this is R. Bambrough, 'Universals and Family Resemblances', *Proceedings of the Aristotelean Society*, vol.LXI, 1960-1, pp. 207-22. While agreeing with the general thrust of Bambrough's argument, my treatment of the issue will be somewhat different.

10. K. Campbell, 'Family Resemblance Predicates', *American Philosophical Quarterly*, vol.2, no.3, 1965, pp.238-44, p.244. Campbell's paper is an attempt to clarify Wittgenstein's doctrine. It is therefore worth noting that it proceeds along very un-Wittgensteinean lines because Campbell takes for granted the idea of a reference class, or extension. In the formal development of his argument Campbell acknowledges that whether a concept has a family-resemblance structure is always relative to the background of linguistic usage – i.e. the taken-for-granted or 'basic' predicates in the language. This important element of relativity is never reconciled with his call to banish family-resemblance concepts from science.

11. L. Fleck, *Genesis and Development of a Scientific Fact*, Chicago, Chicago University Press, 1979. (First published in German in 1935.)

12. Ibid, p.5.

13. Ibid, p.12.

14. Ibid, pp.13-14.

15. Experimentally injecting an animal with *Spirochaeta pallida* and observing the onset of the disease will not prove the point. It is also necessary to prove that the real cause was not introduced along with the suspected cause.

16. Fleck, *Genesis and Development*, p.18.

17. Ibid, p.19.

18. Ibid, p.19.

19. Ibid, p.9.
20. The law of constant proportions had to be established in the face of a host of obscurely understood counter-examples and anomalies such as solutions, alloys and glasses. Only later, after the law had been accepted, did reasons emerge for not counting these cases as compounds. Although these cases came to be understood in a way that reconciled them with the law of constant proportions, other problems emerged, e.g. interstitial compounds. See L. Nash, 'The Atomic-Molecular Theory', in J. Conant and L. Nash (eds), *Harvard Case Histories in Experimental Science*, Cambridge, Harvard University Press, 1966, vol.I, pp.217-321, esp. pp.238-41; and J. Agassi, *Towards an Historiography of Science*, The Hague, Mouton, 1963, esp. pp.58-60.
21. Recall for example the idea popularised by, among others, Otto Weininger: that each human being, and perhaps even each cell of the body, is really a mixture of the pure male archetype and the pure female archetype: O. Weininger, *Sex and Character*, London, Heinemann, 1906 (trans. from the 6th German edn). This example has been specially chosen. Wittgenstein is known to have been greatly interested in Weininger's writing. They were widely discussed in Vienna. See, for example: A. Janik and S. Toulmin, *Wittgenstein's Vienna*, London, Weidenfeld & Nicolson, 1973, pp.71-4, 176; W. Bartley, *Wittgenstein*, London, Quartet, 1974, pp.13-14; A. Janik, 'The Philosophical Sources of Wittgenstein's Ethics', *Telos*, no. 44, Summer 1980, pp.131-44.
22. Fleck discusses this on p.xxvii and pp.112-13 of *Genesis and Development*. A similar thesis and its methodological implications are explored in: H. Collins, 'The Place of the "Core Set" in Modern Science: Social Contingency with Methodological Propriety in Science', *History of Science*, vol. 19, 1981, pp.6-19; H. Collins, 'Understanding Science', *Fundamenta Scientiae*, vol.2, 1981, pp.367-80.
23. A. J. Ayer, *The Problem of Knowledge*, Harmondsworth, Penguin, 1956, p.11.
24. E. Evans-Pritchard, *Witchcraft, Oracles and Magic Among the Azande*, Oxford, Clarendon Press, 1937.
25. 'It is evident that there was a critical difference of viewpoint between Compton and Gray. Gray had argued that any difference in intensity between the primary and secondary beams could only stem from a change in hardness of the radiation in the scattering process. Compton chose precisely this change in hardness as a *criterion* for distinguishing the "truly scattered" radiation from the "fluorescent" radiation.' R. Stuewer, *The Compton Effect*, New York, Science History Publications, 1975, p.139.
26. Cf. *OC*, 98.
27. G. Baker, 'Criteria: A New Foundation for Semantics', *Ratio*, vol.16, no.2, 1974, pp.156-89.
28. Ibid, p.182.
29. Ibid, pp.168-9.

30. E. Specht, *The Foundations of Wittgenstein's Late Philosophy*, trans. D. Walford, Manchester, Manchester University Press, 1963.
31. Ibid, p.165; cf. also pp.154 and 185.
32. "'We decide *spontaneously*" (I should like to say) "on a new language-game'" (*RFM*, III, 23). Cf. also *PI*, II, xi.

Chapter 4

1. Cf. also *NFL*, pp.281 and 307.
2. B. Skinner, 'The Operational Analysis of Psychological Terms' (reprinted from the *Psychological Review*, vol. 52, 1942) in H. Feigl and M. Brodbeck, *Readings in the Philosophy of Science*, New York, Appleton-Century-Crofts, 1953, pp.585-95.
3. It is important for a proper appreciation of Skinner's theory to realise that his operant conditioning is not the same as Pavlov's classical conditioning. It does not, for example, begin with a passive, unconditioned reflex: it begins with an active stream of behaviour or 'operants'. See Skinner's stress on the difference between *elicited* and *emitted* behaviour: B. Skinner, *The Behaviour of Organisms: An Experimental Analysis*, New York, Appleton-Century-Crofts, 1938, pp.19-20.
4. The standard criticism is N. Chomsky, 'A Review of B. F. Skinner's "Verbal Behaviour"', *Language*, vol. 53, no.1, 1959, pp.26-58.
5. Skinner, 'The Operational Analysis of Psychological Terms', p.593.
6. For the claim that Wittgenstein proves no more than that private languages are contingently impossible, see R. Fogelin, *Wittgenstein*, London, Routledge & Kegan Paul, 1976, p.165.
7. E. Durkheim, *The Elementary Forms of the Religious Life*, trans. J. Swain, New York, Collier, 1961, pp.21-33.
8. The original Kantean claim that intuition without thought is not knowledge and 'consequently would be for us as good as nothing' is to be found in his *Critique of Pure Reason*, A.111.
9. It is perhaps significant that Kant did not make his *a priori* apparatus something that could be studied in an empirical psychology of the individual mind. It had a noumenal not a phenomenal existence. This was a wise move. For Durkheim this simply meant that the noumenal was a reified reference to the social – an even wiser move.
10. N. Malcolm, *Dreaming*, London, Routledge & Kegan Paul, 1962: 'if anyone holds that dreams are identical with, or composed of, thoughts, impressions, feelings, images, and so on ... occurring in sleep, then his view is false' (p.52).
11. Ibid. His waking impression is what establishes that he had a dream, and his account of his dream establishes what the content of his dream was (p.79). For further stress on accounts and narrations see, e.g., pp.85-6, 92 and 94.
12. Ibid. Malcolm discusses the work of the psychologists W. Dement, N. Kleitman and G. Ramsey; cf. ch.13.

13. Ibid, p.62.
14. Ibid, p.77.
15. Ibid, p.81.
16. Ibid, p.76.
17. Ibid, p.80.
18. Ibid, p.76. See also p.28, where Malcolm accepts that to use the word 'asleep' to cover hypnotic trances and nightmares 'is to make a natural extension of the use of the word beyond its primary use'.
19. Ibid, p.81.
20. H. Putnam, 'Dreaming and "Depth Grammar"', in R. Butler (ed.), *Analytical Philosophy* (1st series), Oxford, Blackwell, 1966, pp.211-35.
21. Ibid, p.213.
22. Ibid, p.219.
23. Malcolm, *Dreaming*, p.77.
24. Putnam, 'Dreaming and "Depth Grammar"', p.223.
25. Ibid, p.220.
26. P. Feyerabend, 'Wittgenstein's "Philosophical Investigations"', *Philosophical Review*, vol.LXIV, 1955, pp.449-83. The page numbers I cite are from the reprint in G. Pitcher (ed.), *Wittgenstein*, London, Macmillan, 1968, pp.104-50.
27. Wittgenstein's interest in the process of reading may have come from his period as a schoolteacher. Reading is discussed in *PI* I, 156-71 and extensively in the *Blue and Brown Books*.
28. Feyerabend, 'Wittgenstein's "Philosophical Investigations"', p.111.
29. Ibid.
30. A. Melden, *Free Action*, London, Routledge & Kegan Paul, 1967.
31. Ibid, p.169.
32. Ibid, p.169.
33. The outward movement of the dialectic is accomplished by steps of the following kind: 'Our concept of an action is the concept of an action for which the agent may have a reason and a reason of the kind that relates to the social intercourse of agents.' Ibid, p.196.
34. Ibid, p.210.
35. Ibid, p.190.
36. Ibid, p.190.
37. Ibid, p.197.
38. Ibid, p.219.
39. R. Peters, *The Concept of Motivation*, London, Routledge & Kegan Paul, 1960, p.7.
40. C. Wright Mills, 'Situated Actions and Vocabularies of Motive', *American Sociological Review*, vol.5, 1940, pp.904-13. Mills saw his paper as part of a 'major reorientation of recent theory and observation in sociology' (p.904).
41. See, for example, J. Manis and B. Meltzer (eds), *Symbolic Interaction: A Reader in Social Psychology*, Boston, Allyn & Bacon, 1967. It is perhaps significant that when historians and sociologists discuss the problems of imputing motives to historical actors they have no diffi-

culty retrieving Mills's significant paper, or seeing its connection with the Wittgensteinean tradition: e.g. S. Shapin and B. Barnes, 'Darwin and Social Darwinism: Purity and History', in B. Barnes and S. Shapin (eds), *Natural Order*, Beverly Hills, London, Sage, 1979, pp.125-42.

42. Peters, *The Concept of Motivation*, p.155.

43. Melden, *Free Action*, p.184.

44. D. Davidson, 'Actions, Reasons and Causes', *Journal of Philosophy*, vol.60, no.23, 1963, pp.685-700.

45. A simple but cogent argument for this thesis is provided by S. Toulmin, *The Philosophy of Science: An Introduction*, London, Hutchinson, 1965 (7th impression) ch.2.

46. See, for example, S. Toulmin, *Foresight and Understanding: An Enquiry into the Aims of Science*, New York, Harper & Row, 1961, chs 3 and 4 on 'Ideals of Natural Order'; and T. Kuhn, *The Structure of Scientific Revolutions*, Chicago, Chicago University Press, 1962.

47. Melden, *Free Action*, pp.11-17.

48. This example is taken from Toulmin, *Philosophy of Science*.

49. Precisely the same issue is argued out between A. Louch and E. Gellner. The only difference is that the argument is joined at a later stage. Louch – on the anti-positivist side – allows causal knowledge in the social sciences but treats it as a different kind of causal knowledge from that in the natural sciences. He insists that it has an irremediably *ad hoc* character: it is directly ascertained and applies to specific cases. It neither has, nor hints at, generality. Gellner, on the other hand, insists that all causal claims carry an implicit commitment, or reference, to general laws. See: E. Gellner, 'A Wittgensteinean Philosophy Of (or Against) the Social Sciences', reprinted in his *Spectacles and Predicaments: Essays in Social Theory*, Cambridge, Cambridge University Press, 1979, ch.3, esp. pp.72-5; A. Louch, *Explanation and Human Action*, Berkeley, University of California Press, 1966.

50. Melden, *Free Action*, p.72.

51. Ibid, p.116; cf. also pp.109 and 114.

52. Ibid, p.173. Notice the similarity with the phenomenologists and act-psychologists discussed in Chapter 2.

53. C. Taylor, 'Explaining Action', *Inquiry*, vol.13, 1970, pp.54-89. The reference to an original, empirical language is on p.80.

54. Melden, *Free Action*, p.85.

55. Davidson, 'Actions, Reasons and Causes', p.700.

56. J. Conant, 'The Overthrow of the Phlogiston Theory: The Chemical Revolution of 1775-1789', in J. Conant and L. Nash (eds), *Harvard Case Histories in Experimental Science*, Cambridge, Harvard University Press, 1966, vol.1, pp.67-115.

57. See, for example, D. Huff and S. Turner, 'Rationalizations and the Application of Causal Explanations of Human Action', *American Philosophical Quarterly*, vol.18, no.3, July 1981, pp.213-20.

58. M. Black, *Models and Metaphors*, Ithaca, New York, Cornell Uni-

versity Press, 1962; M. Hesse, *Models and Analogies in Science*, Notre Dame, University of Notre Dame Press, 1966, esp. 'The Explanatory Function of Metaphor', pp.157-77; D. Schon, *Displacement of Concepts*, London, Tavistock, 1963.

59. *Explanation* may be represented thus, where the arrow stands for logical deduction:

logically   logically
secondary ⟶ primary
concepts   concepts

Analysis, on the other hand, may be represented thus, where the arrow takes on a meaning which depends on one's view of analysis:

logically   logically
primary ⤍ secondary
concepts   concepts

This claim is argued and illustrated in more detail in D. Bloor, 'Explanation and Analysis in Strawson's "Persons"', *Australasian Journal of Philosophy*, vol.48, no.1, 1970, pp.2-9.

60. Melden, *Free Action*, pp.11-17. Similar arguments about character explanations have been put forward by P. Foot, 'Free Will as Involving Determinism', *Philosophical Review*, vol.LXVI, 1957, pp.439-50. For a reply on behalf of the causalists arguing that Foot has too narrow a conception of causal thinking in science, see M. White, 'Causation and Action', in S. Morgenbesser, P. Suppes and M. White (eds), *Philosophy, Science and Method*, New York, St. Martin's Press, 1969, pp.251-9, esp. p.254.

Chapter 5

1. Cf. *OC*, 47.
2. See, for example, B. Russell, *Introduction to Mathematical Philosophy*, London, Allen & Unwin, 1919; G. Frege, *The Foundations of Arithmetic*, trans. J. Austin, Oxford, Blackwell, 2nd rev. edn, 1959; S. Körner, *The Philosophy of Mathematics. An Introductory Essay*, London, Hutchinson, 1960, chs 2 and 3.
3. Cf. *LFM*, pp.43 and 271.
4. G. Hardy, *A Mathematician's Apology*, Cambridge, Cambridge University Press, 1967 (first printed 1940) pp.123-4.
5. K. Gödel, 'What is Cantor's Continuum Problem', in P. Benacerraf and H. Putnam (eds), *Philosophy of Mathematics, Selected Readings*, Englewood Cliffs, Prentice-Hall, 1964, pp.271 and 272.
6. Cf. *RFM*, I, 130.
7. D. Bloor, 'Wittgenstein and Mannheim in the Sociology of Mathematics', *Studies in the History and Philosophy of Science*, vol.4, no.2, 1973, pp.173-91.

8. 'However queer it sounds, the further expansion of an irrational number is a further expansion of mathematics' (*RFM*, IV, 9).

9. That this is the analogy Wittgenstein had in mind when he spoke of a move into another 'dimension' is clear from the fact that in *RFM* he said the move was 'as it were from the line into a surrounding plain' (*RFM*, IV, 11).

10. In Wittgenstein's text the figures are not numbered.

11. Cf. *LFM*, p.98.

12. B. Russell, *Portraits from Memory and Other Essays*, London, Allen & Unwin, 1956, p.116.

13. G. Frege, *The Foundations of Arithmetic*, trans. J. Austin, Oxford, Blackwell, 2nd rev. edn 1959, sections 7, 9, 10. Frege refers rhetorically to Mill's 'gingerbread or pebble arithmetic' (p.vii).

14. For a detailed discussion of how this theory can be supplemented by sociological considerations and thereby meet Frege's requirements of objectivity, see D. Bloor, *Knowledge and Social Imagery*, London, Routledge & Kegan Paul, 1976, esp. ch. 5, 'A Naturalistic Approach to Mathematics'.

15. C. Boyer, *The History of the Calculus and its Conceptual Development*, New York, Dover, 1959, pp.143-4.

16. Ibid, p.143.

17. Ibid, p.143.

18. The quotation continues, 'It does not establish that they are there; they do not exist until it makes them.'

19. Throughout the remainder of this section I will be following the valuable historical work of Joan Richards J. Richards, 'The Reception of a Mathematical Theory: Non-Euclidean Geometry in England, 1868-1883', in B. Barnes and S. Shapin (eds), *Natural Order: Historical Studies of Scientific Culture*, London, Sage, 1979, pp.143-66.

20. B. Riemann, 'On the Hypotheses Which Lie at the Bases of Geometry', *Nature*, vol.8, 1873, pp.14-17, and 36-7.

21. F. Turner, 'The Victorian Conflict Between Science and Religion: A Professional Dimension', *Isis*, vol.69, 1978, pp.356-76; F. Turner, *Between Science and Religion: The Reaction to Scientific Naturalism in Late Victorian England*, New Haven, Yale University Press, 1974; L. Jacyna, *Scientific Naturalism in Victorian Britain: An Essay in the Social History of Ideas* (unpubl. Ph.D. thesis, University of Edinburgh, 1980).

22. J. Sylvester, Address, in *Report of the Thirty-Ninth Meeting of the British Association for the Advancement of Science*, 1869, pp.1-9, p.8.

23. Quoted by Richards, 'Reception of a Mathematical Theory', p.150, from Whewell's *Of a Liberal Education in General*.

24. Quoted in Richards, 'Reception of a Mathematical Theory', p.154, from H. Helmholtz, 'The Origin and Meaning of Geometrical Axioms', *Mind*, vol.1, 1876, pp.301-21 and 304.

25. Richards, 'Reception of a Mathematical Theory', p.159, from W. Jevons, 'Helmholtz on the Axioms of Geometry', *Nature*, vol.4, 1871,

pp.481-2.

26. W. Cayley, Presidential Address, *Report of the British Association for the Advancement of Science*, 1883, pp.3-37.

27. Quoted in Richards, 'Reception of a Mathematical Theory', p.159, from Cayley, *Report of the British Association*, p.9.

28. Quoted in Richards, 'Reception of a Mathematical Theory', p.162.

29. The point about conceivability and consistency proofs is made by Richards, ibid, pp.154-5.

30. 'One would like to say: the proof changes the grammar of our language, changes our concepts. It makes new connections, and it creates the concept of those connections' (*RFM*, II, 31).

31. This is assuming that the relation between their variables is one of linear regression.

32. K. Pearson, 'Notes on the History of Correlation', in E. Pearson and M. Kendall (eds), *Studies in the History of Statistics and Probability*, London, Griffin, 1970, pp.185-205, first published in *Biometrika* in 1920.

33. Strictly speaking the variables in equation (5) refer to errors, not measurements.

34. Pearson, 'Notes on the History of Correlation', p.188. Pearson is here quoting his own words from 1895.

35. Ibid, p.191.

36. Ibid, p.187.

37. Ibid, p.191.

38. For a clear account of these matters, see D. MacKenzie, *Statistics in Britain, 1865-1930. The Social Construction of Scientific Knowledge*, Edinburgh, Edinburgh University Press, 1981, esp. ch.3 and appendices 3 and 4. I have greatly benefited from MacKenzie's book and have relied on it throughout the whole of the present section.

39. Ibid, esp. p.65.

40. Ibid, p.71. The suggestion here is that Bravais and Galton were working within different 'paradigms' in Kuhn's sense. Bravais was doing 'normal science' within the tradition of error-theory.

41. 'Bravais ... remained blind to the stupendous idea in whose vicinity his mind was hovering ... he might, with one leap of creative imagination, have pounced squarely upon this conception.' H. Walker, 'The Relation of Plana and Bravais to the Theory of Correlation', *Isis*, vol.10, 1928, pp.466-84, p.481.

42. See, for example, the interesting discussions in: K. Mannheim, 'On the Interpretation of "Weltanschauung"', in *Essays on the Sociology of Knowledge*, London, Routledge & Kegan Paul, 1951, ch.II, esp. pp.55-63; H. Garfinkel, *Studies in Ethnomethodology*, Englewood Cliffs, Prentice-Hall, 1967, p.40.

43. Pearson, 'Notes on the History of Correlation', p.189.

44. See MacKenzie, *Statistics in Britain*, ch.3. To make sense of these facts MacKenzie appeals to the notion of social interest. Eugenics, he argues, represented a middle-class ideology. The explanation has been refined in a valuable paper by Searle, who increases the magnifi-

cation and looks at which segments of the professional middle class resisted eugenics. It transpires that it was rejected by those, like social workers, whose interests were not helped by Galton's programme. See G. Searle, 'Eugenics and Class', in C. Webster (ed.), *Biology, Medicine and Society, 1840-1940*, Cambridge, Cambridge University Press, 1981, pp.217-42.

Chapter 6

1. 'I mean: this is simply what we *do*. This is use and custom among us, or a fact of our natural history' (*RFM*, I, 63).
2. Cf. also *RFM*, II, 30 and V, 28.
3. A. Prior, 'The Runabout Inference Ticket', *Analysis*, vol.21, 1960, pp.38-9.
4. Cf. also *RFM*, V, 1-8.
5. N. Belnap, 'Tonk, Plonk and Plink', *Analysis*, vol.22, 1962, pp.130-34. For a valuable further discussion of the ramifications of Prior's paper and the problem of justifying deduction, see: S. Haack, 'The Justification of Deduction', *Mind* vol.85, 1976, pp.112-19; S. Haack, 'Dummett's Justification of Deduction', *Mind*, vol.XCI, 1982, 216-39.
6. Belnap, 'Tonk, Plonk and Plink', p.131.
7. When it is argued that animals can reason, the evidence takes the form of showing that they can combine information in the way summed up by the rule of transitivity. The classic experiments are by Maier. See, for example, N. Maier, 'Reasoning in Rats and Human Beings', *Psychological Review*, vol.44, 1937, pp.365-78. The development of these claims can be followed in any decent textbook on learning-theory.
8. N. Goodman, *Fact, Fiction and Forecast*, Indianapolis, Bobbs-Merrill, 1965, p.67. Similar claims have been made in the theory of rationality. For criticisms similar to those advanced below, see B. Barnes, 'Vicissitudes of Belief', *Social Studies of Science*, vol.9, 1979, pp.247-63.
9. R. Rudner, in P. Edwards (ed.), *The Encyclopedia of Philosophy*, London, Collier-Macmillan, 1967, vol.3, p.371.
10. It is interesting to observe how, in emergencies, philosophers make sudden discoveries. For example, it is discovered that circular arguments are not, after all, things to be avoided. We have seen Goodman invoke the idea of virtuous rather than vicious circles. Similarly Dummett says that circular arguments are fine provided that our aim is to explain rather than persuade – he then proceeds to conflate explanation with justification: M. Dummett, 'The Justification of Deduction', *Proceedings of the British Academy*, vol.LIX, 1973, pp.201-32, p.207. It is also discovered that not all arguments are either deductive or inductive. Deduction can be justified by a new third mode of proof: see J. Bickenbach, 'Justifying Deduction', *Dia-*

logue, vol.18, 1979, pp.500-16. This is, in fact, an interesting line of argument but, on inspection, Bickenbach's new method of proof turns out to be a disguised form of the inductive reasoning, from particulars to particulars, used in science. In other words, he is trying to justify deduction by induction, and this is bound to be too weak.

11. 'It is not a question of *opinion*. They are determined by a consensus of *action*: a consensus of doing the same thing, reacting in the same way. There is consensus but not a consensus of opinion' (*LFM*, pp.183-4). Cf. *OC*, 110, 253.

12. M. Dummett, 'Wittgenstein's Philosophy of Mathematics', *Philosophical Review*, vol.LXVIII, 1959, pp.324-48 (reprinted in G. Pitcher (ed.), *Wittgenstein*, London, Macmillan, 1968, pp.420-47, pp.425-6).

13. Ibid, p.434.

14. Ibid, p.438.

15. B. Russell, *The Principles of Mathematics*, Cambridge, Cambridge University Press, 1903, p.15.

16. C. Lewis, 'Implication and the Algebra of Logic', *Mind*, vol.21, 1912, pp.522-31.

17. Ibid, p.530.

18. Ibid, p.531.

19. Ibid.

20. A. Anderson and N. Belnap, *Entailment. The Logic of Relevance and Necessity*, vol.1, Princeton, Princeton University Press, 1975; A. Anderson, 'An Intensional Interpretation of Truth-Values', *Mind*, vol.81, 1972, pp.348-71; A. Anderson and N. Belnap, 'Enthymemes', *Journal of Philosophy*, vol.LVIII, no.23, 1961, pp.713-23.

21. Anderson, 'An Intensional Interpretation', p.368.

22. This is the position of E. Nelson, 'Intensional Relations', *Mind*, vol.39, 1930, pp.29-453.

23. Anderson and Belnap, *Entailment*, p.296.

24. D. Makinson, *Topics in Modern Logic*, London, Methuen, 1973.

25. T. Smiley, 'Entailment and Deducibility', *Proceedings of the Aristotelian Society*, new series vol.LIX, 1958-9, pp.233-54, p.250.

26. Anderson and Belnap, *Entailment*, p.165.

27. B. Bosanquet, *Logic or the Morphology of Knowledge*, Oxford, Clarendon Press, 1911, vol.I, p.323. (The first edition was in 1888.)

28. F. Bradley, *The Principles of Logic*, Oxford, Oxford University Press, 1922, vol.I, p.130. (The first edition was in 1883.)

29. Ibid, p.139.

30. Ibid.

31. Smiley, 'Entailment and Deducibility', p.233.

32. T. Carlyle, 'Signs of the Times', in his *Critical and Miscellaneous Essays*, London, Chapman and Hall, n.d. (four volumes in two), vol.I, p.104 (this essay was first published in 1829); J. Passmore, *A Hundred Years of Philosophy*, London, Duckworth, 1957, ch.7, 'Some Critics of Formal Logic'.

33. This is the stance taken, for example, by H. Reichenbach, in *Nomo-*

logical Statements and Admissible Operations, Amsterdam, North Holland, 1954, pp.14-15.

34. The critic is J. Bennett, quoted in Anderson, 'An Intensional Interpretation', p.364.
35. See Makinson, *Topics in Modern Logic*, pp.27-41.
36. A measure of the complexity of this relationship may be gathered from the rigorous development provided by A. Church, *Introduction to Mathematical Logic*, vol.I, Princeton, New Jersey, Princeton University Press, 1956.
37. 'There correspond to our laws of logic very general facts of daily experience. They are the ones that make it possible for us to keep on demonstrating those laws in a very simple way (with ink on paper, for example)' (*RFM*, I, 118).

Chapter 7

1. M. Douglas, 'Self-Evidence', in *Implicit Meanings, Essays in Anthropology*, London, Routledge & Kegan Paul, 1975, esp. pp.289, 302-3, and 306-7.
2. I. Lakatos, *Proofs and Refutations, The Logic of Mathematical Discovery*, ed. J. Worrall and E. Zahar, Cambridge, Cambridge University Press, 1976. See also D. Bloor, 'Polyhedra and the Abominations of Leviticus', *British Journal for the History of Science*, vol.11, no.39, 1978, pp.245-72. It is interesting to notice the analogy between anomalies and strangers occurring spontaneously in the patter that accompanies the more formal work of logicians. Makinson, for example, says: 'Different people react in different ways to the Lewis principles. For some they are welcome guests, whilst for others they are strange or suspect.' D. Makinson, *Topics in Modern Logic*, London, Methuen, 1973, p.26.
3. What follows is a simplified version of the ideas that have been developed in: M. Douglas, *Purity and Danger. An Analysis of Concepts of Pollution and Taboo*, London, Routledge & Kegan Paul, 1966; by the same author: *Natural Symbols. Explorations in Cosmology*, Harmondsworth, Penguin, 1973; *Implicit Meanings. Essays in Anthropology*, London, Routledge & Kegan Paul, 1975; *Cultural Bias*, Occasional Paper no.34, Royal Anthropological Institute of Great Britain and Ireland, 1978; also M. Douglas (ed.), *Essays in the Sociology of Perception*, London, Routledge & Kegan Paul, 1982.
4. J. Ben-David, *The Scientist's Role in Society: A Comparative Study*, Englewood Cliffs, Prentice-Hall, 1971; R. Turner, 'The Growth of Professorial Research in Prussia, 1818-1848: Causes and Context', *Historical Studies in the Physical Sciences*, vol.3, 1971, pp.137-82; R. Turner, 'University Reformers and Professorial Scholarship in Germany, 1760-1806', in L. Stone (ed.), *The University in Society*, Oxford, Oxford University Press, 1975, vol.II, pp.495-531.
5. Douglas, *Natural Symbols*, p.88.

6. T. Kuhn, *The Structure of Scientific Revolutions*, 2nd edn, 1970, Chicago, University of Chicago Press, esp. ch.IX.

7. E. Frankel, 'Corpuscular Optics and the Wave Theory of Light: the Science and Politics of a Revolution in Physics', *Social Studies of Science*, vol.6, 1976, pp.141-84.

8. J. Watkins, 'Against "Normal Science"', in I. Lakatos and A. Musgrave (eds), *Criticism and the Growth of Knowledge*, Cambridge, Cambridge University Press, 1970. pp.25-37, 34.

9. It is perhaps not surprising that critics have argued that two paradigms can exist side by side, that not all major change takes place by revolution, etc. If grid-group theory is correct, the growth of knowledge and the attendent patterns of critical argument should have a more complex inner structure and range of variation than Kuhn allows. The fact remains, though, that Kuhn's book is the single most fruitful account of science that we possess. Its real achievement, however, lies in the description of what Kuhn calls 'normal science' rather than in the idea of 'revolution'. See B. Barnes, *T. S. Kuhn and Social Sciences*, London, Macmillan, 1982, section 4.3.

10. A comparable case is the dispute between Karl Pearson and G. Udny Yule over the proper measure of statistical association. See D. MacKenzie, *Statistics in Britain, 1865-1930*, Edinburgh, Edinburgh University Press, 1981, ch.7, 'The Politics of the Contingency Table'.

11. See, for example, the pattern of growth in Euler's formula as it was enriched to take account of ever more complex cases: Lakatos, *Proofs and Refutations*, pp.76-81.

12. K. Caneva, 'What Should We Do with the Monster? Electromagnetism and the Psychosociology of Knowledge', in E. Mendelsohn and Y. Elkana (eds), *Science and Cultures. Sociology of the Sciences*, vol.V, Dordrecht, Reidel, pp.101-31; K. Caneva, 'From Galvanism to Electrodynamics: The Transformation of German Physics and its Social Context', *Historical Studies in the Physical Sciences*, vol.9, 1978, pp.63-159.

13. See the descriptions of the Big Man system in New Guinea: Douglas, *Natural Symbols*, pp.89 ff.

14. I speak from personal experience: C. Bloor and D. Bloor, 'Twenty Industrial Scientists: A Preliminary Exercise', in M. Douglas (ed.), *Essays in the Sociology of Perception*, London, Routledge & Kegan Paul, 1982, pp.83-102. See also the other essays in this volume.

15. See Douglas, *Purity and Danger*, and *Implicit Meanings*, p.283.

16. Douglas, *Implicit Meanings*, p.281.

17. 'I do not explicitly learn the propositions that stand fast for me. I can *discover* them subsequently like the axis around which a body rotates. This axis is not fixed in the sense that anything holds it fast, but the movement around it determines its immobility' (*OC*, 152).

18. R. Metz, *A Hundred Years of British Philosophy*, London, Allen & Unwin, 1938, pp.239-43; J. Mander, *Our German Cousins: Anglo-German Relations in the 19th and 20th Centuries*, London, Murray, 1974.

19. T. Carlyle, 'Novalis', *Foreign Review and Continental Miscellany*, vol.IV, 1829, pp.97-141, p.116.

20. Ibid, p.117.

21. Ibid, p.118.

22. C. Brinton, *The Political Ideas of the English Romantics*, Oxford, Oxford University Press, 1926; A. Cobbam, *Edmund Burke and the Revolt Against the Eighteenth Century: A Study of the Political Thinking of Burke, Wordsworth, Coleridge and Southey*, London, Allen & Unwin, 1929, esp. ch.VI; C. Sanders, *Coleridge and the Broad Church Movement*, Durham, North Carolina, Duke University Press, 1942; R. Harris, *Romanticism and the Social Order, 1780-1830*, London, Blandford, 1969; B. Knights, *The Idea of the Clerisy in the Nineteenth Century*, Cambridge, Cambridge University Press, 1978, esp. ch.II.

23. Coleridge, *Statesman's Manual*, quoted by Knights, *The Idea of the Clerisy*, p.49. For the contrasting economic psychology of the utilitarians see: E. Halévy, *The Growth of Philosophic Radicalism*, trans. M. Morris, London, Faber & Faber, 1952, esp. ch.III.

24. See Coleridge, *2nd Lay Sermon*, quoted by Knights, *The Idea of the Clerisy*, p.66, and the quotation from Coleridge's table talk given in Harris, *Romanticism and the Social Order*, p.227.

25. R. Graves, *Life of Sir William Rowan Hamilton*, London, Longman, 1832, 3 vols; D. Bloor, 'Hamilton and Peacock on the Essence of Algebra', in H. Mehrtens, H. Bos and I. Schneider (eds), *Social History of Nineteenth Century Mathematics*, Boston, Birkhäuser, 1981, pp.202-32.

26. Graves, *Life of Sir William Rowan Hamilton*, vol.II, p.528.

27. P. Rattansi, 'Paracelsus and the Puritan Revolution', *Ambix*, vol.XI, 1963, pp.24-32; P. Rattansi, 'The Intellectual Origins of the Royal Society', *Notes and Records of the Royal Society of London*, vol.23, 1968, pp.129-43; J. Jacob, 'The Ideological Origins of Robert Boyle's Natural Philosophy', *Journal of European Studies*, vol.2, 1972, pp.1-21; J. Jacob, 'Robert Boyle and Subversive Religion in the Early Restoration', *Albion*, vol.6, 1974, pp.175-93; J. Jacob, 'Boyle's Circle in the Protectorate: Revelation, Politics and the Millenium', *Journal of the History of Ideas*, vol.38, 1977, pp.131-40; J. Jacob, *Robert Boyle and the English Revolution. A Study in Social and Intellectual Change*, New York, Franklin, 1977; J. Jacob, 'Boyle's Atomism and the Restoration Assault on Pagan Naturalism', *Social Studies of Science*, vol.8, 1978, pp.211-33; D. Kubrin, 'Newton and the Cyclical Cosmos: Providence and the Mechanical Philosophy', *Journal of the History of Ideas*, vol.XXVIII, 1967, pp.325-46; J. McGuire, 'Forces, Active Principles and Newton's Invisible Realm', *Ambix*, vol.XV, 1968, pp.154-208; M. Jacob, *the Newtonians and the English Revolution, 1689-1720*, Ithaca, Cornell University Press, 1976. These and other studies have been brought together in an important interpretive paper by Steven Shapin which makes explicit their significance for a sociological theory of knowledge. I have relied heavily on Shapin's

paper throughout this section: S. Shapin, 'The Social Uses of Science', in G. Rousseau and R. Porter (eds), *The Ferment of Knowledge. Studies in the Historiography of Eighteenth-Century Science*, Cambridge, Cambridge University Press, 1980, pp.93-139.

28. The classic statement of this position is: P. Duhem, *The Aim and Structure of Physical Theory*, trans. P. Wiener, New York, Atheneum, 1962 (from the 2nd French edn of 1914).

29. R. Boyle, *The Works of the Honourable Robert Boyle*, London, Millar, 1744, vol.I, p.439.

30. C. Hill, *The World Turned Upside Down: Radical Ideas During the English Revolution*, Harmondsworth, Penguin, 1975.

31. Boyle, *Works*, vol.4, p.376.

32. E. McMullin, *Newton on Matter and Activity*, London, University of Notre Dame Press, 1978, p.103.

33. There are, of course, profound historical and methodological problems surrounding the idea of what Newton 'thought'. There seem to be as many Newtons as there are audiences that he was addressing or circumstances to which he was responding. Given a social theory of the nature of the self this is hardly surprising. Nor, as a consequence, is the problem confined to Newton or other historically significant figures, like Darwin; it is completely general. But for the Newton case see S. Shapin and S. Schaffer *'Making Newton; On the Interpretation of Scientific Texts'* (forthcoming).

34. See, for example, the General Scholium to his *Mathematical Principles* given in F. Manuel, *The Religion of Isaac Newton*, Oxford, Clarendon Press, 1974, p.16. See S. Shapin and S. Schaffer, 'Making Newton'.

35. Quoted in Jacob, *The Newtonians*, p.156. The quotation continues: 'I had my eye on such Principles as might work with considering men for the belief of a Deity and nothing can rejoice me more.' It would be a mistake, however, to see this as a generalised expression of piety. Newton was not satisifed with any sincere profession of faith. For him many such professions were no better than atheism, e.g. believing in God as the soul of the world. His aim, like Boyle's, was to direct men's minds to a quite specific conception of God. Only in this way would they draw the desired social and political conclusions from the book of nature.

36. B. Wynne, 'Physics and Psychics: Science, Symbolic Action, and Social Control in Late Victorian England', in B. Barnes and S. Shapin (eds), *Natural order*, London, Sage, 1979, pp.167-86.

37. J. Farley and G. Geison, 'Science, Politics and Spontaneous Generation in Nineteenth-Century France: The Pasteur-Pouchet Debate', *Bulletin of the History of Medicine*, vol.48, no.2, 1974, pp.161-98.

38. The most celebrated cases are the 'German Physics' movement of Stark and Lenard, and the Lysenko affair in Soviet biology. See: A. Beyerchen, *Scientists under Hitler: Politics and the Physics Community in the Third Reich*, New Haven, Yale University Press, 1977, esp. chs 5-8; D. Joravsky, *The Lysenko Affair*, Cambridge, Mass., Har-

vard University Press, 1970. Cases such as these tend to be uppermost in the minds of philosophers who want us to equate social influences with distortions of rationality and with the production of unacceptable, erroneous or unworkable beliefs. To offset the impression that the massive intrusion of political considerations must have bad, rather than good, effects on science, it is worth reflecting on a fascinating paper by Paul Forman: P. Forman, 'Weimar Culture, Causality, and Quantum Theory, 1918-1927: Adaptation by German Physicists and Mathematicians to a Hostile Intellectual Environment', *Historical Studies in the Physical Sciences*, vol.3, 1971, pp.1-115.

39. I owe this argument to Mr. G. Buchdahl.
40. For a valuable survey and analysis of this work, with an extensive bibliography, see S. Shapin, 'History of Science and its Sociological Reconstructions', *History of Science*, vol.XX, 1982, pp.157-211.
41. See F. Turner, 'The Victorian Conflict Between Science and Religion: a Professional Dimension', *Isis*, vol.69, 1978, pp.356-76, for revealing quotations from Galton and Tyndall and Huxley.
42. See, for example: K. Pearson, *The Grammar of Science*, London, A. & C. Black, 3rd rev. edn 1911, ch.IX, 'The Laws of Motion' (first edition 1892); D. Wilson, 'Concepts of Physical Nature: John Herschel to Karl Pearson', in U. Knoepfelmacher and G. Tennyson (eds), *Nature and the Victorian Imagination*, London, University of California Press, 1979, pp.201-15; L. Jacyna, 'Scientific Naturalism in Victorian Britian', unpubl. Ph.D. thesis, University of Edinburgh, 1980, esp. ch.2, 'Causes, and Forces, and Powers'.

Chapter 8

1. Pitkin, for example, claims on p.1 of her book that Wittgenstein offers a 'new perspective'. This theme is reiterated throughout. See, for example, pp.325 and 328. H. Pitkin, *Wittgenstein and Justice*, Berkeley, University of California Press, 1972. It has also been said of Wittgenstein that he is 'outside any specific sociological tradition': see G. Flöistad, 'Notes on Habermas's Proposal for a Social Theory of Knowledge', *Inquiry*, vol.13, 1970, pp.175-98, p.176.
2. K. Mannheim, 'Conservative Thought', in *Essays on Sociology and Social Psychology*, London, Routledge & Kegan Paul, 1953, ch.II. It should perhaps be emphasised that the word 'conservative' as it is used here has no simple application to the categories and labels of present-day, British party politics.
3. W. Walsh, *Metaphysics*, London, Hutchinson, 1963, pp.122-4.
4. J. Nyiri, 'Wittgenstein's New Traditionalism', in *Essays on Wittgenstein, Acta Philosophica Fennica*, vol.28, nos 1-3, 1976, pp.503-12; J. Nyiri, 'Wittgenstein's Later Work in Relation to Conservatism', in B. McGuinness (ed.), *Wittgenstein and his Times*, Oxford, Blackwell, 1982, pp.44-68. I have greatly benefited from reading these papers in the writing of the following section.

5. The literature on German conservative and romantic thought is extensive. Useful and brief accounts can be found in: H. Reiss, *The Political Thought of the German Romantics, 1793-1815*, Oxford, Blackwell, 1955; R. Cardinal, *German Romantics in Context*, London, Cassell & Collier Macmillan, 1975; R. Berdahl, 'Prussian Aristocracy and Conservative Ideology: A Methodological Examination', *Social Science Information*, vol.15, 1976, pp.583-99. Berdahl brings out clearly the basis of the ideology in social interest.

6. Quoted in Mannheim, 'Conservative Thought', pp.128-9.

7. O. Spengler, *The Decline of the West*, trans. C. F. Atkinson, London, Allen & Unwin, 1926.

8. G. von Wright, 'Wittgenstein in Relation to his Times', in B. McGuinness (ed.), *Wittgenstein and his Times*, Oxford, Blackwell, 1982, pp.108-20, p.116.

9. In 1931 Wittgenstein wrote: 'I don't believe I have ever *invented* a line of thinking, I have always taken one over from someone else. I have simply straightaway seized on it with enthusiasm for my work of clarification. That is how Boltzmann, Hertz, Schopenhauer, Frege, Russell, Krauss, Loos, Weininger, Spengler, Sraffa have influenced me' (*CV*, p.19). The first eight names represent authors who mainly influenced Wittgenstein's early work. See: J. Griffin, *Wittgenstein's Logical Atomism*, Oxford, Oxford University Press, 1964; P. Engelmann, *Letters from Ludwig Wittgenstein with a Memoir*, trans. L. Furtmüller, Oxford, Blackwell, 1967; A. Janik and S. Toulmin, *Wittgenstein's Vienna*, London, Weidenfeld & Nicolson, 1973. Sraffa was a Cambridge contemporary of Wittgenstein's whose help is acknowledged in the preface of *PI*. Little has yet been written on the Sraffa-Wittgenstein connection. Further investigation may significantly deepen our understanding of Wittgenstein's relation to the intriguing intellectual climate of Cambridge in the 1930s.

10. Spengler, *Decline of the West*, p.21.

11. Ibid, p.21.

12. Ibid, p.100.

13. Ibid, p.101.

14. Ibid, p.23

15. Ibid, p.59. The whole second chapter of Spengler's book is devoted to the meaning of numbers.

16. Valuable evidence of Spengler's impact in this respect is to be found in P. Forman, 'Weimar Culture, Causality and Quantum Theory, 1918-1927: Adaptation by German Physicists and Mathematicians to a Hostile Intellectual Environment', *Historical Studies in the Physical Sciences*, vol.3, 1971, pp.1-115. For contemporary assessments of Spengler's significance see: E. Troeltsch, 'The Ideas of Natural Law and Humanity in World Politics', in O. Gierke, *Natural Law and the Theory of Society*, trans. E. Barker, Cambridge, Cambridge University Press, 1934, pp.201-22; O. Neurath, 'Anti-Spengler', in M. Neurath and R. Cohen (eds), *Empiricism and Sociology*, Dordrecht, Reidel, 1973, pp.158-213. (first published in 1921).

17. Quoted in R. Rhees (ed.), *Ludwig Wittgenstein, Personal Recollections*, Oxford, Blackwell, 1981, p.128.
18. For example, in the context of educational debate the hierarchy is often upheld by a rhetorical contrast between the symbols of head and hand. See S. Shapin and B. Barnes, 'Head and Hand: Rhetorical Resources in British Pedagogical Writing, 1770-1850', *Oxford Review of Education*, vol.2, no.3, 1976, pp.231-54.
19. See *PI*, I, pp.307-8; *RFM*, II, 18. C. Chihara and J. Fodor, 'Operationalism and Ordinary Language', *American Philosophical Quarterly*, vol.II, 1965, pp.281-95, reprinted in G. Pitcher (ed.), *Wittgenstein*, London, Macmillan, 1968, pp.384-419.
20. P. Winch, *The Idea of a Social Science and its Relation to Philosophy*, London, Routledge & Kegan Paul, 1958.
21. E. Gellner, 'The New Idealism – Cause and Meaning in the Social Sciences', in I. Lakatos and A. Musgrave (eds), *Problems in the Philosophy of Science* (vol.3 of the Proceedings of the International Colloquium in the Philosophy of Science, London, 1965), Amsterdam, North-Holland, 1968, pp.377-406.
22. Two representative papers are: M. Oakeshott, 'The Tower of Babel', *The Cambridge Journal*, vol.2, 1948-49, pp.67-82; and 'Rational Conduct', *The Cambridge Journal*, vol.4, 1950-51, pp.3-27.
23. Winch, *Idea of a Social Science*, p.54.
24. Ibid, p.57.
25. Ibid, p.63.
26. Ibid, p.129
27. Ibid, p.123.
28. Winch is keen to deny any analogy between the exchange of ideas and the interaction of forces in a physical system. Oakeshott shows no such anxiety in the face of similar physical analogies. 'Human conduct' he says 'in its most general character, is energy; it is not caused by energy, it does not express or display energy, it is energy.' ('Rational Conduct', p.22). The significance of Oakeshott's rhetorical identification should be clear in the light of the previous discussion of the spirit-matter hierarchy. Oakeshott is collapsing it in an upward direction.
29. Winch, *Idea of a Social Science*, p.62.
30. Ibid, p.57.
31. Wittgenstein in fact deliberately inverts the metaphor of logical 'seeing' by insisting that in the last analysis 'I obey the rule *blindly*.' (*PI*, I, 219).
32. Winch, *Idea of a Social science*, pp.61 and 62. As evidence for his claim Winch cites E. Levi, *An Introduction to Legal Reasoning*, Chicago, University of Chicago Press, 1949. This fascinating book seems to me to show the opposite of what Winch wants.
33. Wittgenstein does, however, seem to draw the line at machines. Cf. *Z*, 614.
34. Winch, *Idea of a Social Science*, p.62.
35. Ibid, p.63.

36. D. Broadbent, *Perception and Communication*, Oxford, Pergamon Press, 1958, ch.3, esp. p.47.
37. Winch, *Idea of a Social science*, p.87.
38. J. von Uexküll, *Theoretical Biology*, London, Kegan Paul, Trench & Trubner, 1926, esp. ch.V, and 'A Stroll Through the Worlds of Animals and Men', in C. Schiller (ed.), *Instinctive Behaviour. The Development of a Modern Concept*, London, Methuen, 1957, pp.5-80 (first published 1934). N. Tinbergen, *The Study of Instinct*, Oxford, Clarendon Press, 1951, p.37. J. Durant, 'Innate Character in Animals and Man: A Perspective on the Origins cf Ethology', in C. Webster (ed.), *Biology, Medicine and Society 1840-1940*, Cambridge, Cambridge University Press, 1981, pp.157-92.
39. Some philosophers reject such a reading as superficial. They say that the deeper reading of Kant places the *a priori* structure of the mind entirely outside nature rather than making it a phenomenon within nature. There is, however, a long tradition of naturalising the *a priori*. Herbert Spencer and William James, for example, argued in this way: as well as Durkheim and Wittgenstein. For a modern defence of this approach see D. Campbell, 'Methodological Suggestions for a Comparative Psychology of Knowledge Processes', *Inquiry*, vol.2, 1959, pp.152-82.
40. See, for example, K. Lorenz, 'Kant's Doctrine of the A Priori in the Light of Contemporary Biology', in R. Evans (ed.), *Konrad Lorenz: The Man and his Ideas*, New York, Harcourt Brace, 1975, pp.181-217. (The paper was first published in 1941). Uexküll's Kantianism is quite explicit and is closely associated with a characteristic form of relativism. Notice the similarity between what Uexküll says about the self-contained character of each animal's 'self-world' and what Wittgenstein said about the completeness of language-games. The first principle of Umwelt theory is that 'all animals, from the simplest to the most complex, are fitted into their unique worlds with equal completeness'. Uexküll, 'A Stroll Through the Worlds of Animals and Men', p.11.
41. For example, Winch, *Idea of a Social Science*, p.108. See Tinbergen, *Study of Instinct*, p.32.
42. Winch, *Idea of a Social Science*, p.85.
43. For a forceful statement of the dependence of language on prior, non-linguistic adaptations to the material world, see D. Campbell, 'Ostensive Instances and Entitivity in Language Learning', in W. Gray and N. Rizzo (eds), *Unity through Diversity*, New York, Gordon & Breach, 1973, pp.1043-57.
44. 'The philosopher is the man who has to cure himself of many sicknesses of the understanding before he can arrive at the notions of the sound human understanding' (*RFM*, IV, 53). 'The philosopher's treatment of a question is like the treatment of an illness' (*PI*, I, 255).
45. Winch, *Idea of a Social Science*, p.3. Cf. also p.17.
46. Ibid, p.15. Cf. also p.8.
47. Ibid, pp.101-2.

48. Ibid, pp.102-3.
49. Ibid, p.103.
50. P. Ricoeur, 'Husserl and Wittgenstein on Language', in E. Lee and H. Mandelbaum (eds), *Phenomenology and Existentialism*, Baltimore, Johns Hopkins Press, 1969, pp.207-17, p.217.
51. J. Habermas, 'Towards a Theory of Communicative Competence', *Inquiry*, vol.13, 1970, pp.360-75; and 'On Systematically Distorted Communication', *Inquiry*, vol.13, 1970, pp.205-18. For a valuable analysis and clarification see T. McCarthy, 'A Theory of Communicative Competence', *Philosophy of the Social Sciences*, vol.3, 1973, pp.135-56.
52. Habermas, 'Towards a Theory of Communicative Competence', p.372.
53. A similar theory has been offered by Ellis as an 'epistemic' basis for logic. The idea is that if validity is to be defined by assertability rather than truth conditions then, ultimately, validity requires that an inference can be incorporated into an ideally and universally extended system of rational belief. He says, 'a rational belief on a language ... is defensible before an audience of competent speakers. I offer completability through every extension of the vocabulary of the language as my criterion of ultimate defensibility.': B. Ellis, 'Epistemic Foundations of Logic', *Journal of Philosophical Logic*, vol.5, 1976, pp.187-204, p.201. This is just Habermas's image of a totally open and unbounded society expressed in a different idiom. The trouble is that this replaces the myths of Platonism by an equally mythical cosmopolitanism. The truths of logic are just as much beyond our grasp in this myth as in the other. The real epistemic foundations of logic cannot be based on 'every extension' of our vocabulary, but must relate to our vocabulary as it exists here and now.
54. See Oakeshott, 'The Tower of Babel', *Cambridge Journal*, vol.2, 1948-9, pp.67-83.
55. In our free-floating imagination we can, of course, combine ideas in an indefinitely large number of ways and join fragments of all kinds of different social practices. This would suggest that there are, in principle, an infinite number of different ideals of discourse, rather than a small number of archetypes. There must, surely, be some truth in this, but two additional factors must be borne in mind. First, any systematic attempt to sketch out an overall model of discourse and rational conduct must strive to create an appearance of consistency and coherence. Second, if these claims to coherence are going to have any credibility they will have to resonate with the habits of thought and implicit models of conduct in the minds of their intended audience. Taken jointly this means that the ideological traditions that have grown up historically in the inherited culture of that audience will be used as measures of coherence and credibility. If grid-group theory really does pick out the vital variables there would be grounds for suspecting that the four extreme cases would each yield a simple model of a social form that would act as a reference point in the

culture. This point is discussed with reference to the long-standing opposition between conservative and enlightenment ideologies and their relation to the Kuhn-Popper debate in: D. Bloor, *Knowledge and Social Imagery*, London, Routledge & Kegan Paul, 1976, ch.4.

56. Gellner, 'The New Idealism', p.397.
57. For example, the ethnomethodologists, and, B. Latour and S. Wool-gar, *Laboratory Life: The Social Construction of Scientific Facts*, Beverley Hills, Sage, 1979; A. Brannigan, *The Social Basis of Scientific Discovery*, Cambridge, Cambridge University Press, 1981.

Chapter 9

1. Consider the following passage in which Wittgenstein invites us to imagine a tribe who consulted oracles rather than basing their actions and beliefs on the findings of science: 'Is it wrong for them to consult an oracle and be guided by it? – If we call this "wrong" aren't we using our language-game as a base from which to *combat* theirs?' (*OC*, 609). Cf. also *OC*, 610-12. How else could this idea of 'combat' be taken seriously except by appeal to factual data and case studies about the confrontation and conflict of social groups?
2. 'To repeat: don't think, but look!' (*PI*, I, 66).

Index